BLUE SONG

BLUE SONG

St. Louis in the Life and Work of
Tennessee Williams

Henry I. Schvey

UNIVERSITY OF MISSOURI PRESS

Columbia

Copyright © 2021 by
The Curators of the University of Missouri
University of Missouri Press, Columbia, Missouri 65211
Printed and bound in the United States of America
All rights reserved. First paperback printing, 2022.

Library of Congress Cataloging-in-Publication Data

Names: Schvey, Henry I., 1948- author.
Title: Blue song : St. Louis in the life and work of Tennessee Williams /
    by Henry I. Schvey.
Description: Columbia, Missouri : University of Missouri Press, 2021. |
    Includes bibliographical references and index.
Identifiers: LCCN 2020046566 (print) | LCCN 2020046567 (ebook) | ISBN
    9780826222305 (hardcover ; alk. paper) | ISBN 9780826222619 (paperback ;
    alk. paper) | ISBN 9780826274571 (ebook)
Subjects: LCSH: Williams, Tennessee, 1911-1983--Homes and
    haunts--Missouri--Saint Louis. | Saint Louis (Mo.)--Social life and
    customs--20th century.
Classification: LCC PS3545.I5365 Z8337 2021 (print) | LCC PS3545.I5365
    (ebook) | DDC 812/.54 [B]--dc23
LC record available at https://lccn.loc.gov/2020046566
LC ebook record available at https://lccn.loc.gov/2020046567

∞™ This paper meets the requirements of the
American National Standard for Permanence of Paper
for Printed Library Materials, Z39.48, 1984.

Typefaces: Galliard and Abril

This book is dedicated to my loving wife of fifty-one years, Patty, whose patience with my obsession helped me bring this to fruition; and to my children, Aram, Jerusha, and Natasha (and to my grandchildren, Evan, Julian, Livia, Gavi, and Noa). You have brought me joy and inspiration every day.

I also wish to dedicate this book to Cecile Verburg, whose suggestion that this project absolutely needed to be done jump-started it, and to the many gifted students in my Performing Arts Department seminars on Tennessee Williams, who intensified my excitement about the playwright.

Contents

Illustrations

Preface

RESEARCHING AND WRITING this book has led me to the surprising conclusion that my professional life has been intertwined with that of Tennessee Williams for decades. When I arrived in St. Louis in fall 1987 to chair the Performing Arts Department at Washington University, I was generally familiar with the trajectory of the playwright's life and work. I had taught several of his plays during my tenure at Leiden University in the Netherlands, where I began my teaching career, and had directed *The Glass Menagerie* for the Leiden English Speaking Theatre in 1981. From my directorial research, I knew that St. Louis was the city in which Williams had grown up and that he had been unhappy there.

But despite realizing that *The Glass Menagerie* was heavily autobiographical, I had no idea how much Williams's family history had shaped his worldview, or exactly why he felt such strong antipathy toward a city from which I personally had derived so many happy experiences. When I first visited the city in the late 1960s, I found St. Louis (and specifically the warm and generous home of my in-laws) to possess a welcoming calm that was the opposite of my upbringing in New York City.

When I came to work at Washington University nearly twenty years later, I became aware of the playwright's fraught, complicated history with the university: he had begun his studies there as an SNCD (Student Not Candidate for Degree), then had enrolled as a matriculating student in 1936–1937—but had not graduated. Only gradually did I learn that he had left the university under a cloud following a playwriting contest in which the then twenty-six-year-old student (considerably older than his undergraduate

peers and already a produced playwright) received only honorable mention, and that he refused to attend the awards ceremony
in Graham Chapel to pick up his certificate. I also learned that he
failed a course in ancient Greek, something that precipitated his
departure in the summer of 1937.

When I arrived on campus to assume my responsibilities as
chair, I was informed by one of our lecturers that the library's
Special Collections possessed a copy of the one-act that Williams
wrote during his time at the university. It was probably not very
good and had been poorly received, she said, but the play (*Me,
Vashya*) might still be worth looking into.

During the 2003–2004 academic year, Washington University
celebrated its sesquicentennial, and called for projects honoring
distinguished alumni from the school's rich history. Although
Williams had not graduated (he completed his degree at the
University of Iowa in 1938), I proposed an international symposium on his year as a full-time student at Washington University.
The conference, Tennessee Williams: The Secret Year,[1] received
support from the College of Arts and Sciences and was held in
February 2004. The event, including a reception and lectures
by two international scholars,[2] was held in the Art Deco greenhouse in Forest Park known as the Jewel Box. The venue was
chosen because it is mentioned in *The Glass Menagerie* as the
place where Laura spends her time (instead of attending typing
class at Rubicam's Business College, as her mother supposes). In
addition to the scholars, the playwright's brother, Dakin, spoke.
Dakin Williams lived in Collinsville, Illinois, a short distance from
St. Louis, and acted as an informal advisor to our conference.

In conjunction with the conference, I directed a departmental
production of *The Glass Menagerie* in the A. E. Hotchner Studio
Theatre on campus and collaborated with lecturer Shelley Orr to
put on the previously unproduced *Me, Vashya* as a curtain rais-
er.[3] A month after our symposium, I offered a paper on the as
yet unpublished *Me, Vashya* at the Scholars Conference of the
Tennessee Williams Literary Festival in New Orleans in which I
described this production.[4] Most revealing was the fact that while
the one-act seemed banal and melodramatic when read aloud or

staged realistically, it suddenly came alive when played as expressionist fantasy, with Vashya's desk raised on a platform some ten feet above the other actors.

It was during that visit to New Orleans that my connection with Williams grew more interesting than I could have anticipated. As I was browsing in Faulkner House Books in the French Quarter, the store owner showed me a folder of ephemera from Williams's days in New Orleans. To my amazement, there, among a sheaf of miscellaneous photos and documents, was a blue examination book of the kind still used at most universities. The booklet had its author's name ("Th. Williams") written on the cover in pencil, and upon opening it, I realized I was holding the failed Greek-examination booklet that was partly responsible for Williams's leaving the university. Stunned, I opened the pages of the blue book and saw something still more extraordinary: on the page following the exam was an original poem, scrawled in pencil, entitled "Blue Song." An earlier title, I saw, lay underneath but had been erased: "Sad Song." I trembled as I held this piece of literary history in my hands.

While it might appear that the discovery of Williams's Greek examination and "Blue Song" would have been sufficient to lure me to a more intense study of the playwright, an even more curious experience followed. Just weeks after discovering the poem in that New Orleans bookstore, I received a letter from, of all places, Paisley, Scotland, inviting me to visit and speak with a retired American academic who claimed to possess more than a hundred pages of correspondence with Tennessee Williams that had been exchanged during the 1950s.

After seeing a copy of the first letter from Williams and believing the expatriate's account plausible, I traveled to Paisley to meet Konrad Hopkins, a strange and reclusive American who (when we met in person) revealed a bizarre tale: that as a member of the Air Force in his early twenties, he had engaged in a coerced sexual encounter with the then forty-two-year-old playwright in a New York City hotel room while on leave in 1953. Despite this traumatic experience (assuming his story is true), Hopkins worshipped Williams; indeed, he had become completely obsessed with Williams's life and works, and had invited me to Paisley to share the details of his correspondence with the famous writer and in hopes I might turn his letters into a play or a work of fiction.[5] As I examined Konrad's correspondence with Williams in detail, I came to realize that what I was reading was a tale of mutual seduction between the two men, one young and naïve, the other mature and worldly. Konrad was well read, Harvard educated, and profoundly insecure about his homosexuality, which was made worse by his feeling imprisoned in an Air Force base in the deeply conservative South of the early 1950s. Tennessee had come to terms with his sexuality, and was now a tremendously successful writer who was receptive to and intrigued by the young man's literary sensitivity and understanding of his work. The correspondence between the two led to Williams's asking Konrad for a photograph of himself and then playfully guessing the young soldier's height, weight, and shoe size based upon clues from the photo and their correspondence (Williams's guesses were invariably wrong!). However, following their brief tryst in New York during the final rehearsals and the failure of the opening of Williams's new play, *Camino Real*, it becomes clear that Williams loses interest in the young man. Konrad fled New York anxious and needy after a humiliating incident at the Dakota in which Williams and his friend (and former lover) William Inge summarily shoved the coatless young airman out the service entrance of Inge's apartment to avoid being spotted by Tennessee's companion, Frank Merlo.

In the pages of letters that follow, it becomes all too obvious that Williams is looking for an excuse to end their correspondence. Sadly, Konrad is oblivious to the writer's signals. Finally, after Konrad encloses a number of apparently salacious clippings in one of his letters, Williams has had enough: "Your recent enclosures of carefully culled clippings from scandal sheets and snot-grey pseudo-intellectual journals with their painstakingly derisive comments . . . more or less affirms my suspicions that you want to *believe* you like me but really don't!"[6] Soon after this, their correspondence ends.

Not surprisingly, the Paisley experience expanded my interest in Williams to a more nuanced examination of his life, his lesser-known later plays, and even the paintings he devoted so much time to during the final decade of his life in Key West.

In late spring 2016 my wife and I were visited by a friend, the artist Cecile Verburg, who had designed the costumes for my Dutch production of *The Glass Menagerie* back in 1981. Visiting the Missouri History Museum, Cecile inquired where she could buy a book on Williams's relationship with St. Louis. When it was not to be found, I promised to find it for her, but I discovered that no full-length study of that kind had ever been published. It was then that I realized a book needed to be written on the subject. I also realized that my many interactions with Williams's life and work over some thirty-five years had been preparation for just such an undertaking.

As I began the process of researching the subject, I discovered a final bizarre connection between us: Tennessee Williams and I had occupied the same apartment building in New York City, at 15 West 72nd Street. Between July 1965 and June 1968, we lived under the same roof—I as a high school student on the twenty-fifth floor, and Tennessee just eight floors above, on the thirty-third. Why, it was even possible that we had seen one another, or said hello in the elevator!

All these strange, almost eerie connections provided me with what I hope is an interesting story to tell. It is the story of a man who grew up and came of age in the city I loved and he despised. In some strange way, we had almost changed places—I had traveled from New York to St. Louis, while he had left St. Louis behind for the opportunity to create a name for himself in New York. Of course, leaving St. Louis was just the first step on Williams's journey toward becoming one of America's greatest playwrights. He went on to live elsewhere—in places as varied as New Orleans, Provincetown, Key West, and Tangier. But as I came to realize in the course of writing this book, the most amazing thing about his peripatetic life may well have been that he never really left home at all.

Acknowledgments

MANY PEOPLE HAVE been of invaluable assistance in preparing and editing this manuscript for publication. At the University of Missouri Press, I owe special thanks to my editor, Mary S. Conley, and to my copyeditor, Gloria Thomas, for their rigorous and insightful comments and suggestions. A debt of thanks is also owed to Gary Kass, who commissioned the manuscript, and to Deanna Davis, Drew Griffith, and Robin Rennison for all their enthusiastic assistance.

Eric Colleary and Cristina Meisner of the Harry Ransom Center at the University of Texas at Austin have been remarkably generous with their time and energy, as has Dale Stinchcomb of Harvard University's Houghton Library, Jennifer Lee of Columbia University's Butler Library, Lauren Salwasser of the Missouri History Museum, and Joel Minor, Curator of the Modern Literature Collection at Washington University in St. Louis. Thanks also go to Nancy Cambria and Carolann Cole of the University City Schools. Christopher Wait of New Directions Publishing and Cora Markowitz of the Georges Borchardt Literary Agency were most helpful in helping me obtain the rights and permissions to use Tennessee Williams's writings.

Particular thanks also go to a group of amazingly talented research assistants at Washington University: Dan Washelesky, Liam Gibbs, Stephanie Carlson, Alex Knapp, and Myles Hesse.

Artist Jessie Hoagland is due great thanks for her wonderfully inventive and whimsical map, "Tennessee Williams Trail," as is Dan McGuire, whose encyclopedic knowledge of the streets, buildings, and churches associated with the youth of Thomas Lanier Williams is amazing. Without his understanding of the locations Tom Williams knew as a child, this book would have been a lesser thing.

Thanks are due to the indefatigable wizardry of Carrie Houk, Artistic Director of the Tennessee Williams Festival St. Louis, for her passionate advocacy of Williams to St. Louis; and to Liam Otten of Washington University's Office of Public Affairs and Jim Kirchheer of KETC television for their valuable assistance.

I want to thank my dear and always supportive colleagues in the Performing Arts Department at Washington University, especially Pannill Camp, Rob Henke, Carter Lewis, Jeffery Mathews, Paige McGinley, Rob Morgan, Anna Pileggi, Sean Savoie, Andrea Urice, Julia Walker, and Bill Whitaker, for their encouragement and enthusiasm for this project; and to Serena Carvajal, Mary Clemens, Phil Durkee, and the astonishing Cindy Kahn for their administrative assistance. Cindy was assistant on the 2004 international symposium held in the Jewel Box in Forest Park, an event that ultimately led to this project.

This book relies heavily on the many Williams scholars and friends whose insights and perspectives over many years have been invaluable, among them John S. Bak, Chris Bigsby, Robert Bray, Eric Colleary, Gilbert Debusscher, Allean Hale, W. Kenneth Holditch, Michael Hooper, A. E. Hotchner, T. R. Johnson, David Kaplan, Thomas Keith, John Lahr, Jeremy Lawrence, Lyle Leverich, Carmen Marchosky, Tom Mitchell, Annette Saddik, William Jay Smith, and Katherine Weiss.

I owe a considerable debt to the actors and friends who worked with me on a production of *The Glass Menagerie* for the Leiden English Speaking Theatre in the Netherlands. In particular, Marjoleine Huigen, Jenny Mijnhijmer, Jos van der Steen, Rick and Kathy van Vliet, and Cecile Verburg were wonderfully supportive.

In St. Louis, working on the productions of *Me, Vashya* and *The Glass Menagerie*, Lindsay Brill, Emmet Grosland, Laura Harrison, Dan Hirsh, Tommy Honton, Rob McLemore, Tara Neuhoff, and Shelley Orr taught me more about Williams than they can imagine.

Dakin Williams was of indispensable assistance in helping us launch our 2004 symposium on Tennessee's "secret year." His kindness and support were deeply appreciated.

The annual Tennessee Williams Literary Festival in New Orleans has provided me with myriad opportunities to test out my ideas about Williams's work, and I am particularly grateful to Robert Bray's generous stewardship of the Scholar's Conference over decades.

Finally, I want to thank Washington University's Center for the Humanities and the University of Texas at Austin's Harry Ransom Center for generously awarding summer research stipends to assist with my research.

Abbreviations

AG   *All Gaul Is Divided*, in *"Stopped Rocking" and Other Screenplays* (New York: New Directions, 1984).

BIW   *Beauty Is the Word, Missouri Review* 7, no. 3 (1984): 185–95.

CC   *A Lovely Sunday for Creve Coeur*, in *The Theatre of Tennessee Williams*, vol. 8 (New York: New Directions, 1992).

CP   *The Collected Poems of Tennessee Williams*, edited by David Roessel and Nicholas Moschovakis (New York: New Directions, 2002).

CS   *Collected Stories* (New York: New Directions, 1985).

CSH   *Clothes for a Summer Hotel*, in *The Theatre of Tennessee Williams*, vol. 8 (New York: New Directions, 1992).

CttS   *Candles to the Sun* (New York: New Directions, 2004).

CWS   *The Chalky White Substance*, in *"The Traveling Companion" and Other Plays*, edited by Annette J. Saddik (New York: New Directions, 2008).

FK   *Fugitive Kind* (New York: New Directions, 2001).

GM   *The Glass Menagerie*, in *The Theatre of Tennessee Williams*, vol. 1 (New York: New Directions, 1971).

HFH   "His Father's House," *Tennessee Williams Annual Review*, no. 7 (2005): 5–13.

HM   *Hot Milk at Three in the Morning, Missouri Review* 7, no. 3 (1984): 196–200.

HMS   *A House Not Meant to Stand* (New York: New Directions, 2008).

LG   *The Long Goodbye*, in *"27 Wagons Full of Cotton" and Other One-Act Plays* (New York: New Directions, 1966).

M   *Memoirs* (New York: New Directions, 2006).

MT   *The Magic Tower*, in *"The Magic Tower" and Other One-Act Plays*, edited by Thomas Keith (New York: New Directions, 2011).

N   *Notebooks*, edited by Margaret Bradham Thornton (New Haven: Yale University Press, 2006).

NAN   *Not About Nightingales* (New York: New Directions, 1998).

NSE   *New Selected Essays: Where I Live*, edited by John S. Bak (New York: New Directions, 2009).

OE   *The One Exception*, in *"The Traveling Companion" and Other Plays*, edited by Annette J. Saddik (New York: New Directions, 2008).

PT   *The Pretty Trap*, in *"The Magic Tower" and Other One-Act Plays*, edited by Thomas Keith (New York: New Directions, 2011).

SatL   *Summer at the Lake*, in *"Mister Paradise" and Other One-Act Plays*, edited by Nicholas Moschovakis and David Roessel (New York: New Directions, 2005).

SL   *The Selected Letters of Tennessee Williams*, edited by Albert J. Devlin and Nancy M. Tischler, vol. 1, *1920–1945* (New York: New Directions, 2000).

SLS   *Suddenly Last Summer*, in *The Theatre of Tennessee Williams*, vol. 3 (New York: New Directions, 1972).

SND   *A Streetcar Named Desire*, in *The Theatre of Tennessee Williams*, vol. 1 (New York: New Directions, 1971).

SR   *Stopped Rocking* in *"Stopped Rocking" and Other Screenplays* (New York: New Directions, 1984).

SS   *Spring Storm* (New York: New Directions, 1999).

SttR   *Stairs to the Roof* (New York: New Directions, 2000).

SU   *Something Unspoken*, in *The Theatre of Tennessee Williams*, vol. 6 (New York: New Directions, 1981).

TH   *In the Bar of a Tokyo Hotel*, in *The Theatre of Tennessee Williams*, vol. 7 (New York: New Directions, 1981).

BLUE SONG

Introduction

IN 2011, PEOPLE all over the world celebrated the centennial of the birth of the man many regard as America's greatest playwright, Tennessee Williams. Theatre festivals, literary conferences, and special exhibitions abounded, including events in those places most closely associated with Williams's life and career: New Orleans, New York City, Key West, and Provincetown. However, there were also celebrations in less obvious places, such as Austin, Texas, and Nancy, France, while in Paris, *A Streetcar Named Desire* was presented in an avant-garde production at the Comédie-Française—meaning that Williams's masterpiece became the first American play produced there in the history of "La Maison de Molière," founded in 1680.

It was not surprising to see Williams's life and work celebrated in his adopted home of New Orleans, the city he often spoke of as his spiritual home, the decadent, bohemian palace of freedom he discovered was his natural ambience. Just weeks after his arrival in the "City That Care Forgot," Williams wrote his mother revealingly: "I already know twice as many people here as I ever knew in St. Louis" (*SL*, 147). But in contrast to myriad celebrations held around the world, what was perhaps most extraordinary was that there was literally *nothing* done to celebrate Williams's legacy in the place he called home longer than any other: St. Louis, Missouri.

Even today, many inhabitants of St. Louis do not realize that the author of American classics such as *A Streetcar Named Desire* or *Cat on a Hot Tin Roof* spent his formative years in their city. And if they do know about the connection between the writer and St. Louis, their refrain commonly is "Yes, but he hated it here, didn't he?" In the initial year of the Tennessee Williams Festival St. Louis, 2016,

3

residents seemed to think of the playwright as a rude interloper at a private party: since the ill-mannered fellow did not enjoy the food or company, he certainly would not be invited back.[1]

Until quite recently, with the advent of the festival, Williams's reputation has been treated with the kind of snobbery that his mother, Edwina, complained of upon her arrival in the city in 1918—expressing feelings that, as we shall see, she was also not shy about communicating at the time to her two young children, Rose and Tom. However, as this study seeks to demonstrate, Tennessee Williams's history with St. Louis was much more complex than his mother's bitterness or inability to climb the social ladder might suggest. It was even more complicated, perhaps, than the playwright himself understood.

This book is an attempt, not so much to correct the record about Williams's dislike of St. Louis, but to argue that the city was—for a plethora of reasons—absolutely indispensable to his formation and development as a person and an artist. Not only were the years of his later childhood, adolescence, and young adulthood spent there—years of crucial importance to anyone, and certainly to any artist—but Williams remained emotionally tethered to the city for the rest of his life. Indeed, since he is buried in the city's Calvary Cemetery, it may be said that his connections to St. Louis, however unintended, transcend the span of his natural lifetime.

The irony of Williams's burial in a city he openly despised, in a cemetery belonging to the faith to which he had virtually no connection, Catholicism, has been noted by numerous biographers and critics. Yet the location of his final resting place is far more apposite than many suppose, epitomizing the extraordinarily complex relationship between an artist and the city that imprisoned his psyche, even as it paradoxically—and even perversely—nourished and helped him liberate his art. Even when the subject of his work seems to be elsewhere—New Orleans or Mississippi, for example—the world he inhabited and the family he grew up with in St. Louis were never far from his imagination. For better or worse, St. Louis was *always* with him.

This book is not intended as a biography. For the reader interested in taking the remarkable journey into the heart of darkness that was the life of Tennessee Williams (1911–1983), there are several excellent options available.[2] Rather, this study has a more restricted trajectory. Its intention is not to detail a life but to clarify the importance of a city in the life and works of Tennessee Williams. Because so much of this writer's work was forged in a crucible of anger and self-conscious rebellion against both family and home, the role of the despised city of "Saint Pollution,"[3] as he called it, has incorrectly been assumed to be small. However, precisely because Williams needed to escape the hated city to achieve self-actualization as man and writer, the reader of his plays, poems, and stories *must* understand how this particular midwestern city helped shape his vision. St. Louis, for better or worse, cannot be ignored as an indispensable piece of the puzzle of Williams's art. If John Lahr's biography concludes by observing that his entire oeuvre was a "game of hide-and-seek . . . played with the world," then the city in which he lived longer than any other offers a lengthy series of clues along the "trail of beauty" we must follow to find him.[4] As the Williams poem "Cried the Fox," inspired by his early idol D. H. Lawrence, suggests, Williams perceived the artist as something of a trickster, leading the pack of dogs hunting him (his critics and readers) on a wild, anarchic chase:

> I run, cried the fox, in circles
> narrower, narrower still,
> across the desperate hollow,
> kirting the frantic hill
> . . . .
> calling the pack to follow
> a prey that escaped them still. (*CP*, 6–7)

Understanding the role played by the city he grew up in and left (and returned to again and again) is central to our finding where this enigmatic fox is hidden.

Chapter One

Without Contraries Is No Progression

It bore a shield and elevated a sword. The look was fierce and compelling. Who was this stranger, this menacing giant on horseback? Her eyes descended to gaze at the description. *Saint Louis* it said.

Tennessee Williams, "Oriflamme"

"NEVER LET ME catch you stealing again!" These were the first words seven-year-old Tom Williams heard spoken in St. Louis—and they were spoken to him by his own father. Cornelius Coffin Williams, known as C.C., met young Tom and his mother, Edwina, on a sweltering day in July 1918 at St. Louis's Union Station, and as they left the cavernous building and passed a nearby fruit stand, the child snatched at a grape and was immediately slapped and punished for his indiscretion. That slap was not only predictive of the hostile and terrifying relationship with his father that was to ensue in the coming years, it established an animus toward the city that became forever associated with restrictions on his personal freedom. No matter how much he tried to attain freedom in body or spirit in the future, the city's formidable shadow always loomed, reminding Tom of what he tried to leave behind. It is little wonder that his personal motto became "En avant!" Both as a child and as an adult, his life's goal was always to go forward, leaving behind places that restricted his freedom, firstly St. Louis.

This sentiment is reflected in the early short story "Oriflamme,"[1] which concerns a tubercular young woman named Anna confronting the restrictions of the city. After weeks of dangerous illness, Anna awakens with a newfound resolve to flee the "conspiracy of dullness" in the city that has kept her imprisoned "in the economy basement of Famous-Barr," the well-known St. Louis department store where she works (*CS*, 128, 129). The story's narrator informs us that the city has robbed Anna of "the natural anarchy of [her] heart" and has compelled it instead to "wear uniform" (*CS*, 128). In an act of sudden rebellion, Anna splurges and buys a red silk dress, "all wine and roses flung onto her body" (*CS*, 131), which (as suggested by the story's original title, "The Red Part of a Flag") symbolizes her rejection of the uniformity and repression that traps her. Her delirious ascent eventually takes her to the city's summit, "the highest point in the park," where she encounters a fatal antagonist: "The terrible horseman over the heads of people was image enough of what she felt in the city. Her hope had died in a basement of this city. Her faith had died in one of its smug churches. Her love had not survived a journey across it. She would not turn to face the sprawling city" (*CS*, 133).

The gigantic soldier that confronts Anna in an approximation of martial combat is, of course, the commanding equestrian statue known as *Apotheosis of St. Louis*, which is perched atop Art Hill just north of the famed Saint Louis Art Museum, and overlooking the Grand Basin.

After Anna's encounter with the "terrible horseman," symbol of the city of St. Louis, where she feels "her hope had died in a basement," her feverish optimism fades. She goes to a fountain for a drink and finds that, as with the city itself, the fountain is not what it seems; it is just a cement bowl for sparrows that contains "only a few oak leaves disintegrating" (*CS*, 133). Concluding that "even the sparrows find it a false invitation," Anna sits exhausted and, moments later, is transformed into another sort of fountain, the "foam of a scarlet ocean cross[ing] her lips" (*CS*, 133). The conclusion of "Oriflamme" is unmistakable: the poor woman is doomed by the city, and her ability to act on "the natural anarchy of the heart" has proven illusory. The city itself, unmistakably personified by the forbidding architecture of the department store, equestrian statue, and bone-dry birdbath, is the antagonist that kills a free spirit in Williams's story.

Figure 1.
*Apotheosis of
St. Louis*, in
Forest Park.
1906. Official
Photographic
Company.
Identifier:
P0166-595-
4g. Courtesy
of the Missouri
Historical
Society.

Like Anna, who is defeated in her battle to leave St. Louis, Williams waged a lifelong struggle to quash the city's deadening effect on his spirit. The Narrator, Tom, in *The Glass Menagerie*, generally recognized as one of Williams's most autobiographical works, is also bent on escaping the city's confines. He argues to his mother, "Man is by instinct a lover, a hunter, a fighter, and none of those instincts is given much play at the warehouse!" But Tom is restrained from his desire for freedom by his mother, who represents the city's dampening and restrictive code of bourgeois morality: "Man is by instinct! Don't quote instinct to me! Instinct is something that people have got away from! It belongs to animals!" (*GM*, 174).

As Anna does in "Oriflamme," Tom tries to leave the city at the end of the play and is seemingly more successful: "I left St. Louis.

I descended the steps of this fire escape for the last time" (*GM*, 236). However, in both these autobiographical works, real escape ultimately is unachievable. The forces driving the writer to escape, to live by "the natural anarchy of the heart," are insufficient.

Williams was addicted to escaping St. Louis from first to last. It was the great triumph of his life that, unlike his sister, he did manage to literally leave it behind. His career as a writer allowed him to go to New York, New Orleans, Provincetown, Key West, and a host of other places where he flourished for a time. However, it was his life's tragedy that for all his desperate attempts, Tom Williams never really left home. The imagination and willpower that allowed him to devote his life to writing also kept forcing him to return home again in his imagination. The consummate irony of his final resting place is that it underscores the fact that this man who perpetually identified himself with "the fugitive kind," who was always traveling or tormented by demons, had his dead body brought back to St. Louis by his brother. And it is there where he yet lies, beside the graves of his mother, brother, and sister, in Calvary Cemetery.

In the previously discussed poem "Cried the Fox," dedicated to D. H. Lawrence, a writer who more than any other proclaimed the need to obey the animal vitality lying dormant in man, Williams forecast the tragic arc of his entire life.[2] He identified not merely with the fugitive fox that leads hunter and hounds on a frenzied chase, but with the fox itself condemned to return "in circles / narrower, narrower still" until at last its "brush hangs burning / flame at the hunter's door." This image of circularity, of a "fatal returning," offers a central metaphor for the author's life (*CP*, 6–7).

The singular desire that motivated Thomas Lanier Williams in his life and work was to escape the clutches of the city in which he was raised and, to his way of thinking, imprisoned. To this end, he changed his name, altered his birthdate, and tried to live according to his motto, "En avant!" This lifelong aspiration was epitomized by his fervent wish to be buried at sea rather than in the sterile and polluted wasteland where he came of age. Reality, however, proved quite different.

In the early story "His Father's House" (not published until 2005), written from the viewpoint of an adult with the mental capacity of a child, Williams seemed to intuit the terrifying fate that awaited him. The story begins with the boy being sent away from school—"I did not feel that I was like the other boys any more"—and mercilessly taunted by his smaller classmates:

> Why don't you go to school any more? one of them asked me.
>   I didn't know what to say. I only looked down at his shoes that were brightly polished and so much smaller than mine. (HFH, 5)

In his foreword to this undated story, which was signed Thomas Lanier Williams and surely dates from Tom's later St. Louis period, about 1937, Robert Bray connects the story with Williams's painful childhood experience at the Eugene Field Elementary School—a time "when he was ridiculed for his southern accent and somewhat effete mannerisms."[3] But this profoundly disturbing story is more than a recollection of the author's unhappy school days; rather, its grotesque fusion of childhood outcast and deranged, amoral adult suggests that Williams was preternaturally aware of who he was—a child/man whose search for love could never be satisfied, a damaged soul whose memories were dominated by horrific images of domestic violence leading him irrevocably back to the place where he began, a terrifying place fraught with images of violence, madness, and death—"his father's house."

The unnamed boy in the story is "bigger than any of the teachers" and even has whiskers (HFH, 5). Since his mother has been murdered by his absent father, the orphaned boy lives with his uncle. He longs to make sense of the strange world he has been thrust into but is completely unable to comprehend it. He begs to see his father, but is told by the uncle (who keeps a whip close at hand to control the boy's animalistic impulses) that the father "is like a wild beast. He would tear you to pieces with his hands!" (HFH, 6). Like the savage but guiltless creature in Mary Shelley's *Frankenstein*, who has similarly been abandoned by his father/creator, the boy is at once innocent and capable of destruction. Told that his father loved his mother but has cut her to pieces with an axe, he laughingly asks, "Was that the way I was born?" The question is met by a slap across the face and the uncle tells the boy, "Get out, you monster" (HFH, 7).

The boy meets a girl in the street, and he experiences sexual desire, but, again like Shelley's creature, he is unable to comprehend or articulate his feelings: "Holding her in my arms was strange. It was like wanting to eat but having no mouth to put food in" (HFH, 7). Having experienced rejection by the girl, he seeks out death by attempting suicide through slashing his wrists but is rescued by his uncle. The boy's response is, "You should have let me die. . . . There is another sore inside of me that the doctor cannot sew up" (HFH, 8). Following the attempted suicide, he is brought to a priest, who teaches him about Jesus Christ and the crucifixion. The boy is excited beyond all measure: "I would like to have been there! . . . I would like to have driven the nails!" he says (HFH, 8).

When he informs his uncle that he wishes to go to the country to learn to "build something with [his] hands" (HFH, 9), his uncle takes him to a vacant plot of land formerly owned by his father. He provides the boy with a black servant, Jim, to cook his meals and assist him in his secret desire to build. As Jim cooks their supper, the boy finds a pile of rusted tools in the barn and works fanatically all night to complete a project that is "hidden like a picture in one man's brain that no other man could see" (HFH, 10). In the morning the boy has finished and wakes Jim up to show him what he was wrought. When Jim comes out to view the work, an enormous cross, the boy beats him with the hammer and nails him, still living, to the cross. The description of Jim's crucifixion combines grisly horror and childlike innocence in equal measure:

> But he couldn't get loose. Only his blood could get loose. His blood was not black like his skin. His blood was red and it splashed in little fountains from his hands and feet, shining in the sunlight and splattering over the little blue and gold flowers that covered the earth. (HFH, 12)

The next day, the boy enthusiastically presents his accomplishment to the uncle ("I've made the black Christ!") and is immediately taken away to an asylum: "The house looked big and dark as though one could get lost in it and never find his way out. The windows were covered with bars. I didn't want to go into this house of my father's. I lay down in the garden and began to cry." The story concludes with the uncle dragging the boy from the garden and uttering the final, chilling words, "Every man must live in his father's house!" (HFH, 13).

Combining horror story, fairy tale, and parable, "His Father's House" is a revealing examination of a mind that is naïve and savage in equal measure. It is written with a remarkable simplicity of tone, mirroring the boy's deranged, damaged perspective. And while the story offers some specific images directly from the writer's own childhood (the girl instructing the awkward boy to dance is clearly derived from the lessons his older sister, Rose, provided him as a child) and adolescence—the foreboding image of the sanitarium, his father's violent temper, and the threat of physical abuse—it more accurately conveys the young writer's premonition of his St. Louis years as a road inevitably winding back to a place of anxiety, violence, and inchoate fear: "his father's house."

* * * * *

From a very young age, Tom Williams disliked the place he would later call "Saint Pollution." Coming from tiny, rural Clarksdale, Mississippi, at age seven, he found the large manufacturing city polluted and noisy. Lest we think Williams's reference to Saint Pollution was mere hyperbole or a reflection solely of the writer's emotional state, it should be noted that during this time St. Louis was one of the most polluted cities in the entire country due to its heavy reliance on bituminous (soft) coal for heat, business, and transport. While an 1893 ordinance forbade the emission of thick gray smoke within corporate limits, the regulation was essentially ignored, even after the passing of a smoke ordinance in 1937 created a Division of Smoke Regulation in the city's Department of Public Safety. Despite a number of attempts to eliminate the problem, including the mayor's appointment of his own secretary to oversee the issue, it was only after disaster suddenly struck in the form of "the day the sun didn't shine" (November 28, 1939) that real change was initiated.

On what became known as "Black Tuesday," a meteorological inversion trapped coal emissions close to the ground, blanketing the entire city in black smoke, a condition that recurred on several days in the following weeks.

Figure 2. "Saint Pollution." St. Louis at midday on the infamous "Black Tuesday," November 28, 1939. Identifier: N14587. Courtesy of the Missouri Historical Society.

This dramatic event, during which streetlamps were required all day, accompanied by a series of blistering articles in the *St. Louis Post-Dispatch*, finally led to the prohibition of burning the cheap, soft coal.

In his poem "Demon Smoke," written in 1925 at age fourteen while he was attending Ben Blewett Junior High, Williams describes the

crash and clap of Olive Street
Where nature and man's work compete
For mastery in the dingy sky;

Where clouds of smoke
And jets of steam
Defy pure air and sunlight's gleam. (*CP*, 214)

Later, in the autobiographical story "Portrait of a Girl in Glass," Williams depicts a character based on his sister opening a window to view the stars; but "as usual during Saint Louis winters," he writes, the sky was "completely shrouded by smoke" (*CS*, 114).

The narrative arc of Williams's life might be interpreted as one long attempt to leave this "demon smoke" behind, but it was only partly the city's polluted atmosphere that was to blame for his dread of the place. His true antagonists lay not in the physical city but within his own family. Prior to the move to St. Louis in 1918, C.C. Williams had been constantly on the road, a traveling salesman selling clothing in towns throughout the Mississippi Delta for a Knoxville clothing manufacturer. Cornelius's absence allowed the family to live in harmony under the benevolent roof of Edwina's parents' rectory, where the children, Rose and Tom,[4] were spoiled as rector Walter E. Dakin's grandchildren. Indeed, Williams biographer Lyle Leverich describes Tom growing up more as "a minister's son than the son of a traveling salesman, whom he scarcely recognized as a father."[5] Once C.C. received a promotion to work in St. Louis for the International Shoe Company and stayed at home full time, however, the Williams family experienced life together for the first time. Lacking the Dakins' emollient influence, the atmosphere immediately changed into one of perpetual fear and anxiety for both children.

Hostilities between husband and wife that had lain dormant in the Dakin rectory in Clarksdale now were overt. During the period Williams called St. Louis home, from 1918 to 1938, the family moved nine times; but wherever they moved, they remained unhappy. C.C.'s drunkenness, gambling, and penury were constant topics of violent disagreement—along with his vocal complaints about his wife's aversion to anything having to do with sex. However, if C.C. dominated "almost everyone who entered his limited sphere of influence," as Leverich notes, the great exception was the tiny

Figure 3. The "happy" family in St. Louis. Photo reference: MS Thr 553 (42). Courtesy of the Harvard Theatre Collection, Houghton Library, Harvard University.

Miss Edwina, "his indomitable mate," and so the antagonism went on unabated.[6]

While the geographic distance from Clarksdale to St. Louis was only some 350 miles, the shift in the children's lives was seismic. Gone was the serenity and security of a tiny, rural village in the deep South, and in its place was a huge, polluted metropolis in the Midwest. Then known as "Shoe City," St. Louis was the nation's shoe manufacturing capital, and the International Shoe Company, where C.C. had been hired to run the Friedman-Shelby division, was the largest shoe manufacturer in the world. As the Williams family emerged from the vaulting brick edifice of Union Station that July morning in 1918, they would have been greeted by the unfamiliar stench of coal dust and smoke, and the alien sight and sound of

Figures 4a, 4b. A tale of two cities: the Clarksdale, Mississippi, train station in 1918, the year Tom left Mississippi (courtesy of the Mississippi Department of Archives and History), and St. Louis's majestic Union Station, ca. 1930s (photograph by Russell Froelich, identifier: N34529, courtesy of the Missouri Historical Society).

motorcars. It is not unlikely that Edwina and Tom felt they had been uprooted from paradise to be transported into hell.

Born in Ohio, Edwina Dakin was a lively, intelligent, and beautiful girl, and she grew into one of the most eligible debutantes in Columbus, Mississippi. She quickly took on the privileged status

Figure 5. Edwina Dakin Williams in 1936. Courtesy of the Tennessee Williams Collection, Harry Ransom Center, University of Texas at Austin.

of a southern belle, and it was a role she not only accepted and learned with alacrity but continued to perform for the rest of her life. Indeed, she modeled it so well that her son was able to use her speech and mannerisms to depict the southern belle par excellence Amanda Wingfield in *The Glass Menagerie*, a role his mother never acknowledged as even remotely resembling herself. In her memoir *Remember Me to Tom*, Edwina describes her first meeting with Laurette Taylor, the legendary actress who created Amanda first in Chicago, then later on Broadway:

I entered Laurette's dressing room, not knowing what to expect, for she was sometimes quite eccentric. . . . Before I had a chance to get out a word, she greeted me.

Well, how did you like you'seff, Miz' Williams? she asked.

I was so shocked I didn't know what to say. It had not occurred to me as I watched Tom's play that *I* was Amanda.[7]

Figure 6. Laurette Taylor as Amanda in the Broadway premiere of *The Glass Menagerie* in 1945. Taylor's inscription on the photo reads: "I led the cottillion [*sic*]—I won the cake walk prize—and wore this dress to the governor's ball—when I was a girl in Blue Mountain." Laurette Taylor Papers, Harry Ransom Center, University of Texas at Austin.

Twenty years after the show's opening in 1944, Edwina was still protesting: "I think it is high time the ghost of Amanda was laid. I am *not*
Amanda. I'm sure if Tom stops to think, he realizes that I am not. The
only resemblance I have to Amanda is that we both like jonquils."[8]

Her vehement protests to the contrary, it is obvious that not only
was Edwina the prototype for Amanda Wingfield but her habit of
relentless conversation was something that even Tom's friends were
aware of. One of Williams's closest friends at Washington University
was Clark Mills McBurney (who had already published under the
name "Clark Mills" by then), and in recalling a visit to their home,
Mills observed,

> Mrs. Williams *never stopped talking*. It was a nightmare, just
> yammer, yammer, yammer, to the point you were ready to
> go through the ceiling. From the distance, it had its comical
> aspect, but close up, watch out: It was absolutely destructive.
> Mrs. Williams as a social figure had an element of lunacy about
> it—it had no connection with reality except in a grotesque
> way—all that talk about her elegant past and their southern
> gentility. I couldn't find any redeeming quality in her at all. To
> me, the word *nightmare* is strictly applicable, because she *was* a
> nightmare.[9]

Another close friend from their days at Washington University was
the distinguished poet William Jay Smith. Smith (who in his nineties
wrote a memoir about Williams's poetic gifts, *My Friend Tom*) noted
that Edwina "presided over [her home] as if it were an antebellum
mansion":

> A busy little woman, she never stopped talking, although there
> was little inflection or warmth in the steady flow of her speech.
> One topic, no matter how trivial, received the same emphasis
> as the next, which might be utterly tragic. I had the impression
> listening to her that the words she pronounced were like the
> red balls in a game of Chinese checkers, all suddenly released
> and clicking quietly and aimlessly about the board.[10]

Figure 7. Doting mother
and son in Clarksdale,
Mississippi. Photo
reference: MS Thr
553 (2). Courtesy of
the Harvard Theatre
Collection, Houghton
Library, Harvard
University.

Despite his mother's deleterious effects on his and his sister's lives,
Williams probably would have acknowledged that his mother's love
of language and histrionic delight in extravagant storytelling were
deeply embedded in his own nature from early on. Williams also
took from his mother her inveterate disdain for St. Louis, particularly St. Louis society, which was based largely on her failure to find
a social position equivalent to what she possessed in Columbus and
Clarksdale as the rector's beautiful daughter. She instilled in both

her older children the notion that St. Louis was a snobbish place from which they all had been excluded as southerners:

> Social status in St. Louis depended on how much money you possessed. This was not true of the Mississippi and Tennessee towns where we had lived. There you could have very little money and still hold a superior place in the community. . . . The line was quite impassable; you were either born to the purple or you were not. Which, of course, was rather unfair if you didn't happen to inherit the proper social niche.[11]

It is striking that Williams seems to echo his mother's accusations about St. Louis in his own description years later of the family's move from Westminster Place to their residence on South Taylor:

> It was a radical step down in the social scale, a thing we'd never had to consider in Mississippi; and all our former friends dropped us completely—St. Louis being a place where location of residence was of prime importance. That, and going to a private school and belonging to the St. Louis Country Club or one of nearly corresponding prestige; attending Mahler's dancing classes and having the right sort of car. (*M*, 14)

It is difficult to read these words from mother and son without concluding that Tom was raised predisposed to find St. Louis an unpleasant place to live. Indeed, in 1947, years after he had become famous, he still maintained his antipathy for St. Louis, calling its inhabitants "cold, smug, complacent, intolerant, stupid and provincial" in an interview in the *St. Louis Post-Dispatch*.[12]

In her memoir, Edwina chronicles the family's many relocations, ending with her triumphant move (buoyed by half of the royalties from *The Glass Menagerie*) into a home of her own, just off upscale Wydown Boulevard on Arundel Place in the posh suburb of Clayton, "beyond the city line":

> Those first years in St. Louis were hard on us. We could not afford to buy a house in an exclusive neighborhood so we kept

trying to find roomier apartments, and houses for rent. We made nine moves in St. Louis—they say three moves is equal to a fire—before I bought the home where I now live on Wydown Boulevard in Clayton, a few houses beyond the city line, just west of Forest Park.[13]

Although the emotional contents of *The Glass Menagerie* reflect psychological realities that Tom undoubtedly felt, the Wingfields' tenement dwelling does not accurately reflect the Williams family's socioeconomic status in St. Louis, which was not one of poverty. Their apartment at 4633 Westminster, the family's second home in St. Louis, may have *seemed* to be in "an ugly region of hive-like apartments," as Edwina describes it, but even she was forced to concede that it "was no tenement. . . . No doubt, to an eight-year-old

Figure 8. *St. Louis Post-Dispatch* interview in which Williams calls the people of St. Louis "Cold, Smug, Complacent," December 22, 1947. Courtesy of the *St. Louis Post-Dispatch /* Polaris.

boy suddenly cut off from the spaciousness of a house and garden, the apartment loomed grim. It was long and narrow, six rooms and a bath, and Tom said he was allotted the worst room, . . . but at least he had a room of his own."[14]

In diametric contrast with his mother's and his own descriptions of their St. Louis years, the playwright's recollections of his earliest years in Mississippi read like an account of prelapsarian paradise. In her memoir, Edwina quotes from a "scrap of paper" on which an adult Tom "had written a few sentences about his early life":

Before I was eight my life was completely unshadowed by fear. I lived in a small Mississippi town. My mother and sister and I lived with our grandparents while my father travelled around the state, selling clothing to men. My sister and I were gloriously happy. We sailed paper boats in wash-tubs of water, cut lovely colored paper-dolls out of huge mail-order catalogs, kept two white rabbits under the back porch, baked mud pies in the sun. . . . And in the evenings, when the white moonlight streamed over our bed, before we were asleep, our Negro nurse Ozzie, as warm and black as a moonless Mississippi night, would lean above our bed, telling us in a low, rich voice her amazing tales about foxes and bears and rabbits and wolves that behaved like human beings.[15]

These recollections—harsh and unforgiving when considered in contrast to St. Louis, romanticized when referencing life in the South—reveal the polarity upon which the writer's life and personal mythology were forged. This idealized vision of the South is especially fascinating in light of the fact that just two years prior to their move to the Midwest, Tom had contracted Bright's disease, an acute form of nephritis from which he nearly died but which goes virtually unmentioned in his remembrance of life in the South. His mother, however, remembered: "For the better part of two years Tom could not use his legs. . . . That disease was a fearful thing. . . . I bought him a toy called the Irish Mail which permitted him to steer himself around the room without putting pressure on his legs."[16]

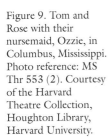

Figure 9. Tom and Rose with their nursemaid, Ozzie, in Columbus, Mississippi. Photo reference: MS Thr 553 (2). Courtesy of the Harvard Theatre Collection, Houghton Library, Harvard University.

The "sweet half-imaginary world in which my sister and our beautiful black nurse Ozzie existed" is rhapsodically described in *Memoirs* as being "separate, almost invisible to anyone but our little cabalistic circle of three" (11). But omitted from this reflection is the fact that Tom felt a deep sense of shame for his responsibility for Ozzie's abrupt departure. In the summer of 1916, just before she left for her annual trip home, Tom, then just five, called her "a big black nigger." Ozzie never returned to the Williams family.[17]

Although out of proportion with the time he actually spent in the South (especially in comparison with the decades in which he was living in or closely associated with St. Louis), Williams apparently needed to insist that Mississippi was in fact not merely the place of his birth but his *home*. It has been observed that "southerners have a sense of place, and a sense of place gives you a sense of self."[18] Williams required the sense of self that belonging to the South offered him. The location of course provided him with many of his greatest characters, but it also gave those characters an exotic past and a sense of history suggesting that, no matter how pitiful or downtrodden their present circumstances, there was once a time when things were different. Amanda (channeling Edwina Williams) reminds Jim O'Connor of this sense of loss in *The Glass Menagerie*: "Well, in the South we had so many servants. Gone, gone, gone. All vestige of gracious living! Gone completely! I wasn't prepared for what the future brought me" (*GM*, 204). In describing the tragic loss of Belle Reve in *A Streetcar Named Desire*, Blanche DuBois paints a similar picture of irretrievable loss: "The four-letter word deprived us of our plantation, till finally all that was left . . . was the house itself and about twenty acres of ground, including a graveyard, to which now all but Stella and I have retreated" (*SND*, 284).

As Kenneth Holditch argues, "The further removed he was from his childhood in Mississippi, the more those early years seemed transformed for him into an ideal time, an innocent and painless existence in which contentment was the order of the day."[19]

* * * * *

When asked in an onstage interview in New Orleans in 1978 what had originally sent him to the Crescent City, Williams replied simply, "St. Louis," later comparing the journey that led him to the exotic French Quarter as being like that of "a migratory bird going to a more congenial climate."[20] German behavioral scientists use the term *Zugunruhe* to describe a pattern of extreme restlessness in caged birds. These domestic species demonstrate their desire for migration by fluttering from one side of the cage to the other, emulating their wild species. Like these birds' instinctive need, a frantic restlessness was an essential part of Williams's makeup.

Immediately prior to his discovery of New Orleans, Williams's life was at its nadir. After failing to graduate from Washington University in St. Louis, he finally received his BA from the University of Iowa at age twenty-seven, and while convinced that his vocation was as a writer, he had neither job nor prospects, and following graduation he was right back where he had started—in dreaded St. Louis, at home, living with his parents. He briefly attempted to land work with the Federal Writers' Project in Chicago, but when that did not materialize, he returned home, looking for a job in radio that likewise proved unobtainable. Living in the city he despised, listening to his parents endlessly quarreling over money, sex, and his father's concealment of a bottle behind the tub in the bathroom, he wrote, "I feel uncomfortable in the house with Dad when I know he thinks I'm a hopeless loafer—Soon as I gather my forces (and I shall!) I must make a definite break—because this stagnation is debilitating my will—making me weak and timid again" (N, 125). He needed to escape, but it seemed impossible. Again referencing the wild birds that were to become such a ubiquitous symbol throughout his work, he wrote, "Surely I won't stay on here when I'm regarded as such a parasite—Now is the time to make a break—get away, away—I have pinned pictures of wild birds on my lavatory screen—Significant— I'm anxious to escape—But where & how?— . . . What a terrible trap to be caught in!" (N, 127).

In addition to life with a bullying, abusive father and a prim, puritanical mother, another shadow loomed—the specter of Rose, now diagnosed with dementia praecox, as schizophrenia was often still called then, and confined to a mental institution in Farmington, Missouri, seventy miles south of St. Louis. A visit to Rose in the sanitarium shortly before his departure for New Orleans completed the picture of unremitting horror from which escape was the only possible solution:

She is like a person half-asleep now—quiet, gentle and thank God—not in any way revolting like so many of the others—She sat with us in a bright sunny room full of flowers—said "yes" to all our questions—looked puzzled, searching for something— sometimes her eyes filled with tears—(So did mine)—Only the little dog stirred her. (N, 129)

Waking from this living nightmare into the freedom of the French Quarter must have been a jolt, offering both exhilaration and confusion. Traveling by bus, Williams headed south in December 1938, eyeing a possible job with the Works Progress Administration (WPA) in New Orleans, but, like his previous experience trying to relocate in Chicago, his efforts to find government work there once more proved illusory: "Oh, God, did I ever try to make that scene in Chicago and New Orleans and was I ever slapped down!"[21] On his way to New Orleans, he spent a night with his beloved grandparents in Memphis (where the Dakins had moved from Clarksdale) and the following morning mailed several scripts to a playwriting contest run by the Group Theatre in New York for writers under twenty-five. Employing the name "Tennessee" for the first time, he also deducted three years from his age of twenty-seven to maintain eligibility for the contest. Later, Williams justified the fabrication in words that reflected on his years in St. Louis; the three years were compensation for the nearly three years of "hard labor" he had endured (1932–1935) at the International Shoe Company when his father forced him to withdraw from the University of Missouri after he failed a compulsory class in the Reserve Officers' Training Corps (ROTC). Not until illness intervened in the form of nervous collapse had he been able to resign.[22] These acts of deliberate self-fashioning mean that Williams was expunging (or attempting to expunge) the identity of "Tom from St. Louis" and replacing him with a new and younger version of himself, "Tennessee Williams from Memphis." Like that of F. Scott Fitzgerald's character who leaves James Gatz behind to renew himself as Jay Gatsby, Williams's new identity "sprang from his Platonic conception of himself."[23]

And then there was New Orleans. The young man who had boarded the bus in St. Louis "dressed in a neat conservative suit, polished shoes, dress shirt and a tie" descended in New Orleans and registered himself at a rooming house using the name "Tennessee."[24] A mere three hours later, Williams had an astonishing presentiment of what the city might be able to offer: "I am delighted, in fact enchanted with this glamorous, fabulous old town. I've been here about 3 hours but have already wandered about the Vieux Carré and noted many exciting possibilities. Here surely is the place I was made for if any place on this funny old world" (*N*, 131).

His short story "In Memory of an Aristocrat" (written around 1940, but unpublished until it appeared posthumously in *Collected Stories* in 1985) is perhaps Williams's most thoroughgoing celebration of the life he discovered there. Nearly every aspect of the bohemian world is touched upon in this story—musicians, fortune tellers, cheap seafood, and the "boiling human sea" of Mardi Gras; small-time crooks who earn their money "conking queers" at night; prostitutes, painters, and impoverished writers like the author himself; and Quarter Rats, defined as "all those persons, creative or otherwise, who have wandered into the Quarter and remained there more or less permanently because of the fact that it is the cheapest and most comfortable place in America for fugitives from economic struggle" (*CS*, 80).

Irene, painter and prostitute, is the eponymous aristocrat of the story's title. An artist whose pictures "hit you right smack between the eyes with the force and precision that only comes from the fury of a first-rate talent" (*CS*, 85), Irene defines the bohemian ideal that Williams discovered in the city, and her savage rebellion against the elite at the Annual Spring Display forms the story's climax. Her paintings are brutally rejected for exhibition, her canvases "turned to the wall as though they stood there in shame" (*CS*, 88). Seeking to retrieve them before they are burned, she instigates a scuffle with the art world elite, and the ensuing pandemonium is comparable to an outbreak of plague.

Charges are filed against Irene, and although they are subsequently dropped, when the narrator returns to the Quarter the following spring she has vanished, and all that is left of her violent struggle against bourgeois respectability is a scrawled message on the wall of the studio bequeathed to her by the story's youthful narrator: "There is only one true aristocracy, . . . the aristocracy of passionate souls" (*CS*, 92). This, succinctly, was the truth Williams discovered in New Orleans.

But despite his immediate attraction to the city's magic, Williams's first visit to New Orleans lasted less than two months. He and Jim

Parrott, a musician friend, fled the city just at the start of Mardi Gras
on February 20, 1939, heading west toward California in Parrott's
jalopy. Why Williams left so quickly after discovering the French
Quarter's allure is something of a mystery, but a clue may be found
in a letter he later wrote to his agent, Audrey Wood: "I don't like
the crumby sort of Bohemian studio life that an impecunious writer
is subjected to in a large city—I got too much of that in the 'Vieux
Carré' and it's taken five months of California sunlight to fumigate
my soul" (*SL*, 179). Perhaps the Quarter was a bit *too* stimulating
for a writer beginning to discover both his vocation and his sexual
identity. The Quarter's "rotten-sweet odor . . . / so much like a
warning of what he would have to learn," powerfully described in
the poem "Mornings on Bourbon Street" (*CP*, 72–73), suggests
that despite its appeal, New Orleans was also threatening, its casual
hedonism diametrically at odds with the moral strictures he was just
beginning to try to leave behind in St. Louis.

In his journal, Williams describes a "rather horrible night" of an
"amorous advance" with "picked up acquaintance Doug" that left
him "sick at the stomach—Purity! Oh God—it is dangerous to have
ideals" (*N*, 153), suggesting that the newly birthed Tennessee was
still engaged in a struggle for supremacy with the Tom he had left
behind. For a sexually inexperienced young man raised in a puritanical, middle-class home by a mother for whom physical touch
was anathema, the charged atmosphere of New Orleans left him
completely confused about who he really was: "Am I all animal, all
willful, blind, stupid *beast*?" he wrote. "*Is* there another part that is
not an accomplice in this mad pilgrimage of the flesh?" (*N*, 133).

His first visit to the city may have been brief, but its allure brought
him shortly back. He returned in 1941, portentously alluding to the
Lawrence-inspired poem "Cried the Fox," quoted above:

The Second New Orleans Period here commences.
The much-bedeviled pilgrim—the fox who runs in circles—has
returned to one of those places that failed him (?) before.
He still looks for sanctuary.
Still hopes some new move will appease his unrest. (*N*,
231–33)

But this second stay did not simply "appease his unrest"; rather, Williams scholar Allean Hale notes, it turned into a remarkably productive period during which he completed "two long plays, at least eight one-acts, nine stories, and some New Orleans verse."[25] Within days of his first arrival in the city in late 1938, Williams had sent his grandmother a postcard with a map of the Quarter, enthusiastically writing her that his slogan "Meals for a Quarter in the Quarter" had been adopted as advertising copy for a new restaurant: "I serve as waiter, cashier, publicity manager, host— . . . sometimes dishwasher" (*N*, 136). He also noted that he had begun a new play about life in the Quarter. But by one week later, the Eat Shop had closed and his writing was faring no better: "I write badly or not at all—Started a marvelously promising new play last week—but can't seem to get going on it—Dull, dull!—I sit down to write & nothing happens. Washed up?" (*N*, 139).

That play, although begun back in January 1939, was not completed until 1977, as *Vieux Carré*. During a gestation of nearly four decades, New Orleans packed Williams's psyche with its singular characters and experiences, of which *A Streetcar Named Desire* is the epitome—a perfect symbiosis of city and artist. Reflecting in *Memoirs*, "I know of no other city where it is better to have a skylight then [*sic*] New Orleans," Williams remembered that he wrote *Streetcar* under ideal conditions while seated at a long refectory table in a third-floor study while the clouds, "fleecy and in continual motion," hung just overhead. In New Orleans, then, Williams felt close enough to think he could touch the clouds (*M*, 109). How very different from life in St. Louis, where the ubiquitous air pollution rendered the sky all but impossible to see.

It is tempting to look at the work of an artist only through the polish of what he allows us to know he discovered and created, not through what he discarded or rejected. However, as William Blake wisely observed in *The Marriage of Heaven and Hell*, "Without contraries is no progression. Attraction and Repulsion, Reason and Energy, Love and Hate, are necessary to Human existence."[26] The playwright owed an enormous debt to the "demon smoke" he inhaled at 6254 Enright Avenue in St. Louis. As will be evident, the obstacles he faced in St. Louis were every bit as meaningful to his achievement as his discovery of that miraculous skylight at 722 Toulouse Street in New Orleans. The two elements were equally necessary to make him the playwright he eventually became.

Chapter Two

A Fatal Need

The South once had a way of life I am just old enough to remember—a culture that had grace, elegance . . . an inbred culture . . . not a society based on money as in the North. I write out of regret for that.

Tennessee Williams

THE DUELING MYTHOLOGIES between a romanticized childhood "unshadowed by fear" in the deep South and a boyhood and adolescence spent in St. Louis beneath the penumbra of eternally quarreling parents, a doomed sister, and his tormented self defined the way Tennessee Williams perceived the world. When success did arrive—in stunning fashion—with the breakthrough of *The Glass Menagerie* in 1945, Williams brought along with him not merely his battered old typewriter but a deeply embedded narrative of who he was and how he managed to survive. Accordingly, two decades of his boyhood and adolescence in St. Louis were virtually expunged. For example, the playwright's biography in the Broadway *Playbill* for *Menagerie* read as follows:

TENNESSEE WILLIAMS was born in Columbus, Miss., in 1914 and lived in Episcopal rectories in the Mississippi Delta until he entered high school. He then became a typist for a large shoe concern, and he worked until he had saved up enough to go to college. He attended three universities—the U. of Missouri, Washington U. (St. Louis) and the U. of Iowa, where he got his degree in 1938.[1]

The only strictly accurate statements above are the place of his birth and the names of the universities he attended. The notion that he grew up in Episcopal rectories in the Delta until high school and the implication that he worked as a typist until leaving for college were, like the fictitious birth date of 1914, attempts at the creation of a Horatio Alger myth of a boy who left the Mississippi Delta and miraculously found himself on the Broadway stage. Such revisionist history is, of course, relatively harmless—but Williams's inaccurate narratives about his life before reaching the pinnacle of success have led the general public and even much of the critical establishment to take him at his word, resulting in the promulgation of a fable at the expense of the truth about where he spent so many of his formative years. If St. Louis may be accurately conceived of as the site of Williams's traumatic wound—his boyhood and adolescence under the thumb of a bullying father, with the care of a smothering mother, and affected by the unease of a mentally fragile sister—then the critic's responsibility should be to interrogate and mitigate false or misleading narratives. In the words of one of Williams's early mentors, D. H. Lawrence, "Never trust the artist. Trust the tale. The proper function of a critic is to save the tale from the artist who created it."[2]

Decades after reaching the highest levels of artistic celebrity, Williams remained loath to record or fully acknowledge his past. Following the publication of the playwright's deeply personal *Memoirs* in 1975, Washington University alumnus Shepherd Mead (author of *How to Succeed in Business Without Really Trying*, upon which the famous musical comedy was based) took Williams gently to task for one particular omission from his book: "He hides almost nothing in this extraordinary book of some 250 pages. . . . Everything is there, everything but that one unspeakable secret: he went to Washington University."[3] Mead was the editor of *The Eliot*, Washington University's literary magazine, to which Williams contributed many poems over a number of years before, during, and for some time after his time at the university. Williams was also on the staff while he was a student there.

The reasons for the playwright's reticence are not difficult to surmise. Aside from the unhappy circumstances of his departure from

Washington University, the image of a virtually unknown youth from tiny Clarksdale named "Tennessee" was bound to generate a more spectacular sensation than the arrival of Tom Williams, a young man from a middle-class family in the industrial Midwest. For a Broadway audience, Tennessee Williams's emergence from the Mississippi Delta evoked the world of William Faulkner's Yoknapatawpha County, antebellum mansions, cotton gins, Spanish moss, and cotillions. The association would also likely have resonated with viewers who had seen *Gone with the Wind* sweep the Oscars just a few years before. And such associations with a time of lost gentility and refined manners were echoed in the speech of that prototypical southern belle Amanda Wingfield, a woman who (like his mother, Edwina) was capable of making only angel food cake:

Gone, gone, gone. All vestige of gracious living! Gone completely! I wasn't prepared for what the future brought me. All of my gentleman callers were sons of planters and so of course I assumed that I would be married to one and raise my family on a large piece of land with plenty of servants. But man proposes—and woman accepts the proposal! (*GM*, 204)

St. Louis, by contrast, was a dirty metropolis, and, at the time of Williams's arrival, the fourth largest city in America, following New York, Chicago, and Philadelphia. It was best known for its shoe factories, heavy industry, breweries, and smog.

St. Louis also had a reputation for something else, however; and it was that from which the young Thomas Lanier Williams undoubtedly derived great, if unacknowledged, advantage: it had what social historian David Loth described as "the best city school system in the midwest, and by several years of national ratings it was considered one of the best school systems in all America. High school teachers quite regularly had doctorate degrees from the best universities in the country."[4]

Williams began his St. Louis years inauspiciously at the Eugene Field Elementary School, an enormous, ugly redbrick structure with the look and feel of a Dickensian prison, replete with two menacing watchtowers looming above the roof.

Figure 10. With its two prisonlike watchtowers, the Eugene Field Elementary School, where Tom was bullied as a child, was an intimidating structure. Photograph by George Stark, ca. 1900. Identifier: N33211. Courtesy of the Missouri Historical Society.

During his two years there, Williams felt so frightened that the words *public school* were enough to terrify him:

> I was scared to death of everyone on earth and particularly of public school boys and public school teachers and public school principals. That name, public school, kept stabbing at my guts till I wanted, as old as I was, to sit down and cry.[5]

At Eugene Field, Tom was teased by other children and embarrassed by his teachers for his distinctive southern accent: "Anybody can tell you're from the South—you're slow as molasses in January," they would say to him.[6] However, by age thirteen he was able to take full advantage of St. Louis's progressive educational system at Ben Blewett Junior High School. Blewett, a school for pupils in grades seven through nine, offered new educational opportunities he would never have been exposed to at school in the Mississippi

Delta. Blewett emphasized citizenship, student government, and school activities; it was a place where the students were subdivided into smaller groups based on intelligence, educational background, environment, and psychological testing. The school even had its own biweekly newspaper, *The Junior Life*, and it was there that the fourteen-year-old Williams had the thrill of seeing his name in print for the very first time with a first-person story, unsurprisingly titled "Isolated," in the November 7, 1925, issue. It was at Blewett that he began writing poetry, including the socially committed protest poem "Demon Smoke," and "Old Things," a moving portrait study of the survival of memory amid old age and physical decay:

> Old things—sallowed and hallowed,
> Grayed in the gloom;
> Things from the old life
> In the dusk of their tomb.
> This is the place for him and his dreams,
> His old gray head bowed over the remnants
> > Of days that are dead. (*CP*, 213)

In another (undated) early poem, "Look Both Ways Crossing Streets," Williams foreshadows his later work by satirically caricaturing his mother's well-known verbosity—a motif obviously suggestive of things to come:

> Now and then, with a dull resentment—
> With a weary, baffled sigh—I hear my heart enquiring why
>
> Every school day of the year
> Mother's voice I used to hear
>
> With such acute concern repeat,
> "Now, Tom, look both ways crossing streets!" (*CP*, 215–16)

Fifty years later, Williams still voiced resentment toward "Miss Edwina," whom he ridiculed as "a little Prussian officer in drag." Yet he also acknowledged her vast influence upon him: "She contributed a lot to my writing—her forms of expression, for example. And that underlying hysteria gave her great eloquence."[7]

During his deeply formative experience at Ben Blewett, where he chose as his eighth-grade electives Latin and art, and cited his planned curriculum for high school as "Classical," Williams began to catch a glimpse of his future vocation. And, following a single semester spent at Soldan High, the family moved again, to an apartment on Enright Avenue in University City, allowing Tom to enroll at the prestigious University City High School, where his literary credentials were burnished even brighter.[8]

Despite a rather mediocre academic record, Williams began to achieve literary celebrity while at University City High School. He published a short piece in the men's pulp magazine *Smart Set* and won third prize and five dollars. The piece is remarkable for its chutzpah as well as its imaginative reach. Responding to the

Figure 11. In the "Aud" at Soldan High School, Blewett Junior High and Soldan High pupils listen to a concert by the St. Louis Symphony, ca. 1933. Identifier: P0900-14648-01-8n. Courtesy of the Missouri Historical Society.

magazine's prompt "Can a Good Wife Be a Good Sport?" the sexually inexperienced sixteen-year-old wrote a letter masquerading as advice from the perspective of a dissatisfied husband who has decided to recount "[his] own unhappy experiences" in the hope of "present[ing] convincing answers" to others (*NSE*, 223). The aggrieved, hapless husband concludes that since his wife's being a "good sport" has led her to vices such as "drinking, smoking, and petting—staying up all night with boys at cabarets," he cannot support the notion that she can possibly be "that kind of 'good sport'" (*NSE*, 224). For this entry, Williams received tangible proof of his literary ability in the form of his cash prize, always important for a young man facing opposition from a penurious, judgmental father. While there is no record of what Cornelius's stunned response might have been, his sister, Rose, wrote, "Tom you are a wonder—simply wonderful and I'm proud to death of you," and his grandfather Dakin, while expressing pride in his grandson's accomplishment, shared with him, "*I* ruined my mind and memory by reading too much *trash*. . . . I have suffered all my days on account of it."[9] Furthermore, the rector warned his grandson, "*If* you continue to write to such magazines use a nom-de-plume instead of your own name" (*NSE*, 290).

The following year, 1928, Tom accompanied his beloved grandfather on a European tour with Reverend Dakin's parishioners. Prior to his departure, one of his teachers pushed him to keep a diary of his travels, initiating a habit he maintained for the rest of his life. After the trip, the teacher encouraged him to publish his travelogues in the *U City Pep*, the school's newspaper. Tom then acquired "a certain position among the student body, not only as the most bashful boy in school but as the only one who had traveled abroad" (*M*, 23). The trip lasted from the beginning of July to early September and included visits to London, Amsterdam, Cologne, Venice, Pompeii, and Paris, and Tom's notes from the trip provide ample evidence of the young man's maturing powers of observation and expression. These essays clearly demonstrate his command of language, as well as the benefits provided by the superior educational system he was exposed to in St. Louis.

Figure 12. Tom at fifteen, photograph dated May 1926. Courtesy of the Tennessee Williams Collection, Harry Ransom Center, University of Texas at Austin.

One particular essay in the *U City Pep* foreshadows the mature author's interest in the macabre and ghostly. Of a visit to the famous crypt in Rome, Tom notes in "The Tomb of the Capuchins" the feeling that "spirits of the dead can rise to avenge themselves for insults or indignities," describing in highly theatrical terms the vision spread out before him:

> Here, before our eyes, is a vast assemblage of those dead beings which in our early and timorous childhood we have fancied to be lurking in the depths of our blackest closets. . . . Here, in short, are those gruesome things which heretofore we have never been permitted to see except in our dreams. (*NSE*, 225)

When he returned to school after the trip abroad, Williams had already become a celebrity—he was by then a published author! A story he had submitted prior to the European trip had been accepted for publication by the pulp magazine *Weird Tales* in its August 1928 issue and was available on newsstands before his return. The story, titled "The Vengeance of Nitocris," for which the seventeen-year-old received thirty-five dollars, featured this bit of lurid copy for the prospective reader:

*Weird revenge was taken by
the sister of the Pharaoh on
those who had murdered him—
a true story of old Egypt*[10]

Based loosely on a story from Herodotus, "The Vengeance of Nitocris" is set in ancient Egypt and chronicles Queen Nitocris's grisly revenge for the untimely death of her brother, Pharaoh Osiris. The queen invites her royal brother's murderers to a lavish feast held in an underground chamber, then opens the sluice gates to the Nile, drowning them all. When confronted by the families of those she has killed, she cleverly eludes retribution by incinerating herself on a bed of burning coals. Although intentionally melodramatic and written in a deliberately archaic style ("Hushed were the streets of many peopled Thebes" [*CS*, 1]), "The Vengeance of Nitocris" anticipates many of the writer's central preoccupations, including a quasi-incestuous love between brother and sister and a fondness for spectacular, often horribly violent denouements. In the future, these would include cannibalism ("Desire and the Black Masseur," *Suddenly Last Summer*), rape (*A Streetcar Named Desire*), castration (*Sweet Bird of Youth*), and burning alive (*Auto-da-Fé*, *Orpheus Descending*). The connection between the adolescent story and everything that followed did not escape Williams's own attention. In an essay that served as the foreword to *Sweet Bird of Youth*, he observed, "If you're acquainted with my writings since then, I don't have to tell you that ["The Vengeance of Nitocris"] set the keynote for most of the work that has followed" (*NSE*, 94).

In his senior year at University City, Williams was invited to join the *Pep* staff and on the strength of the essays he published documenting his European travels was even invited to keep writing for the newspaper following graduation. Williams was now a published author, and (thanks in no small measure to the educational opportunities at University City High School) his ambition and reasons for optimism were considerable. In a letter to his grandfather, Williams describes his graduation tuxedo (purchased for him by his grandparents) and the prom he will attend. He also mentions his intention (no doubt pleasing to Reverend Dakin) to continue the study of

Figure 13. University City
High School graduation
photo of Thomas Lanier
Williams. Courtesy of
the Tennessee Williams
Collection, Harry Ransom
Center, University of Texas at
Austin.

Latin, so that he would have four full years under his belt before
starting college. Finally, in the same letter, Tom reveals his intention
to enroll in courses in shorthand and typewriting at a local business
college—all in preparation for entering the University of Missouri
in the fall. Despite the family's countless moves, and the anxiety of
growing up amid his parents' acrimony, at the time of his graduation
from the St. Louis public school system Tom Williams was clearly on
an upward trajectory toward success.

* * * * *

The roller-coaster decade spanning Williams's enrollment as a freshman at the University of Missouri–Columbia in 1929 through his
departure for New Orleans in late 1938 was the most formative
decade of the playwright's life—both emotionally and artistically.
While the decade was dominated by feelings of anxiety, inertia, and
depression, it also contained moments of inspiration and exhilaration. There were long stretches where he felt imprisoned and captive

to his family, but also periods where he felt the stimulation of like minds and tasted real artistic freedom for the first time. All these things happened during the decade when Williams considered St. Louis his home. It was the place he set out from, and the place to which (however grudgingly) he returned. For better or worse, St. Louis was the fixed point on the compass of his life. However unhappy he may have been during much of that time and however much he longed to escape, St. Louis was the tether that tied him to his parents, to his sister, and even to himself.

Perhaps the most remarkable thing about this decade of change was how conventionally it began. The last thing anyone would anticipate when viewing the arc of Tennessee Williams's career or life would be that this shy, diffident young man would be eager to join a college fraternity or that he would so enjoy becoming a pledge. But that is exactly what happened in October 1929, when he took the highly unusual step of writing a buoyant letter addressed to *both* his warring parents:

Dear Mother and Dad,

I have some very big news for you in this letter. I have just pledged the Alpha Tau Omega. They invited me to supper last night and afterwards took me up to the council chamber where I was asked to join the Frat, and offered a pledge pin. I have never accepted anything with more alacrity. I have been over to the A.T.O. house several times and I liked the fellows there a great deal. They are just completing a new chapter house— one of the finest on campus. I don't think I could have made a better Frat. (*SL*, 32)

Not only did Williams join the Alpha Tau Omega house, he took considerable pleasure in his involvement in fraternity life, lending credence to Allean Hale's observation that the "Columbia years were perhaps the most normal in his life."[11]

Williams enrolled in the university's prestigious School of Journalism, and the normally introverted young man actually went to dances and double dated with fraternity brothers, ran cross-country

for the ATO team, and bought riding breeches and took equitation—
he even participated in intramural wrestling as "Tiger" Williams.
The slight, 120-pound flyweight posted the following demand on
the ATO bulletin board prior to his bout with a couple of Missouri
farm boys: "Williams Ultimatum: Liquor! Liquor! Must have liquor
for my bout with the aggressive agrarians."[12]

Despite these apparently successful attempts at blending in with
normal fraternity life, Williams remained what he had been, a perpetual observer at heart. Since he had already won writing prizes in
high school, the University of Missouri's newspaper published an article on him headlined "Shy Freshman Writes Romantic Love Tales
for Many Magazines." The story was published in October 1929,
just after he entered the university, describing him as "intending to
be a journalist after his graduation from college," while offering this
prescient portrait:

> It bothers Mr. Williams to have anyone ask him questions about
> himself. He is little more than five feet tall. He has clean cut
> features and smooth brown hair. His eyes, which have a look
> that seems thousands of miles away, add to the unapproachable
> and reserved appearance which he presents. He is equally as
> reticent and shy as he appears.[13]

In *Memoirs*, Williams elaborates on this characteristic shyness: "I was
a very slight youth. I don't think I had effeminate mannerisms but
somewhere deep in my nerves there was imprisoned a young girl,
a sort of blushing school maiden much like the one described in a
certain poem or song 'she trembled at your frown.' Well, the school
maiden imprisoned in my hidden self, I mean selves, did not need a
frown to make her tremble, she needed only a glance" (17).

Much of Williams's incentive in joining ATO and trying to pass
himself off as a typical college freshman was to please his father, a
man he never succeeded in pleasing. Edwina notes in her memoir
that C.C. blamed Tom for everything, even that he "[sat] writing all
night and [ran] up the light bill."[14] Cornelius was a military man to
his core; he attended the Bell Buckle Military Academy in Tennessee
(describing it as "a school for bad boys"[15]), studied law for two years

at the University of Tennessee, then enlisted in the service for the Spanish-American War. Convinced that Edwina was spoiling his son and turning him into a sissy, C.C. terrorized both Tom and, with even more tragic consequences, his older sister, Rose.

Hoping to save him from his mother's deleterious influence, Cornelius was only too pleased to remove Tom from Edwina's reach when the time came for him to attend college, although she insisted on personally escorting him to Columbia to select "what she regarded as a suitable boarding house" for him to live in until he got settled.[16] The school required a course in ROTC, which appealed to C.C. as the ideal way of hardening his dreamy son. Meanwhile, Cornelius took pains to separate Tom from his first girlfriend, Hazel Kramer. Behind his son's back, he pressured Hazel's grandfather to make sure she and Tom attended different colleges so that the two would not spend more time together after high school graduation. While it is unclear exactly why C.C. disapproved of Hazel's companionship, he was aware that his son was always surrounded and being spoiled by women (his mother, his beloved grandmother, Rose) and was suspiciously lacking in male companions. Instead of participating in sports, he was compulsively scribbling in his room. For his father, Tom's relationship with Hazel, much like his son's incessant writing, seemed unmanly and impractical, something to be discouraged.

In fairness to Cornelius Williams, it ought to be noted that the collapse of the New York Stock Exchange hit on the 29th of October, just one month after Tom enrolled at Mizzou. The fact that C.C. allowed his son to stay in school while so many others forced their children to withdraw during the Great Depression certainly speaks to his credit. That he also encouraged his son to join the fraternity may be attributed both to his own vanity and to his hope for his son's emancipation from his mother. C.C. even wrote to a pair of young cousins at the ATO chapter at the University of Tennessee, where he had studied, encouraging them to advocate for his son's acceptance at the Columbia chapter, arguing that his boy was "descended from the Williamses and Seviers of East Tennessee, was a published writer and a traveller of the world."[17]

Once a member of ATO, Tom arranged to have his notoriously penurious father pay his expenses. In an ingratiating letter to his father, he wrote, "A non-frat man is practically 'out of it' in Columbia. . . . In business and social life after you are out of the University, belonging to a fraternity is still a very big asset" (*SL*, 32). Evidently, this strategy worked, at least for a while.

Williams's interest in members of his own sex was still of course a secret in those days, and in all probability his sexual preference was a secret he kept even from himself. Some forty-five years later, in his unabashedly outré *Memoirs*, Williams described in some detail his attraction to an ATO brother he calls "Smitty." Whether real, invented, or an amalgam of several boys is unclear, although it is quite possible that, as biographer Lyle Leverich surmises, Smitty was "a wishful feeling in the recesses of Tom's mind and a figment of Tennessee's imagination."[18] Williams admitted that his infatuation provided no "outlet for the physical side of the attachment, at least none that led to a release" (*M*, 31), and he was apparently never suspected or subjected to the ultimate disgrace in those days of being labeled a "fairy" by his fraternity brothers.

At the time Williams entered college, he was still in love with Hazel, who was two years younger, and on his first night in Columbia, Tom even wrote a letter from the boardinghouse to her, proposing marriage. Hazel, then a high school senior who may or may not have known about the plot her grandfather and Tom's father had hatched opposing the couple's plan to attend the University of Missouri together, wrote back saying they were far too young to consider marriage. Nevertheless, Williams called Hazel "the great extrafamilial love of my life" (*M*, 15).

Williams quickly lost interest in journalism. His first assignment was a report on the costs of local produce, and he had nothing but contempt for writing about the weights of hens, sour cream, and cheese. His second proved even more disastrous. Required to write an obituary of the wife of one of the university's professors, Williams carelessly reported that the person who had died was the professor himself, not his wife. Not surprisingly, he was immediately dismissed from the college paper. "They fired me, of course," Williams said. "I couldn't take journalism seriously."[19]

While journalism did not maintain his interest, writing did. Encouraged by an English professor, Robert Ramsay, Tom submitted his first play, *Beauty Is the Word*, to the university's Missouri Workshop Theatre during the 1929–1930 academic year, and this was followed in 1931–1932 by *Hot Milk at Three in the Morning*. Neither play won awards, but both short one-acts are revealing about the ways in which St. Louis had imprinted itself on the playwright's consciousness, foreshadowing so many later preoccupations. Gore Vidal observed that "Tennessee is the sort of writer who does not develop; he simply continues. By the time he was an adolescent he had his themes" (quoted in *BIW*, 186). This trenchant observation reveals why the term *juvenilia* is really not a meaningful or helpful distinction in examining the work of Williams. His writing follows a thematic continuity from first to last, irrespective of his age; Williams's earliest works are preoccupied with many of the same concerns as his later ones. Although his formal mastery evolved, there is a powerful through-line that connects such early works as *Beauty Is the Word* and *Hot Milk* with later achievements; this continuity is based on rebellion against both the place in which he came of age—St. Louis—and the people to whom he was most deeply bound—his parents.

Beauty Is the Word may be didactic and naïve in its advocacy of the primitive power of art and its celebration of the senses in overturning religious hypocrisy and outmoded beliefs, but its Romantic vision is entirely consistent with more sophisticated later works such as *Summer and Smoke, You Touched Me!* (the adaptation of the D. H. Lawrence story "You Touched Me," which Williams coauthored with Donald Windham), *Eccentricities of a Nightingale*, and the story "The Yellow Bird." The predicate for all these works (and others as well) is the same—outrage against the bourgeois repression of human instincts and the hypocritical attitudes he found in his own home, specifically in the person of his mother. These are cleverly satirized in the early poem discussed above, "Look Both Ways Crossing Streets":

With perfect filial subjection
I would glance in each direction,
. . . .
By virtue of this curious habit
I grew to be a model Babbitt,

With a wifey and a kiddie,
And a home just out of city.
Lots of shrewd wit beneath my hat,
Behind my belt, a little fat. (*CP*, 215–16)

Beauty Is the Word was apparently prompted by Williams's reading of the life of Percy Bysshe Shelley in 1928, but what made Shelley resonate for Williams in the first place was the poet's steadfast opposition to religion. Shelley arrived at Oxford University in 1810 and was expelled the following year by the university registrar for his obstinate refusal to answer questions and to disavow his publication *The Necessity of Atheism.*

Williams's play is set on a South Pacific island, where a missionary couple are engaged in trying to convert the natives to Christianity, essentially by blotting the joy from the indigenous people's lives. The opening stage directions depict the mission house where they reside as "depressingly sombre"; Mabel is sewing heavy black garments as coverings for the unclad bodies of the local inhabitants, while her husband, Abelard (ironically named after the Medieval French philosopher who saw *doubt* as the key to wisdom), fills the mission house with "Biblical quotations of a stern and threatening nature" (*BIW*, 187). The pair have taught the natives about the devil and the dangers of hell, but nothing about beauty—a word that is literally unknown to them. By comparison, their niece, Esther, appreciates and is able to celebrate the local customs, recognizing that "this is a land of freedom and joy" (*BIW*, 189). Faced with a rebellion from the indigenous people, Esther begins a dance to preach the "Gospel of Beauty" and by so doing prevents a planned attack from happening. The play is a straightforward plea for the power of art as a celebration of life in the face of a dreary and dogmatic adherence to religion.

Hot Milk at Three in the Morning, written during Tom's junior year at Mizzou, is even more rooted in the young man's experience of his home in St. Louis. The play concerns a married couple with a new baby trapped by poverty and unhappiness in an unspecified "Eastern city" (*HM*, 196). The brief play (so short it is more of a sketch than a one-act) is written entirely from the husband's perspective, and the opening stage directions clearly evoke Cornelius Williams's powerful, destructive presence entering the family's home:

> A door is opened and closed; footsteps sound; there is another impact with furniture accompanied by the sound of falling and shattering glass and a man's fierce, necessarily indistinguishable oath; a hand is laid violently upon the knob. . . . the door, thrown open, hits against and over-topples a piece of furniture; the man utters another oath under his breath. The door is slammed shut and the light is switched on. (*HM*, 196)

In his autobiographical essay "The Man in the Overstuffed Chair" (written in 1960), which serves as the preface to *Collected Stories* (1985), Williams describes C.C. in strikingly similar terms, entering the house "as though . . . with the intention of tearing it down from inside" (*CS*, vii). Near the end of the essay, he forgives the man who caused him so much hurt, suggesting that his father's cruelty toward him was born from feelings of pent-up frustration: "My father, Cornelius Coffin Williams, the Mississippi drummer, . . . was removed from the wild and free road and put behind a desk like a jungle animal put in a cage in a zoo" (*CS*, ix–x). In *Hot Milk*, the young father's rage is similarly a direct result of his lost freedom. Clearly echoing Tom's father's feelings of loss of freedom at moving from the road to a desk job, the young man, Paul, laments the loss of agency he once had as a lumberjack with an axe ("I tramped from Massachusetts to Oregon, and I tramped from Oregon to Alaska") before being turned into "a mill hand! A wage slave! A chained animal!" with "a skinny, yellow cat of a wife" and a bawling baby. In a remarkable stage image, even a loaf of bread mocks the man's captivity; it has a "thick, not-quite-amputated slice lopping from the end of it," giving it "the grotesque semblance of sticking out its tongue at the room and its abject occupant" (*HM*, 196). The man's anger and sense of pent-up frustration are the play's sole subjects; his wife, by contrast, is a woman whose once youthful charm has vanished into "the pathos of frailty," and her sickly yellow face "bears a look

of peevish stupidity" (*HM*, 197). At the end of the play, Paul forces
his wife out of the room and prepares to follow his dreams. He hears
the whistle of a passing train and is about to step over the threshold
into freedom when the baby's cry forces him to stop. As the cries
grow more shrill and insistent, the man reaches for a glass of hot
milk and his head sinks to his chest. The ecstatic smile that Paul wore
moments before as he approached the doorway now vanishes as he
sips his hot milk and resigns himself to his fate. Although rudimen-
tary (the play was expanded into the one-act *Moony's Kid Don't Cry*
in 1936 and became the first of Williams's plays to be published, in
1940), this little work is an agonizing portrait of the need to escape
the confines of home. This remained one of the playwright's most
ubiquitous themes.

Although a middling student at the University of Missouri, with
grades in the C+/B- range, Williams was on track to graduate until
his father discovered that he had failed ROTC in the spring of his
junior year, bringing disgrace upon the family name. Recalling that
the country was still feeling the ill effects of the Great Depression,
Edwina notes that "Cornelius was not about to put out one more
cent for Tom's education." As a result, her gifted son was conscripted
into the "world of dusting shoes, typing out factory orders and haul-
ing around packing cases stuffed with sample shoes, the world of his
father."[20] Sadly, after he departed Columbia, there were signs his creative work was appreciated there. One poetry editor wrote to inform
him that the next issue of his magazine had already been filled but
thanked him "for letting [them] see the exceptionally good poems"
and encouraged him to submit his work in future; and Professor
Ramsay wrote him, "Your absence from the University this year has
been a matter for real regret to all of us who knew the excellent work
you did here . . . especially in the field of creative writing."[21]

Despite encouraging signs of literary success at the university,
being forcibly removed from Columbia at the end of his junior year
must have been absolutely devastating. Leverich describes Williams's
circumstances poignantly as follows: he was "no longer a precocious
child, [he was now] a young adult confined to the same prison as
C.C., his jailer. Confinement was what he most feared, the feeling of
suffocation, and the agony he felt was the worst he had ever known."[22]

That dread of confinement, of suffocation, expressed so viscerally in *Hot Milk*, remained with him throughout his life, occasioning the horrible irony that this man who always feared suffocation died in New York's Hotel Elysée in 1983 with the cap of a medicine bottle lodged in his throat.

A detailed portrait of the agony the young man must have endured during his *saison d'enfer*, while he worked at the International Shoe Company as a clerk, appears in the unpublished short story "Stair to the Roof," which exists in several unnumbered, undated drafts at the Harry Ransom Center at the University of Texas at Austin. Running through all the versions is a common thread: a young writer has been obliged to leave school and suffers as he is forced to work in a shoe or shirt factory. In one of these drafts, Williams delineates the repetitive, mind-numbing routine of the "little key-puncher":

> Now I am going to tell you the story of a little man that wanted escape and how he got it. There ought to be a lot of other people in this story but there is only room for the little man. His name was Thomas but he never outgrew Tommy. That was probably why his position in the office never changed. When his father took him out of college ten years ago and got him this job he started typing factory orders and he continued typing them till the end. Typing factory orders goes like this. You insert a sheet of paper, form No. 246-M, in your "ditto" machine, an ordinary typewriter with larger figures and a duplicating ribbon. In spaces provided for these items at the top of the sheet, you write the name of the factory, the index number of the order, the date, the number of cases and the number of dozens. Then you skip down a couple of spaces and type the run of sizes, 5 1/2 to 8, 12 to 2, 6 1/2 to 11 1/2, depending on whether the shoes are intended for men, women or children. Then the monotony begins in earnest. . . .
>
> This is what Tommy did for ten years, five and a half days out of every week and sometimes six.[23]

Although Williams actually only worked at the International Shoe Company on Washington Avenue for something under three years, as opposed to Tommy's ten, it is clear that he saw this period of his life as one of unending imprisonment after his time at Mizzou. Release, however, came suddenly and without warning. Following an evening with Rose downtown at the Loew's State Theatre to watch *The Scarlet Pimpernel*, Williams suddenly began suffering heart palpitations and lost the feeling in his hands on the return streetcar ride. Rose brought Tom to St. Luke's Hospital, where he stayed for a week. When he was released, the doctor insisted on complete bed rest, offering him as "a twenty-fourth birthday gift . . . permanent release from the wholesale shoe business in St. Louis" (*M*, 39).

Rose, beset by a series of ailments and unable to either hold a job or attend school at this time, somehow managed to maintain a sense of calm while admitting her younger brother to the hospital. In the words of her mother, she "sailed magnificently through the crisis," only to suffer nervous collapse afterward: "She lost control of her senses, wandering from room to room in a panic. She woke up her father screaming in terror, 'You're going to be murdered! We're all going to be murdered!' It was as though Tom's slight breakdown had destroyed the slender thread by which she had been hanging on to a reality she could no longer grasp."[24]

At the time of his collapse, Williams was working on a short story, "The Accent of a Coming Foot," in which there is a young poet who has dropped out of college. The story's poet, Bud, is described as "floating out upon the cold lake of his loneliness further and further from the friendly shore" (*CS*, 34). Bud's sister chronicles his increasingly bizarre, aberrant behavior: "Most of the time he's up there in the attic by himself, pounding away at that old typewriter of his that he got from the junk shop, not even bothering to put on his clothes. . . . I tell you he doesn't act civilized anymore. . . . He shaves about once every week, he never combs his hair and seems like Mother just has to *make* him take a bath! Can you imagine that?" (*CS*, 36–37).

What makes "The Accent of a Coming Foot" so extraordinary is the fact that Williams tells the story of the poet's collapse through his girlfriend's eyes. Bud has failed to meet Catharine at the train station as planned, and so she has gone back to Bud's house to wait for his return, along with his mother and sisters. The drama in the story is wholly contained within Catharine's mind, as she nervously waits with Bud's sister Cecilia.

Williams employs the image of a coiled spring to ratchet up the story's tension as he depicts Catharine's soaring anxiety while listening to Bud's sister's description of a young man for whom she herself clearly feels great affection. The story's true subject, then, is not Bud, but Catharine, who desperately longs to reconnect with the lonely, isolated boy. At the beginning of the story, as Catharine heads back from the train station, her internal state is compared to "a relentless crank winding up inside of her some cruelly sharp steel spring whose release would certainly whirl her to pieces." As she enters Bud's home and finds him absent, "the spring had to go on winding itself still tighter till heaven knows what might happen" (*CS*, 32). With each intimation of Bud's arrival, the spring grows tighter and tighter, until it has "coiled itself too tight this time. She wouldn't be able to bear the intolerable moment of his birth in her presence again" (*CS*, 40). The story's effect is to re-create Catharine's growing anxiety and increasing psychological paralysis, but the story's final moments deny the reader any sort of release.

Bud is the precise age of Williams at the time of writing (twenty-four) and the portrait of this lonely boy is clearly a self-portrait, although Bud himself scarcely enters the frame of the story; we catch only a glimpse of him in the final moments before he turns away, leaving Catharine (and the reader) unfulfilled and agitated, wondering if it will be "at all possible to reach him again. Perhaps these cold waters [have] closed completely, this time, over his head" (*CS*, 35).

When at the end of the story Bud does finally make his appearance, Catharine is trapped midway on the staircase, unable to descend or to return upstairs. She cannot even articulate what she wishes to say, literally appearing to age before our eyes; she cannot "speak the gay words of greeting nor touch the red cherries that [tremble] on her hat's brim. She [stands] with her head held stiffly, like a haughty old dame glaring down the straight line of her nose at some impertinent intruder" (*CS*, 41). As a result, Bud, now in the doorway, bows slightly from the waist "as though this house were a bathroom which he [has] inadvertently entered at the wrong moment, finding Catharine unclothed or in an unfortunate pose" (*CS*, 41). He then vanishes from her sight—presumably forever.

The bibliographical note in Williams's *Collected Stories* for this story from the unpublished collection "Pieces of My Youth" describes a note from Williams found with the manuscript that intimately interrelates this story's terrible anticlimax with his own imminent breakdown, which he describes as a "cardiac seizure":

> It was immediately after the conclusion of this story, one of those which I wrote in the evenings after my days at the Continental Branch of the International Shoe Company in St. Louis, that I suffered my first heart attack. As I rose from my worktable in my cubbyhole room in the apartment we were crammed into at 6254 Enright St. [*sic*], in the unfashionable suburb of University City, I found that my heart was pounding and skipping beats. Something more than cups of black coffee, something too close to myself in the character of Bud and the tension of Catharine, triggered this first cardiac seizure. (*CS*, 571)

The story's title alludes to the Emily Dickinson poem "Elysium is as far as to," which examines the mix of emotions of joy and dread felt at moments of intensely fraught emotional anticipation. The title appears in the poem's second stanza, capturing perfectly Williams's evocation of the precarious balance between bliss and terror at moments of heightened tension:

> What fortitude the Soul contains,
> That it can so endure
> The accent of a coming Foot—
> The opening of a Door—[25]

This terrifying story reveals not merely the mindscape of a writer's inner anxiety but also his profound resentment toward the joyless existence he was leading at this time in the "cubbyhole room" of the bleak Enright apartment. The description of Bud and his sister Cecilia's home is clearly modeled on the author's feelings toward the

Williamses' dwelling, anthropomorphized into a demonic presence suggesting Poe's "Fall of the House of Usher": "It was uncompromisingly ugly. . . . it seemed to pucker its yellow face malevolently against the young green gesture of returning spring. Its walls groaned and its windows shrieked a loud denial to the playful wind, and through its dark rooms the echoing rain was transposed to such a dismal minor key that to Catharine it sounded like the sly laughter and whispering of ghosts" (*CS*, 34).

* * * * *

Following the "cardiac seizure" in spring 1935 that allowed Williams to leave International Shoe, doctors discovered him to be seriously underweight and in generally poor health. As would happen often in his life, his grandmother Dakin ("Grand") came to his rescue, inviting him to Memphis to recuperate for the summer. The visit in Memphis proved enormously beneficial to him both physically and artistically. As chance would have it, a neighbor of the Dakins', Dorothy Shapiro, belonged to a small local theatre company called the Garden Players. Williams and Shapiro collaborated on the writing of a play, *Cairo, Shanghai, Bombay!*, which was performed on July 12. The play may have been a simple comedy about two sailors on a date with a couple of "light ladies," but it offered Williams the pleasure of seeing and hearing an audience respond to his words on stage for the first time. The impact of this moment was extraordinary, and in a letter to his mother written the following month, his protective feelings toward his newly discovered vocation are apparent. Politely, but firmly, Williams asked his mother *not* to visit him and her parents in Memphis, clearly frightened of upsetting his newfound equilibrium. "I am just beginning to feel human again after this long period of nervous prostration," he wrote. "The sun and fresh air have helped me tremendously. . . . I'm anxious to enjoy this southern atmosphere as long as possible" (*SL*, 79). As he did so often in his life, Williams connected the "southern atmosphere" in the company of his grandparents with health, as opposed to the deleterious, bleak Midwest associated with his mother's possible re-entry into his sphere.

When he did return to St. Louis after the visit, he felt physically refreshed. However, since Cornelius refused to send him back to the

University of Missouri, he remained in captivity at home, though, given the seriousness of his medical diagnosis, he was under no pressure to return immediately to International Shoe, allowing him freedom to write. Additional motivation came in the form of a new home—the family had finally left the ugly apartment on Enright and leased a quiet two-story home at 6634 Pershing Avenue. In a letter to his grandparents, he wrote,

> The house is perfectly lovely, even prettier than I expected. It is in Colonial style throughout. The living room is gorgeous. It is one of the most charming small homes I've ever seen. We found everything in perfect order, the grape arbor loaded with ripe grapes and the rose garden in full bloom. The place seems so quiet and spacious and dignified after our sordid apartment-dwelling that it doesn't seem like we're the same people. (*SL*, 80)

Of course, the people were the same, with or without a grape arbor. Before long, Williams once again felt the toxicity of his home environment encroaching on his sanity. On August 10 of the following year, he complained in a notebook, "My situation now seems so hopeless that this afternoon it seemed there were only two possible ways out—death or suicide." He now felt, "I hate this house and today I hate everyone in it. . . . If I could get my money out of the bank I think I would go off somewhere—anywhere—just to be out of this poisonous place" (*N*, 49).

Shortly after this entry, Tom and his brother, Dakin, were able to take a two-week holiday on Lake Taneycomo in the Ozarks. But after they returned to St. Louis following the idyllic reprieve from the family, Williams wrote of a palpable alteration in perspective he had felt as the city drew near: "Two glorious weeks of sun, water and starlight now gone. Like a jewel in the drab setting of my usual life. It was all pure light. Hardly a shadow except toward the end when I felt St. Louis creeping closer. I won't write about it in detail. It doesn't need writing about. It couldn't be forgotten ever" (*N*, 51). Following this dispiriting critique, he wishfully added that perhaps St. Louis was not really his home—the wider world was. But even

Figure 14. Dakin and Tom poolside. Courtesy of the Tennessee Williams Collection, Harry Ransom Center, University of Texas at Austin.

marking this crucial distinction between the place in which he actually resided and the outside world he longed for, the grim vision of St. Louis still felt unassailable:

The world is my home—not my single cramped unhappy place. But just the same I've got to stay here or so it seems and being here is very miserable. I hate brick and concrete and the hissing of garden hoses. I hate streets with demure or sedate little trees and the awful screech of trolley wheels and polite, constrained city voices. I want hills and valleys and lakes and forests around me! I want to lie dreaming and naked in the sun! I want to be free and have freedom all around me. I don't want anything tight or limited or constrained. (*N*, 51)

Figure 15. Brookings Hall, the main administration building at Washington University,
1 Brookings Drive. Sievers Studio, November 5, 1931. Identifier: P0403-03985-08-8n.
Courtesy of the Missouri Historical Society.

In some ways, this insight from the twenty-five-year-old Williams
is illustrative of his entire life's rhythm, even after supposedly departing St. Louis and his parents' home for good. Escape followed
by return—followed in turn by another relentless attempt at escape.
From wherever he stood, the next voyage was always on the horizon.
"En avant" was always the inevitable next step.

Now that he had returned from his vacation and had had more
than a year off—from working, not from writing, his father began
demanding to know when he would get a job. However, salvation
arrived just weeks later, in mid-September, in the form of a miraculous gift: "Yesterday my sainted Grandparents sent me a check
for $125 to pay my tuition at Washington University. So now it is
definitely decided that I am to go there—I want to make every day
of it *count*—since my lovely grandparents have sacrificed so much to
send me" (*N*, 53).

*First Row—*WILLIAMS, FERRING, THYSON, KEALHOFER, SCHWEIG, GUIDRY.
*Second Row—*CLARK, LORENZ, DUSARD, EXTEIN, PICKERING, HOTCHNER.

Figure 16. Tom (*front row, far left*) with the staff of *The Eliot*, Washington University's literary magazine. Washington University Photographic Services Collection, Washington University Libraries, Julian Edison Department of Special Collections.

The prospect of returning to college at twenty-five was both exhilarating and daunting. He would be much older than his undergraduate peers, and he had been away from school for four years. Nevertheless, the time at Washington University proved truly inspirational in many ways, regardless of how disastrously it ended. There, he would meet two important companions who shared his love of writing and literature and who undoubtedly influenced the trajectory of his work. Whatever else he might have felt about returning to the classroom, these friendships and what he learned about his craft as a writer were vital in developing the arc of his career. Indeed, it may be said that it was during this time—the time he was at Washington University—that Williams truly became a poet.

The two young men he befriended at Washington were Clark Mills and William Jay Smith, at the time just a freshman but destined to one day become Poet Laureate of the United States, or as it was formerly called, "Consultant in Poetry to the Library of Congress." Together they fashioned a poetry club that Williams fondly called the "Literary Factory."

The charismatic, tall, and handsome Mills in particular made a powerful impact on Tom, introducing him to both left-wing politics

Figures 17a, 17b. Tom's Literary
Factory friends, Clark Mills McBurney
(*left*) and William Jay Smith (*below*).
Detail of Mills from a group photo of
the staff of *The Eliot*, from Washington
University Photographic Services
Collection, Washington University
Libraries, Julian Edison Department of
Special Collections. Photograph of Smith
courtesy of the poet's son, Gregory
Smith.

and the wonders of French symbolist poetry. Mills possessed a contagious enthusiasm for nearly every subject, and Smith recalled that "Clark told us how from an early age books had been part of his life," although he, like Tom, had a father convinced that "book learning" was a waste of time. Smith also remembered how Mills classified everyone he met "according to whether or not he or she had a soul," and years later Williams himself tenderly recalled, "It was Clark who warned me of the existence of people like Hart Crane and Rimbaud and Rilke, and my deep and sustained admiration for Clark's writing gently but firmly removed me from the obvious to the purer voices in poetry."[26]

The three friends began meeting at the Williamses' new home on Pershing Avenue, with Williams ironically enough, as Smith recalled, claiming his father's faded blue overstuffed chair and "assuming the

Figure 18. A scene from Molière's *Les Fourberies de Scapin* at Washington University in 1937. In this French Department production, Williams played the old father (*fourth from the right*). His good friend William Jay Smith played Scapin (*center*). Seventy-four years later, Williams's own *Streetcar Named Desire* became the first American play to be performed at the legendary "House of Molière," the Comédie-Française in Paris. Photo reference: MS Thr 553 (30). Courtesy of the Harvard Theatre Collection, Houghton Library, Harvard University.

direction of our literary gathering." While Mills set the exploratory tone of the meetings, Smith maintained it was Williams who gave the group its dynamism.[27] Mills described in detail the "fanatical and inexhaustible energy" of Williams's approach: "His persistence was almost grotesque. It was Dionysian, demoniac. He wasn't aiming basically at material success. He wrote because it was a fatal need."[28]

The fact that writing was a "fatal need" for Williams is not merely central to understanding both his life and his work, it pinpoints the extraordinary importance of the legacy of these St. Louis years. The educational advantages Williams received at Ben Blewett Junior High and University City High School, combined with his three years at the University of Missouri, provided him with a strong foundation, and it is fair to say that this foundation was built upon during the frenetic and productive days of the three friends' Literary Factory meetings. Mills was witness to many of Williams's early attempts at playwriting, and saw firsthand his unique approach to dramatic composition: "The way Tom learned to write a successful play was by first attempting countless versions that he then discarded, finally arriving at one he felt might be accepted. *That* was his greatness, as I saw it—what set him apart."[29] Mills also described Williams's process as having sudden bursts of lightning, dynamically charged bolts of electricity:

> He would do, say, a half page or two pages, and it was fast—he was fast on the typewriter—he would be operating as if blindly. He was never sure where he was going but when he got there— when he finished the passage and it might not be right—he'd toss it aside and start all over again. While he would do the whole business over, it would go in a different direction. It was as if he was throwing dice—as if he was working toward a combination or some kind of result that wouldn't have *any* idea what the right result might be but would recognize it when he got there.[30]

If we accept the fact that St. Louis was the bane of Williams's existence, we must also understand that at the same time, it was his wellspring in the sense that this was the place where everything came together to produce his unique approach to writing. So many things coalesced at the same time—his profound unhappiness living at home, his feeling of impotent imprisonment at the shoe factory, his growing despair over his sister's worsening condition—and then all these deleterious aspects of his life were suddenly illuminated and brought to new life by the group he formed with Mills and Smith to produce a writer of genius. As when irritants work their way into the oyster, and the oyster secretes its defense mechanism in the form of layers and layers of nacre as coating, so Williams's creative process was his own protective secretion against the many irritants and threats to his life. He wrote compulsively, desperately— vanished into his writing—and this "fatal need" to escape his daily reality ultimately sealed him off against the destructive aspects of home and family. It also, it must be admitted, sealed him off from other people. As the dying painter Mark expresses it in *In the Bar of a Tokyo Hotel*, written some thirty years later, "After the work, so little is left of me. To give to another person" (*TH*, 28). Each of his works, and in particular his plays (as is apparent from their volumi- nous drafts in manuscript form), provided him with layers of nacre insulating him against these wounds. They also made "normal" hu- man contact impossible. In the extraordinary essay "Comments on the Nature of Artists with a Few Specific References to the Case of Edgar Allan Poe," written for Professor Wilbur L. Schramm's course Comprehensive Survey of English Literature at the University of Iowa in the fall of 1937, Williams appears to have understood that his calling left him "completely unsatisfied with the usual acts of living" (*NSE*, 254). Although this essay is classified as "juvenilia" in *New Selected Essays: Where I Live*, the piece speaks eloquently to the twenty-six-year-old playwright's self-conception, presaging the torment of his final years with terrifying accuracy: "The energy of an artist is something that possesses him rather than something he possesses. It is a 'volunté': an unleashed force." Comparing the art- ist with the prophet Daniel, who was miraculously saved from the lions' den by an act of God, Williams claims that "it takes something nearly as unexpected to preserve the artist from dismemberment in the physical cell which he is forced to occupy with his savage beasts" (*NSE*, 254).

Even then, Williams somehow intuited that he lived in perpetual danger of self-destruction; he might "lead his beautiful feline pets through graceful routines that will make the big tent resound with his acclaim," but "no matter how beautifully they are trained to perform," his creations were "potential destroyers" that might turn against him in an instant. And for the artist unable to harness his creative gifts, these untamed beasts, craving the red meat of his art, "will take out their vitality on him: they will make him sickly, neurotic or utterly mad" (*NSE*, 254).

* * * * *

On the morning of Monday, May 31, 1937, near the end of his first (and only) full academic year at Washington University, Williams woke up with a feeling of melancholia he frequently described as the "blue devils."[31] He was miserable, clueless about his future. His notebooks at the time offer a remarkably detailed portrait of a young man on the very brink of collapse—insecure, anxious, and depressed. He was still at home with his nagging mother and alcoholic, bullying father. His beloved sister had grown increasingly unstable and erratic, and had been moved from the psychopathic ward at Missouri Baptist Hospital to St. Vincent's, a Catholic convalescent home in St. Louis. By the end of July, she would be moved again, to Farmington (Missouri) State Hospital as Case Number 9014 with the following diagnosis: "Dementia Praecox (Schizophrenia) Mixed Type, Paranoid Predominating." Her admission report noted "delusions of sexual immorality by members of the family. . . . The patient has periods of great excitement and confusion."[32] Dakin observed of Rose prior to her transfer to Farmington, "My sister was a raving maniac at the time and had no thought pattern at all. It was very unnerving to go there and hear your sister screaming incoherently like a wild animal."[33]

In addition to Rose's worsening condition and his own profound unhappiness, Williams learned of the recent suicide of a neighbor, Roger Moore, a deeply gifted young man who had received both a Rhodes Scholarship and a Ph.D. in political science from Yale. Moore had run for mayor of University City, and suffered a nervous breakdown shortly after losing the election. He was being treated in the same sanitarium as Rose, and he deliberately jumped in front of a truck just outside it. Williams's extraordinary response to Moore's

Figure 19. Rose outside of St. Vincent's Sanitarium. Courtesy of the Tennessee Williams Collection, Harry Ransom Center, University of Texas at Austin.

death reveals something of his own depressed mental state: "Ghastly! I doubt that I shall ever do that. Having no self respect one doesn't have the pain of losing it. I am so used to being a worm that the condition seldom troubles me" (*N*, 87).

Academically, at this time he was in the middle of studying for his final examinations. He notes in the same entry that he has just completed two "easy" finals, in the classes Problems in Philosophy and the American System of Government. Unfortunately, he received grades of D on both. He had spent the previous weekend revising a short one-act play then called "Escape" about a young man on vacation so horrified by the idea of returning home to the city and to his parents' dissolving marriage that he takes his own life by drowning in the one place he still feels completely free, the lake.[34] In a notebook entry a month earlier, April 25, 1937, Williams confessed his own suicidal impulse, referring to the play: "The boy in it is *me*. More than any other character I've ever created except of course that he was capable of violent action and I am not" (*N*, 85).

Even in courses where he might have been expected to excel, he was doing poorly. For example, he also received a D in Professor Otto Heller's General Literature III course, Principles and Problems of Literature. For this class, Williams had written a twenty-three-page essay (now housed at the Ransom Center), "Birth of an Art (Anton Chekhov and the New Theatre)," on the title page of which Professor Heller, a highly respected German émigré scholar who had taught for decades at Washington University, wrote, "Page numbers? This paper in no way fulfills the requirements of a term paper as indicated repeatedly." He followed this with "All of this, or nearly all, was written without reference or relation to literary standards and criteria as studied in the course. O.H." (*NSE*, 292). The effect of such pedantry on Williams's delicate psyche in the midst of his other vicissitudes cannot be overestimated.

Twenty-six years old, he still had not completed his undergraduate degree, and was facing failure once again. The previous fall, there had been such hope when he received the tuition money from his "sainted Grandparents," allowing him to complete his degree by attending Washington University. Now, however, as he awoke on this Monday morning, life was closing in: "Monday. Never woke in more misery in all my life. Intolerable. The brilliant earth mocks my fear. Children and birds sing. People speak in casual voices. The poplar leaves shine. Yet I up here in this narrow room endure torture God help me! Please! I've got to have help or I'll go mad. What is this a punishment for? What? Or is it all blind, blind without meaning!" (*N*, 89).

That afternoon, Williams sat staring at his doom—a final examination in ancient Greek class that he knew he had no chance of passing. In the previous day's journal he had written, "Tomorrow Greek final which I will undoubtedly flunk." And then, after taking a break, he had added the following note: "Greek final tomorrow but no studying done. Can hardly blame myself, my nerves are in such rotten shape" (*N*, 89). He scrawled his name, "Th. Williams," on the cover of the blue book that lay before him and tried unsuccessfully to concentrate on writing translations from Greek into English, and from English into Greek. As he suspected, he failed the examination.

Fearing that this failure would only confirm his father's estimation of him as a worthless sponge, and that his grades would repay his grandparents' generous support with yet another unequivocal flop, he turned over the leaves of his Greek examination booklet to the last one and began to write words on the blank page. The poem, scrawled in pencil, was initially entitled "Sad Song," but the word *Sad* had been erased and replaced by *Blue*. Perhaps more than anything else he wrote during this terribly unhappy period of his young adulthood, "Blue Song" tells the story of the utter despair Williams felt in St. Louis. Here is the poem in full:

Blue Song

I am tired.
I am tired of speech and of action.
If you should meet me upon the
street do not question me for
I can tell you only my name
and the name of the town I was
born in—but that is enough.
It does not matter whether tomorrow
arrives anymore. If there is
only this night and after it no
morning it will not matter now.
I am tired. I am tired of speech
and of action. In the heart of me
you will find a tiny handful of
dust. Take it and blow it out
upon the wind. Let the wind have
it and it will find its way home.[35]

The poem reveals a young man whose spirit is inert and whose heart has been broken ("In the heart of me / you will find a tiny handful of / dust"), who can "tell you only my name / and the name of the town I was / born in." These lines indicate a desire to eradicate all reference to a present, in favor of a distant, far happier past. In Williams's case, this meant returning in his mind to his birthplace in Columbus, Mississippi, and to the early years when he and Rose

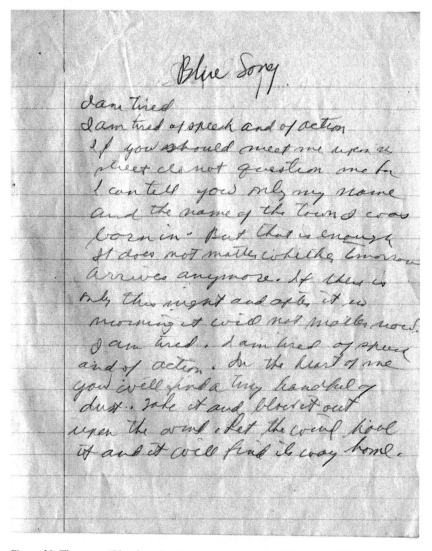

Figure 20. The poem "Blue Song," written on the last page of Tennessee Williams's Greek-exam blue book (1937). Tennessee Williams Collection, Washington University Libraries, Julian Edison Department of Special Collections.

played innocently in their grandfather's rectory in Clarksdale. In the poem's final lines, the poet wishes for self-annihilation—calling out for the wind to take the handful of dust that will somehow "find its way home."

This short, unhappy, and discarded lyric offers a remarkable snapshot into Williams's pivotal St. Louis years. A brief moment, it nonetheless sheds light on so much that both preceded and followed it. As a result of his failure in Greek, Williams received word from the registrar that he would not be able to graduate in June. He would need to pass ancient Greek, and take another (dreaded) term of physical education. And all this had to be explained to his parents and grandparents.

As bad as this situation was, something far worse was about to descend. The end of that same week brought the news that Williams—by far the oldest and most experienced writer in Professor William G. B. Carson's playwriting class, English 16—had not been selected among the three winners of the one-act playwriting competition, which brought with it a cash prize and production of one's play. The cash prize, in particular, might have redeemed his family's faith in his talent. Instead, his notebook entry for Friday, June 4, reveals the unmitigated rage he felt, born from his deep shame at not being one of those selected: "Never a more ignominious failure! My play for English 16 rejected for presentation—given fourth place—Went to Carson's office this morning and he gave me the news—without any apparent compunction—But why should I expect sympathy from anyone—especially a Washington University Professor—the stronghold of the Reactionaries!" (*N*, 89). Not surprisingly, Williams chose not to attend the awards ceremony at the university's Graham Chapel, nor did he collect his honorable mention certificate. If the playwright's testimony more than a decade later is to be believed, he apparently went to Professor Carson's office and vented his rage, surprising even himself with his vehemence.[36]

Although unable to permanently leave the city until December 1938, following the completion of his degree from the University of Iowa, the failure to be selected as one of the three winners in Professor Carson's class drew a bold line underneath the St. Louis chapter of Williams's life. When he returned to the city afterward, it was as a visitor rather than as a son or family member returning home—if the word *home* may be applied to what Williams felt about the city he grew up in and where he came of age.

* * * * *

Williams's submission to the English 16 competition had been a one-act entitled *Me, Vashya*, which was loosely based on the career of the arms manufacturer Sir Basil Zaharoff (1850–1936). When Williams read it aloud in class, the play must have seemed both pretentious

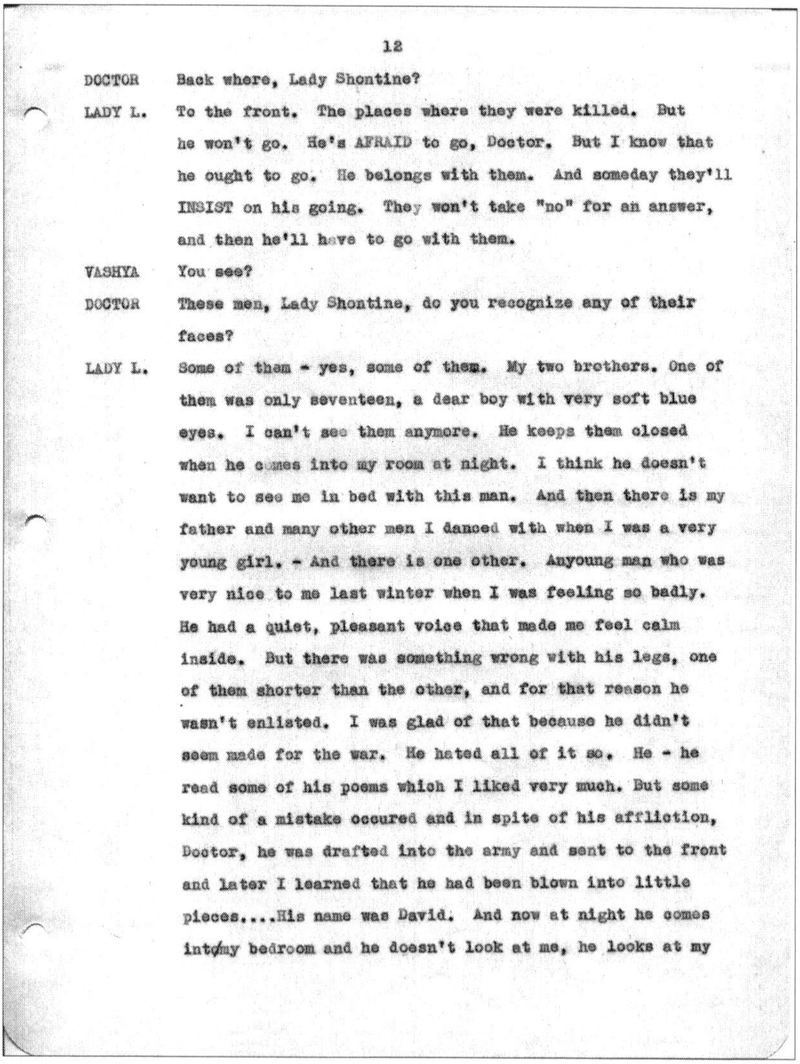

12

DOCTOR   Back where, Lady Shontine?

LADY L. To the front. The places where they were killed. But
         he won't go. He's AFRAID to go, Doctor. But I know that
         he ought to go. He belongs with them. And someday they'll
         INSIST on his going. They won't take "no" for an answer,
         and then he'll have to go with them.

VASHYA   You see?

DOCTOR   These men, Lady Shontine, do you recognize any of their
         faces?

LADY L. Some of them - yes, some of them. My two brothers. One of
         them was only seventeen, a dear boy with very soft blue
         eyes. I can't see them anymore. He keeps them closed
         when he comes into my room at night. I think he doesn't
         want to see me in bed with this man. And then there is my
         father and many other men I danced with when I was a very
         young girl. - And there is one other. Anyoung man who was
         very nice to me last winter when I was feeling so badly.
         He had a quiet, pleasant voice that made me feel calm
         inside. But there was something wrong with his legs, one
         of them shorter than the other, and for that reason he
         wasn't enlisted. I was glad of that because he didn't
         seem made for the war. He hated all of it so. He - he
         read some of his poems which I liked very much. But some
         kind of a mistake occured and in spite of his affliction,
         Doctor, he was drafted into the army and sent to the front
         and later I learned that he had been blown into little
         pieces....His name was David. And now at night he comes
         intomy bedroom and he doesn't look at me, he looks at my

Figure 21. Typescript page from Williams's play *Me, Vashya* (1937). Courtesy of the William G. B. Carson Papers, Washington University Libraries, Julian Edison Department of Special Collections.

and absurdly melodramatic to his undergraduate classmates. One student in the class, the novelist, playwright, and Ernest Hemingway biographer A. E. Hotchner, remembered the stifled laughter that accompanied Williams's reading. When he was finished, Hotchner recalled, "Tom rose slowly from his seat, suffused with anger, and left the room. None of us ever saw him again." Another classmate, the painter Martyl Schweig, remembered that the much older Williams "did not sit with the class but to the left of Professor Carson facing us," and that "he wore the very same brown suit all year. . . . it was purple and shiny at the elbows and seat. My recollection of his droning voice and boring play [is that they] prompted me to do my next class' homework during the reading."[37]

It is easy to understand why *Me, Vashya* was so poorly received by Williams's classmates, and why this one-act about an international armaments dealer, portrayed as a petty tyrant sitting at a desk embellished with a large bust of Caesar, Napoleon, or Mussolini and twirling a globe, might well have aroused their ridicule. In the play, Vashya profits from selling munitions to both sides in an unnamed global war. He has risen from a life of abject poverty, he has gone from a "common peasant who roasted his naked back pitching wheat" to someone able to command the respect of heads of state. The play was likely intended as expressionist fantasy rather than the realistic piece the students assumed. At the play's conclusion, the audience discovers that the doctor who has come to treat Vashya's insane wife (whom he keeps locked in their bedroom) has in fact smuggled in a revolver to her so that she can assassinate him. The final moments of the play depict Vashya pleading for his life as his wife calmly shoots him in revenge for the countless young men he has sent to their deaths: "They come into the room and stand around the bed and ask for HIM. They want HIM to go WITH them. He SENT them there. He's their LEADER they say, and they want him to go back there with them."[38]

However, if the play does feel contrived or melodramatic, there was another component—unrelated to either its subject matter or style—that neither Professor Carson nor Williams's undergraduate classmates could possibly have understood: this one-act of madness and murder, apparently so removed from a typical undergraduate's experience, contained a remarkable portrait of Williams's sister, Rose, then experiencing her own terrifying descent into madness.

The catastrophic reception of *Me, Vashya* and his failure in Greek may have brought to an end Williams's academic career at Washington University. But his feelings of humiliation, failure, and resentment remained with him for the rest of his life. No matter where he traveled, no matter what honors came his way or what he accomplished, St. Louis always reminded him of his own insufficiency and failures, and of what he had left behind in the form of his broken Rose.

Chapter Three

Have You Ever Seen the Skeleton of a Bird?

IT IS NOT often that any of us can pinpoint when a career begins, that moment we discover who we are or what our vocation is meant to be. In the case of Tennessee Williams, we can label it precisely. On July 12, 1935, Thomas Lanier Williams became a playwright. Following two months during which, he admitted (in a letter to Pulitzer Prize–winning novelist Josephine Johnson), "I've hardly touched my typewriter, . . . since my heart and nerves have been playing these disturbing tricks on each other" (*SL*, 76), Williams was engaged in a collaboration on a little one-act with Dorothy Shapiro, a young neighbor of the Dakins' in Memphis. The play's subject was trivial, and concerned two young sailors on shore leave. The facts that the play (*Cairo, Shanghai, Bombay!*) was staged by the small theatre group the Garden Players under the direction of Arthur B. Scharff and that it was seen "on the great sloping back lawn of a lady named Mrs. Rosebrough" (*M*, 41) are equally insignificant. However, the occasion of the play's performance was momentous enough that exactly thirty-five years later, the playwright remembered, "The laughter, genuine and loud, at the comedy I had written enchanted me. Then and there the theatre and I found each other for better or worse. I know it's the only thing that saved my life" (*M*, 41–42).

Returning to St. Louis after an extended stay with his grandparents at their home in Memphis, Williams became affiliated with a community theatre group, the Mummers, and their charismatic director Willard Holland. Astonishingly enough, Williams's initial connection with the theatre company was made through his mother. Just prior to his departing for Memphis that April, Edwina Williams had noticed an advertisement for a one-act play contest at the Webster

Groves Theatre Guild and encouraged her taciturn, diffident son to submit something. Tom had sent them a short play called *The Magic Tower*, about a young couple: Jim, an impoverished painter, and Linda, a vaudeville actress who has given up her life on stage to live with Jim in a rundown attic the two idealize as their "magic tower." While the specific location of their garret goes unmentioned, it is obviously St. Louis. "I never look out of the window if I can help it," Linda says, mirroring Williams's perpetual view of St. Louis as a place where the sky can never be seen. "It's all so hopelessly ugly out there, those awful billboards and filling stations and delicatessens!" (*MT*, 14). Like Tom, Jim longs for a life outside the city's confines: "I've never been outside this city. I've grown up in the middle of it. All this ugliness" (*MT*, 15).

While Jim goes to see a well-connected art dealer about representing his work, two sleazy friends from Linda's vaudeville past visit her, attempting to lure her back to the stage. Linda is forced to defend her husband against her friends:

> LINDA: He's an artist, you nut! Haven't you heard of an artist before?
> MITCH: Sure, an artist is a guy that's out of a job and don't give a damn. (*MT*, 28)

After initially seeing their blandishments about returning to her former profession rejected, the two eventually persuade Linda she is holding her husband back. When Jim returns from the art dealer with his hopes dashed, he turns on his wife, repudiating their idealistic fantasy of the magic tower. There is nothing to eat in the house, and the lovers who once imagined their squalid home as "surrounded by wonderful green forests" (*MT*, 14) and themselves surviving on a diet of "nightingales['] tongues" (*MT*, 23) now face harsh reality. "Do you think we can EAT each other? . . . Come down to earth, woman! . . . Magic tower, boloney! It's Mrs. O'Fallon's attic that we're up in! Mrs. O'Fallon's lousy, leaking attic!" (*MT*, 36).

Linda is now convinced she is an impediment to Jim's professional success, and the one-act concludes with Jim asleep on the couch while Linda quietly slips back to her former life. As she leaves, she vocalizes her sadness with a few lines reminiscent of *The Glass Menagerie*'s poignant lyricism: "There's a funny little slice of moon coming out. Right over the Fix-it Garage. It looks like a yellow dancing slipper" (*MT*, 38).

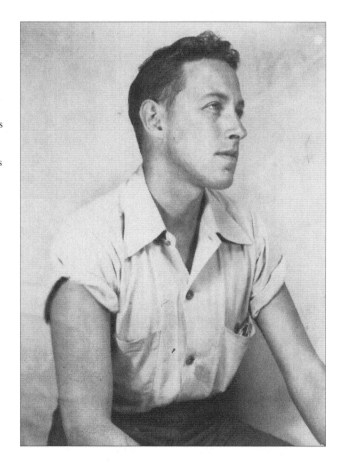

Figure 22. The young poet, Tom at age twenty-four. Courtesy of the Tennessee Williams Collection, Harry Ransom Center, University of Texas at Austin.

The Magic Tower won Williams the Webster Groves Theatre Guild prize. More importantly, it caught the attention of Holland, who telephoned Williams. In the playwright's recollection in the essay "Something Wild . . . ," the conversation went this way: "I hear you go to college and I hear you can write. . . . Then he asked me: How do you feel about compulsory military training?" (*NSE*, 45).

The Mummers' next offering was to be the St. Louis premiere of Irwin Shaw's short anti-war play *Bury the Dead*, to be produced on Armistice Day. Holland needed a short curtain-raiser to fill out the program. Williams assured Holland, "I . . . left the University of Missouri because I could not get a passing grade in the ROTC. Swell! said Holland, you are just the guy I am looking for. How would you like to write something against militarism?" (*NSE*, 45). As a result, Holland commissioned Williams to write a short skit, which would be called *Headlines*, to fill out the evening. Although Williams thought his curtain-raiser (now presumed lost) was "a piece of hack work" (*N*, 65), the commission began a relationship with Holland and the Mummers that not only would determine the earliest stages of Williams's life in the theatre but even more crucially would help the young writer formulate his aesthetic principles.

In "Something Wild . . ." (written a decade later, by which time Williams was famous) Williams describes the Mummers as nothing less than "[his] professional youth," admitting he had been "spawned" by the theatre group; "but," he said, "like most offspring, once I departed from the maternal shelter, I gave it scarcely a backward glance" (*NSE*, 44, 43). It was with the Mummers in mind, under the direction of Holland (who starred in several of the group's productions), that Williams crafted his first full-length plays: *Candles to the Sun*, *Fugitive Kind*, *Not About Nightingales*, *Spring Storm*, and *Stairs to the Roof*. In "Something Wild . . ." Williams is careful to distinguish the Mummers from the typical "Little Theatre" groups proliferating in America at the time. Whereas the Little Theatres were "eminently respectable, predominantly middle-aged, and devoted to the presentation of Broadway hits a season or two after Broadway" (*NSE*, 44), the Mummers provided something quite different and often shocking. Their approach to theatre was political, subversive, or, as Williams succinctly describes it, "disorderly" (*NSE*, 44). In his reminiscence, he lovingly writes,

> Now let me give you a picture of the Mummers! Most of them worked at other jobs besides theater. They had to, because The Mummers were not a paying proposition. There were laborers. There were clerks. There were waitresses. There were students. There were whores and tramps and there was even

a post-debutante who was a member of the Junior League of St. Louis. Many of them were fine actors. Many of them were not. . . . But what they lacked in ability, Holland inspired them with in the way of enthusiasm. I guess it was run by a kind of beautiful witchcraft! It was like a definition of what I think theater is. Something wild, something exciting, something that you are not used to. Offbeat is the word. (*NSE*, 45)

In this same essay, Williams uses the Mummers' philosophy of theatre to express his definition of art as "a kind of anarchy." Unlike art that conforms to society's values, true art, Williams argues, offers "benevolent anarchy in juxtaposition with organized society. It is benevolent in the sense of constructing something which is missing, and what it constructs may be merely a criticism of things as they exist" (*NSE*, 43). He concludes the essay with an idea that suggests how the Mummers helped fashion his credo about the role of art in society: "The biologist will tell you that progress is the result of mutations. Mutations are another word for freaks. For God's sake let's have a little more freakish behavior—not less" (*NSE*, 47). This last sentence is vital to understanding just how much Williams took from the Mummers' legacy in the years and decades to come. His work, from first to last, is a celebration of the outsider, the dispossessed, and the freakish against what society deems "normal" behavior. Perhaps just as important as the Mummers' artistic philosophy was something else Williams jotted down in his notebook on the morning of the performance of his *Headlines*—there was "nothing snotty or St. Louis 'Social'" about the Mummers (*N*, 65).

The Mummers' productions may not have always succeeded, Williams reminds us, and Holland himself was unprepossessing, with a high-pitched, nervous voice, but never once did they produce anything that "didn't deliver a punch to the solar plexus" (*NSE*, 45). While most theatre audiences today do not think of Williams as a politically engaged writer, his early involvement with the Mummers suggests otherwise; he began his career indebted to popular traditions of 1930s American "Proletarian Theatre" modeled on productions by the Group Theatre in New York, including Clifford Odets's seminal play *Waiting for Lefty*.[1]

In a 1966 interview Williams was asked whether he would write directly about the social unrest sweeping the country. He responded, "I am not a direct writer. . . . I am always an oblique writer, if I can be; I want to be allusive; I don't want to be one of those people who hit the nail on the head all the time."[2] However, some years later, following the Watergate scandal, he confessed that despite their obliquity, "all [his] plays have a social conscience."[3]

This dialectical relationship between allusiveness and indirectness, on one hand, and socially committed theatre on the other may be traced back to the origins of Williams's development as an artist during his years in St. Louis, a period that forced him to come to grips with derelicts and outcasts he would famously describe as "the fugitive kind." Indeed, Williams implicitly yoked the isolation and misery he felt in his personal life with the economic plight of the miserable and dispossessed people he saw living in encampments around the Mississippi riverfront. While Williams's great contribution to the American theatre has generally been regarded as his uniquely poetic voice—a voice described by Arthur Miller as having "lifted lyricism to its highest level in our theatre's history"[4]—there is also a fundamental symbiosis in his work between the lyrically personal and the socio-poetical.

Ironically, given the group's left-wing, "disorderly" approach to theatre, the Mummers performed in rented space in the fashionable Wednesday Club (where Edwina Williams had been denied membership, fueling her resentment toward the city's supposed snobbishness), located on the same street (Westminster Place) as the Williams family's second home in St. Louis and just around the corner from Eugene Field Elementary School, where little Tommy was bullied as the kid with the funny southern accent. It was at the Wednesday Club where Williams's first full-length plays were performed, and indeed, given the large cast size of these early plays (nearly all boast a cast of more than twenty), it is clear that Williams was writing for a particular group of actors, including Holland himself, who performed the part of the radical activist Birmingham Red in *Candles to the Sun*, the first of Williams's plays to be performed by the Mummers, in 1937.

Figure 23. Program for *Candles to the Sun*, Tom's first production with the Mummers. Courtesy of the Tennessee Williams Collection, Harry Ransom Center, University of Texas at Austin.

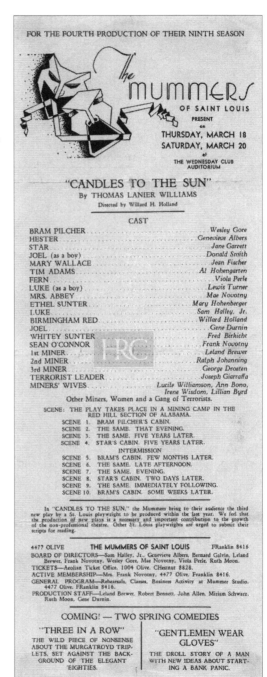

While *The Magic Tower* was an intimate play, dramatizing Williams's internalized frustrations at establishing his identity as an artist in urban St. Louis, *Candles to the Sun* reached into a world that was completely unknown to the inexperienced young writer. The plot was borrowed from a one-act play entitled *The Lamp*, written by Joseph Phelan Hollifield, whom Williams's grandfather Dakin knew in Memphis. Little else is known about Hollifield, except that he sent Williams his one-act play based on a strike by coal miners in Alabama with the instruction that he make whatever use he could of the material: "I just hope you will be able to do something with The Lamp. It is the only thing I have ever done that I feel is worth anything at all. Whatever you do with it will be all right, I'm sure."[5]

The play examines a family of miners in Alabama coal country and the impact of a strike on their lives. The opening scene is eerily reminiscent of the peasants around a table in Vincent van Gogh's *Potato Eaters* in its stark simplicity and atmosphere of dire poverty. It is morning, and the Pilcher family eats their humble meal of mush and coffee in near total darkness. Indeed, as Williams's friend William Jay Smith, who attended one of the two performances of the play, observed, *Candles to the Sun* "must be read as an extended study of light and dark, both inside and outside the characters and the setting."[6]

The opening scene establishes the play's basic conflict, between the darkness of the mines and the light of the world above. The darkness below is personified by Bram Pilcher, the "Old Man of the Mines," whose wife, Hester, accuses him of being "a natcheral born slave" (*CttS*, 7). Hester has encouraged their two children to rise up and escape into a different world. The setting, characters, and dialogue are astonishingly well-grounded in the world of Alabama coal mining. Indeed, when the play was reviewed in the *St. Louis Post-Dispatch*, the reviewer lauded it as one of the Mummers' strongest offerings to date, praising in particular the uncanny accuracy of its idiom: "[The] writing is rarely unsteady and his play has an emotional unity and robustness. It stands on its own feet. Its characters are genuine, its dialogue of a type that must have been uttered in the author's presence, its appeal in the theater widespread."[7] The reviewer, of course, had no way of knowing that Williams had never been to Alabama, let alone set foot in an actual coal-mining community. Indeed, even a planned research trip to mines in neighboring Illinois never took place.

The play's plot revolves around the horribly exploitive working conditions endured by the miners and their response to them. Hester's hopes that her children will have a life outside the mines are destroyed. As conditions worsen, the revolutionary Birmingham Red foments a strike but is ultimately murdered by a gang trying to suppress the strikers. The metaphor suggested by the title, *Candles to the Sun*, is profoundly ambiguous. It may allude to the human need to search for a greater ideal than mere self, to the dichotomy between an individual's need for freedom and collective responsibility to a larger cause, or it can be read ironically, suggesting the utter futility of such aspiration. In several instances in the play, an individual's desire to escape or elude destiny is thwarted, suggesting less social activism than a universe governed by determinism. Hester's failed dream of seeing her children escape the mines is mirrored in the desperate, futile desire of her daughter-in-law, Fern, to have her own son, Luke, attend college instead of laboring in the darkness below, and individual dreams are shattered and hopes sacrificed. Even Birmingham Red, the play's spokesman for the necessity of revolutionary activity to bring about the greater good, is destroyed, in a fiery inferno. At the end of the play, the labor strike is settled but the resolution of strife feels less important than the tragedy of individual destinies. The Old Man of the Mines has grown blind and demented. His mind gone, Bram fumbles his way back to the newly opened mines, asking in vain for milk for his coffee, pointing up the play's juxtaposition of the darkness of the mines with the vain search for light that haunts so many of the characters. Luke was once full of promise, but now his name ironically suggests loss of light and his failed rebirth.[8] Luke has spent his mother's savings (intended for his college tuition) to help feed the miners during the strike, and now seems condemned to spend the rest of his life working below. Star, Hester's rebellious daughter, whose longing for Birmingham Red was the one redemptive thing in her life ("I wanted to get in front of your hands and feel them poundin' me down, down,"), sees her lover murdered and at the end of the play plans to buy herself "a new silk kimona" (*CttS*, 107), suggesting she will now waste her powerful sensuality in a brothel. Fern, exhausted, sinks into a rocker bathed in sunlight, wearing black calico and a "tired smile" as the play ends. She has failed in her quest to liberate Luke from the mines, but a shaft of "thin, clear sunlight pale as lemon-water" comes through the windowpanes (*CttS*, 104): the young Williams resisted an overly simple tragic conclusion, thus reminding us of the remarkable subtlety of his sensibility in matters pertaining to visual images on stage. The strike may indeed have been settled, but the end of the play reveals a scene of terrible human waste, suggesting exhaustion, enervation, rather than a simplistic clarion call to mount the barricades, like that of Odets's *Waiting for Lefty*.

Candles to the Sun borrowed from the genre of labor melodrama to create something more symbolically complex and satisfying than a predictable plea for social action. And of course there was Williams's innate command of character and dialogue; in Holland's words, "His people were really fantastic. You could take a page or pages of dialogue he wrote, give them to an actor, and just put a spotlight on him, and anyone who just happened to walk into the theater couldn't turn away from the strength of it."[9]

Williams's next play, *Fugitive Kind* (1937)—also written for and produced by the Mummers—was inspired by the gangster film tradition so popular in the 1930s, as exemplified by films such as *The Petrified Forest* (1936), which, like Williams's play, ends in a violent shoot-out between "G men" and a gangster—in the movie, Duke Mantee, played by Humphrey Bogart as a violent yet strangely sympathetic killer.

Like *Candles to the Sun*, *Fugitive Kind* has a cinematic quality and is comprised of eight scenes (each with its own title). However, unlike *Candles*, the location is the playwright's own immediate world. St. Louis was then in the immediate aftermath of the Great Depression, and after leaving the University of Missouri at the end of the spring term in 1932, Williams's daily commute by streetcar from his parents' apartment at 6254 Enright Avenue in University City to the International Shoe Company at 1501–1509 Washington

Avenue would have brought him in proximity to the groupings of squalid shacks known as "Hoovervilles," where multitudes of homeless men and women lived in direst poverty along the Mississippi riverfront. His friends in this period were socially active and often affiliated with radical groups. Williams's close friend and fellow Washington University student Clark Mills was a member of the left-wing John Reed Society and worked on the proletarian literary magazine *The Anvil*. Williams also consorted with a group of young artists and activists who met on Saturdays at the Old Courthouse on the St. Louis riverfront. Led by Jack Conroy, the Marxist author of *The Disinherited* (1933) and editor of *The Anvil*, the group included Wally Wharton and Joe Jones, the latter an artist who offered free art classes for the unemployed.

Fugitive Kind is set in the lobby of a "flophouse in a large Middle Western city" and is filled with numerous specific references to St. Louis, including the Eads Bridge, the riverfront, Market Street, and the Hoovervilles he had seen on his daily trek from the city's West End to International Shoe. In his opening stage directions, Williams makes it clear that St. Louis itself is the play's true antagonist, a feeling Williams knew from bitter personal experience: "A large glass window admits a skyline of the city whose towers are outlined at night by a faint electric glow, so that we are always conscious of the city as a great implacable force, pressing in upon the shabby room and crowding its fugitive inhabitants back against their last wall" (*FK*, 3). As one of the many minor denizens of the flophouse observes, "This town's a jinx. I don't like this town. Look out there, that dirty ole muck, that slimy creepin' ole fog all a time—gits down under yer skin, makes yuh sick" (*FK*, 43).

Although written amid the sweltering heat and humidity of a St. Louis summer in 1937, *Fugitive Kind* is set at Christmas, with frequent references to a blanket of snow that both conceals the city from view and mocks the characters' futile attempts at escaping it. As gangster Terry Meighan puts it, the snow "covers things up! Makes everything look clean an' decent an'—stuff like that!" However, it becomes apparent that the blanket of snow that appears to blot out the corrupt world is only a whited sepulcher. As Meighan says, "God's asleep. . . . He's tired of looking at the nasty mess we've made of ourselves. He's pulled down a big white shade to cover us up. Now our stink can't reach his nostrils" (*FK*, 130).

A metaphor for the collection of society's impoverished fugitives, the flophouse is overseen by Glory Gwendlebaum, adopted daughter of its Jewish proprietor. Glory acts as both ingénue (the role assumed by Bette Davis in *The Petrified Forest*) and tough-as-nails gatekeeper of the refuge for the homeless and desperate. As the playwright explains in his stage directions, "In dealing with these men she has acquired a hard, shrewish manner. . . . But off her guard she is graceful and relaxed and has . . . charm and softness" (*FK*, 3–4). The imprint of the Mummers' social aesthetic is everywhere apparent in this play, both in the large cast size (twenty-seven in the published version) and in the relentless attack on bourgeois society. In addition to Glory (idealistically named after the American flag by her immigrant father), the central characters include Texas, a lanky drifter who plays guitar with the hope of picking up loose change; the fugitive gangster Terry Meighan, who commands the center of the plot and becomes Glory's lover; and Gwendlebaum's son, Leo, a radicalized university student who has recently been expelled for his left-wing writings. All three men are at war with the city, and all three are clear projections of discrete aspects of the author's own psyche, radically in conflict with St. Louis himself.

Texas is not central to the plot (although the archetype will return in future plays as the key figure of the martyred artist—most memorably as Val Xavier in *Orpheus Descending*), but his guitar provides important counterpoint to the clichéd Christmas music. At one point, Texas asks Glory to switch on the radio, but when he hears a church choir singing "Carol, Brothers, Carol" he suddenly shouts "SHUT IT OFF!" before collapsing into a chair and kicking over the checkerboard on which he has been playing. The stage directions at the end of this scene are particularly revealing: "With a single violent motion, he kicks the board off the bench, scattering the checkers, and swerves about, facing the audience, and flings his head in his hands" (*FK*, 47). Later in the play, Texas rails against the mechanistic world that threatens to destroy his art, a theme Williams will return to in more mature work: "Radios an' electric-victrolas, machine music, that's all they want, these lousy clip-joints around here! What chance does a flesh'n blood artist got against them?" (*FK*, 62). In the somewhat later play *Stairs to the Roof* (1941, first produced in 1947) we will again hear the playwright's rage against a mechanistic, dehumanizing world that, for Williams, epitomized the St. Louis he knew.

Terry Meighan is *Fugitive Kind*'s central character, a gangster on the run from the law, angry at the world that has cast him out: "You tell your kid brother for me that the world's a hopeless case. . . . the only cure is the axe!" (*FK*, 65). Near the end of the play, we hear his backstory as the orphan of a consumptive mother: "I never had a chance to learn much. Barely to read and write. I had to make money somehow. God, but it made me sick to see mother go into the back room at night with men she'd picked up on the street! Hear them laughing in there!" (*FK*, 101). While the above quotation indicates that much of Terry's dialogue echoes the clichés of the gangster-film genre, as the play moves toward its predictable shoot-out in the flophouse his language is elevated to a new level, rising to an aria that transforms gangster-speak into poetic diction:

> Listen how quiet it is now. The bells've stopped ringing. It's so quiet you can almost hear the snow fall. It makes a sound like cat's feet walking on velvet. Even softer than that. It makes a sound like your breath does coming in and out of your body. There's nothing sweeter than that. . . . look out there and see for yourself. There's nothing but snow. . . . And look how thick it's falling. You can't hardly see the cathedral. (*FK*, 120)

Leo, Glory's twenty-one-year-old brother, is the most interesting character in the play—precisely because his presence in this familiar world of outcasts and gangsters is so unexpected, just as the lonely intellectual Squire (played by Leslie Howard) is alien to the world of *The Petrified Forest*. Texas introduces Leo as someone who "writes poetry an' stuff. Goes to college," to which another of the derelicts replies, "Sissy, huh" (*FK*, 14). Like Texas and Terry, Leo decries a system that destroys people's humanity, and he has been expelled from the university for sentiments very like those that Williams had begun to be exposed to by left-wing friends (including Clark Mills)

at *The Anvil* or at the Blue Lantern Tavern near the Eads Bridge.
Leo, we are told, has written "Bolshevistic stuff," along with a term
paper titled "Fascism and the ROTC" (*FK*, 38).

After a confrontation with his heavily Yiddish-accented father in
which he refuses to "kow-tow to the reactionaries" (*FK*, 82), Leo
flees and considers attempting suicide by throwing himself off the
Eads Bridge. At the time he was writing this play, Williams himself
was plunged into virtually an identical crisis. On June 4, 1937, after
receiving a mere honorable mention in a Washington University
contest for his play *Me, Vashya* (discussed in chapter 2), Williams
scribbled words in his notebook nearly identical to Leo's: "Why
should I expect sympathy from anyone—especially a Washington
University Professor—the stronghold of the Reactionaries!" (*N*,
89).

When his contemplation of suicide is interrupted by a cop, Leo
claims to be watching the river. When the cop sarcastically tells him,
"The river don't need any watching," the young man replies, "Yes, it
does. It's running away as fast as it can and I'll be damned if I blame
it. Who wouldn't want to be running away from this lousy town"
(*FK*, 126). And so Leo returns home, having discovered his poetic
identity through his very desperation and sense of isolation and difference from others (a clear reflection of the author's own sense of
his otherness in middle-class St. Louis and his sense of restoration to
health following the "cardiac arrest" that led to his resignation from
International Shoe in 1935):

> Too many streets, too many people. I got all confused. It didn't
> look that way from the streetcars when I was going to school in
> the mornings. It looked like I belonged to it then. The people's
> faces looked like mine and they seemed to be doing the kind
> of things that I could be doing. But that was all a mistake, an
> optical illusion. I found out when I tried to get out there and
> be like they were. —I didn't belong. (*FK*, 127)

Fugitive Kind has usually been considered an "apprentice" work,
presumably because of its plot and clichés borrowed from gangster
films: "I'm not asking for a handout. I don't expect nothing for

nothing from nobody!" (*FK*, 72). However, such a designation fails to acknowledge the play's remarkable sophistication in modulating the stylistic shifts from realism to expressionism in ways that clearly anticipate Williams's more mature, nonrealistic work. The play's opening stage directions point directly to this sophistication: "When lighted the set is realistic. But during the final scenes of the play, where the mood is primarily lyrical, the stage is darkened, the realistic details are lost—the great window, the red light on the landing and the shadow walls [*sic*] make an almost expressionistic background" (*FK*, 3).

A second argument for seeing *Fugitive Kind* as something more substantial than juvenilia is the way Williams creates the illusion of a complete world peopled by dozens of wonderfully idiosyncratic minor characters, each demonstrating the playwright's remarkable gift at creating an individual with a simple brushstroke. In addition to numerous transients of various ethnicities, there is a dying consumptive and his Swedish companion; a lunatic schizophrenic who takes pleasure from lighting women's hair on fire; a janitor who is desperate for snow so he can clear the streets and earn money in the fashionable West End—but by the time it falls he has pawned his shovel for drink; a cocaine-addicted prostitute; and various society matrons from the Junior Welfare League, do-gooders who want to "help the homeless" over Christmas. Each of these figures is brought to life with distinctive and illuminating character traits and speech patterns the variety of which is amazing, considering that the play's author was a middle-class young man with virtually no firsthand knowledge of the "fugitive kind" except for the people he may have met or seen going to and from his job at International Shoe.

Typically, by the time *Fugitive Kind* appeared, Williams was already well into his next play, provisionally titled "April Is the Cruelest Month." By the fall of 1937, Williams had left Washington University in St. Louis and was in the process of finally completing his bachelor's degree in theatre at the University of Iowa. Holland, although still technically in charge of the Mummers, was living in Hollywood, looking for an agent and taking screen tests in the hope of becoming a film actor. While Holland was away, the board of the Mummers discontinued paying his salary. Although they eventually offered to rehire him provided that he abandon his "dictatorial" ways, the group never rebounded. As a result, two additional works from this period that Williams attempted to submit to Holland for production with the Mummers, *Spring Storm* (the title eventually given to "April Is the Cruelest Month") and *Not About Nightingales*, disappeared from view and went unpublished and unperformed until long after Williams had died. Manuscripts for both plays were discovered in the Tennessee Williams Collection in the archives of the Harry Ransom Center at the University of Texas at Austin.[10]

Shockingly, *Not About Nightingales*, this searing and profoundly intense work, was only produced some sixty years after its composition—when the National Theatre of Great Britain in conjunction with Houston's Alley Theatre brought it to the stage for the first time. Williams's comments from late 1938 on the play's fate are painful to read: "Dec. 5 or 6—Monday—Blue Monday—N.A.N. is tucked away in the desk with so many other derelict scripts." Yet, reflecting his lifelong custom, the very next sentence optimistically adds, "And I have started a new one" (*N*, 129).

Both *Spring Storm* and *Not About Nightingales* speak powerfully to the playwright's artistic and personal connections to St. Louis during these critical, formative years of his artistic development. It must be underscored that both are important plays in their own right, and both illuminate not only Williams's St. Louis years but the trajectory of his artistic development.

Williams had written *Nightingales* after returning to St. Louis in the spring of 1938 following the completion of his degree at Iowa, where he benefited from that university's connection with the Federal Theatre Project, one of many Depression-era plans under the WPA. Williams had taken a seminar class in documentary drama taught by department chair Professor Edward C. Mabie that revolved around contemporary social issues, known as "the Living Newspaper." In this type of play, writers brought to the stage a news story, composing scenes by linking together various headlines or through the use of an announcer. Thus, these were plays that basically illustrated a story in theatrical terms, as the term *Living Newspaper* conveys. Among other projects for this class, Williams wrote a sketch called

"Quit Eating," a dramatization of a hunger strike at Statesville Prison in Illinois protesting parole policies.

Although Williams had finally completed his college degree (nine years after first enrolling as a freshman at the University of Missouri in 1929), his parents chose not to attend his graduation and his father maintained that his son's "next job [would] be in the army," Edwina told her parents.[11] Williams tried to land a job in Chicago with the WPA's Federal Writers' Project but was unsuccessful. The Mummers, for whom he had written both *Candles to the Sun* and *Fugitive Kind*, had disbanded, and his few close friends had either left for graduate school or, in the case of Clark Mills, taken a job teaching French at Cornell University. His sister had been committed to an asylum. He was stuck back in St. Louis with his impossible family and no job prospects. Then, in early September, he came across the following article:

> One day late in August, 650 inmates of the Philadelphia County prison in Holmesberg [*sic*], PA., struck against a monotonous diet of hamburger and spaghetti, refused their supper. Three days later the naked, tortured bodies of four prisoners were found in an airtight cell. They had been scalded to death.
>
> An investigation was launched. Prison guards and officers were arrested. The American public was shocked to learn that "hot steam treatment" had been given 25 unruly prisoners.[12]

The Living Newspaper techniques Williams had worked on at Iowa and the socially committed theatre practiced by the Mummers (clearly evidenced in both *Candles to the Sun* and *Fugitive Kind*) were to find cohesion in a new play about inmates who were subjected to torture in the Philadelphia prison. The play also built on the popularity of crime dramas depicting prison life, such as *The Big House*, directed by George W. Hill in 1930.[13]

The plot of Williams's play follows the published accounts of a sadistic prison warden (Boss Whalen in the play) who responds to the prisoners' hunger strike in protest of the prison diet by subjecting some of them to horrific torture in a steam room ironically named the "Klondike," literally roasting the men alive. The prisoners' leader is a hardened criminal, Butch, who conceals a razor blade to intimidate his fellow inmates (both name and character were taken from Wallace Beery's character in *The Big House*, also named Butch and carrying a concealed sharp instrument, in his case a knife). As the play builds to its melodramatic climax, Butch and the Boss have a confrontation in which Butch kills the warden.

A second plotline concerns a convict known as Canary Jim, a figure who is entirely Williams's invention (as well as his alter ego); he appears neither in newspaper accounts of the strike nor in Hill's film. Jim is used by Boss Whalen to spy on the other prisoners in return for better personal treatment and the possibility of early parole. He has also used his privileged position in the prison hierarchy to better himself by reading and editing a prison monthly he sarcastically describes as "extolling the inspirational quality of prison life" (*NAN*, 11).

As the play opens, a young woman, Eva, arrives at the prison to apply for a secretarial job and meets Jim as she waits to be interviewed by the warden. Jim and Eva develop an emotional connection leading to romance, while the warden manipulates Eva into "cooking" the prison's books, attempting to exploit her for sex. She does not submit to his advances but is nonetheless strangely attracted by Boss Whalen's power. The play culminates with Jim and Eva conspiring to expose the barbaric and inhumane treatment at the prison to end the authoritarian reign of terror imposed by Whalen. After Butch (the sole survivor of the Klondike massacre) is released, Jim helps him free the other prisoners and lock one of the guards in the Klondike: "Sometimes even hell breaks open and the damned get loose" (*NAN*, 154). As the newly released prisoners encircle Boss Whalen, Butch whips him to death. Troopers now storm the prison, but Jim eludes them by removing his shoes and jumping from the window of the island fortress into the sea—whether to death or freedom, we are not told. The play concludes with a scene (mirroring the play's opening) in which the cruise ship *Lorelei* sails past, narrating via loudspeaker the story of the impregnable, "escape-proof" prison to a group of dancing tourists. The sound of the *Lorelei*'s music and dancing are juxtaposed with the final visual image of Eva holding

Jim's shoes following his escape, reinforcing the ambiguity regarding his drowning as the play ends.

What such a summary fails to illuminate is the way Williams transcends the newspaper account of the deadly Pennsylvania prison massacre, moving beyond the sensational headlines to create a personal narrative of entrapment and escape mirroring his own interior longings. Ostensibly a socially committed work about a hunger strike and the need for prison reform, *Nightingales* is actually much more—a profoundly autobiographical play about the playwright's desperate desire to escape his own prison: St. Louis.

Whereas with some writers it may be a questionable tactic for critics to rely upon biographical data to gain insight into their work, in the case of Tennessee Williams it is absolutely essential. As the character Mrs. Venable (closely based on Edwina Williams) says of her poet son in *Suddenly Last Summer* (1958), "The work of a poet is the life of a poet, and—vice versa, the life of a poet is the work of a poet, I mean you can't separate them" (*SLS*, 352). In *Not About Nightingales*, the plot of prisoners hoping to escape from a torturous prison run by an authoritarian "boss" resonated not merely as a work of social justice—the script is dedicated to "the memory of Clarence Darrow, The Great Defender," who had died that March—but as a reflection of Williams's own life crisis in 1938.

The most significant addition to the story of the Klondike massacre is the character of Canary Jim, and it is his struggle toward freedom that transforms this play from clichéd crime melodrama into a work about an individual's search for freedom. Recalling that Williams's original title was "The Rest Is Silence," alluding to the final words of Shakespeare's Hamlet, we are reminded that Jim is one of many heroes (particularly in these early plays) who are, as the playwright felt himself to be, trapped in a hostile world and looking for a means of escape at any cost.

We first meet Jim through the eyes of Eva, when she is a newcomer seeking work at the prison. He introduces himself as being self-educated, having started "[his] present career" (i.e., as a criminal) at the age of sixteen (*NAN*, 10). Interestingly, it was at that same age that Williams's own career began, not in crime but in writing:

at sixteen he wrote his first work for prize money (his essay from an unhappy husband in *Smart Set*) and at seventeen his first paid short story, "The Vengeance of Nitocris," published in *Weird Tales* in 1928. Jim is editor of a prison monthly called *The Archaeopteryx*. The mention of this "extinct species of reptile-bird" is the first of several references to birds and flying in this play about individuals who are, both literally and figuratively, caged. Not only is Jim known by his fellow convicts as "Canary Jim" (referencing his position in the prison hierarchy as a "canary," or snitch) but he falls in love with a woman (Eva Crane) also named after a bird. Even the opening scene alludes to the ubiquitous bird imagery in the play, as Mrs. B, who has come to see the warden about her imprisoned son, notices a spot on Eva's hat: "It's those pigeons, the little rascals!" (*NAN*, 3).

Images of entrapment and flight are integral to the play's development. Early on, Butch tells Jim that if they were not separated by bars "there'd be yellow feathers floating all over Hall C!" (*NAN*, 37). And toward the end of the play, Jim opines, "Canaries never get out of their cages, do they Eva? . . . Naw, they die in 'em—singin' sweetly till doomsday!" (*NAN*, 125).

The imagery of birds and flight in *Not About Nightingales* is taken to its climax when Jim (tormented by his knowledge of what Boss Whalen is planning to do to the prisoners, yet aware that if he publicizes the facts, he will lose any chance of parole) suddenly rips a page out of a book he is reading and throws it to the floor. Referring to the poem on the page, John Keats's "Ode to a Nightingale," he tells Eva, "Those literary punks ought to spend a few years in stir before they select their subjects" (*NAN*, 98). Jim is presumably reflecting upon the lines in Keats's poem that suggest flight from bitter reality by following the nightingale's song:

> Fade far away, dissolve, and quite forget
>> What thou among the leaves hast never known,
> The weariness, the fever, and the fret
>> Here, where men sit and hear each other groan.[14]

Jim reflects upon the fact that "if [he] wrote what [he] wanted to write" (i.e., revealing the horrors inside the prison), he would be stuck inside its walls "till Klondike becomes an ice-plant." If he remains silent and waits until he obtains his parole to write, however, he announces that his subject matter will not be "about nightingales!" (*NAN*, 99). The implication is that "sissy stuff" and lyrical reflections should take a back seat to writing that is committed to advancing social change.

Williams's close friend and occasional collaborator Gore Vidal had a special nickname for him: the Glorious Bird. In his introduction to Williams's *Collected Stories*, Vidal reflects, "I had long since forgotten why [I gave him that name] until I reread the stories. The image of the bird is everywhere. The bird is flight, poetry, life. The bird is time, death." Vidal concludes this appraisal by quoting from Williams's story "The Knightly Quest": "Have you ever seen the skeleton of a bird? If you have you will know how completely they are still flying" (*CS*, xxi). In Williams's play *Orpheus Descending* (1957), about a young, charismatic stranger exotically dressed in a snakeskin jacket and carrying a guitar who arrives unexpectedly and upends normal life in a small, southern town, the character Val Xavier (named after Williams's ancestor Valentine Xavier) suggests the powerful correspondence between birds and freedom throughout the playwright's work: "You know they's a kind of bird that don't have legs so it can't light on nothing but has to stay all its life on its wings in the sky?"[15]

The name "Glorious Bird" is particularly appropriate with reference to *Not About Nightingales*, a play that celebrates the author's desperate need to write as an antidote to imprisonment. Early in the play, Jim observes that the notion of human isolation and solitude are universal: "Ev'ry man living is walking around in a cage. He carries it with him wherever he goes and don't let it go till he's dead. Then the walls come to pieces and he stops being lonesome" (*NAN*, 37). One may conclude from this that writing for Williams was a method by which the prison walls of his life were at least partially torn down.

In the play, it is Eva who reminds Jim that Keats's own life tragically ended at only twenty-five years (close to Williams's age as he began writing the play) and that his poetry is not effeminate whining but represents a way out of prison. Quoting from the sonnet "When

I have fears that I may cease to be," Eva tells him, "[Keats] was like you, Jim. He got out of his prison by looking at the stars. He wrote about beauty as a form of escape" (*NAN*, 100).[16]

Williams's notebooks reveal his profound personal identification with Keats and the ideas generated by his poetry at about the time he wrote *Not About Nightingales*. On October 16, 1937, he made an entry in which he quotes directly from Keats's letters to his friend Charles Brown, written shortly before his death in February 1821:

> Notes from John Keats letters—"Is there another life? Shall I awake and find all this a dream? There must be, *we cannot be created for this sort of suffering.*"
> (I wish that I shared this belief)
> "I wish for death every day and night to deliver me from these pains and then I wish death away for death would destroy even those pains which are better than nothing."

Then, in a truly astonishing passage, Williams addresses Keats directly—almost as a lover—uniting with the Romantic poet in a quasi-mystical bond:

> Keats, did God pity you and love you as much as I? You will be always remembered—I will be forgotten—if only we could stretch out our hands across these dark spaces of death and time—clasp hands and walk into the dark together—why must our . . . lives be so separate—so lonely? I am not *one*—now I am you and all the others—I have broken the walls of self—I have become a part of you all—lost myself in you—no, I am not afraid now! I do not ask for your pity—pity is a poor thing— give me your love—and go with me bravely dear companions— bravely together—the dark has no peril that love and courage cannot face when friends walk together! (*N*, 109)

Both the title of the play and the references to Keats's brief life, suffering, and poetic works suggest that in this prison play, Williams was indeed not writing about nightingales (in the sense of indulging in Romantic escapism), but was probing the deepest recesses of his own subconscious fears and desires for release through the power of art.

In none of Williams's source material about the Holmesburg Prison riots is there reference to an inmate's escape, nor is there any reference to water surrounding the prison. The actual prison at which the riots occurred was built in 1896, and it was in constant use until 1995.[17] An aerial map of the site shows that the structure is completely landlocked, and that Jim's final escape or death by drowning was clearly Williams's invention.

Early in the play, Butch observes that "there's a window in Boss Whalen's office from which a guy could jump right into the Bay." Butch adds that he would like to "kill two birds with a stone" by killing the warden and escaping through the window. However, the convict is unable to swim and is consequently frightened of the water, to which a fellow inmate adds, "Nobody's ever swum it yet." Thus, despite the forbidding surroundings, the playwright indicates at least a hint of possible escape.

Edwina Williams recalls in her memoir, "I marvel that [Tom] ever learned to swim because when he was a boy, one summer at a resort on the [Meramec], his father tried to teach him by throwing him into the river and Tom nearly drowned." To offset this first, traumatic experience with water, she notes, "I sent him to the Lorelei, a pool in St. Louis, where he learned to swim."[18] No matter what the cause, swimming became a passionate refuge for Tom while growing up in St. Louis. It was the only physical exercise he pursued, and something he continued to engage in until the end of his life. As one biographer put it, "He seemed to understand that it was this regimen more than anything that kept him alive" in the face of his many excesses and addictions.[19] Most important, swimming afforded Tom an avenue of escape. At the end of *Not About Nightingales*, when Boss Whalen has been killed and thrown out the window, Jim observes, "There's water out that window. I can swim" (*NAN*, 161). Although Eva tells him "there's not a chance that way," Jim hears the music coming from onboard the cruise ship (significantly named the *Lorelei*!) and imagines his possible rescue. The German Romantic poet Heinrich Heine wrote his famous poem "Die Lorelei" (1824) with the Lorelei anthropomorphized as a siren, sitting on the cliff above the Rhine and combing her golden hair, distracting unwitting seamen with her beauty and song, luring them to crash on the rocks. For Williams, however, the Lorelei Natatorium at 4525 Olive Street represented not fatal temptation but welcome refuge, and the cruise ship whose music reaches Jim's ears at the end of the play represents not the siren's song of death, but hope and the possible opportunity for rebirth.

In a one-act that had undergone numerous revisions just a few months earlier, *Summer at the Lake*, Williams similarly invokes the image of water as a haven for the disenfranchised on a more personal level. Originally titled "Escape," the play consists almost entirely of a volatile exchange between a mother, Mrs. Fenway, and her seventeen-year-old son, Donald; or more accurately, it consists of Mrs. Fenway talking *at* her son. The dialogue between the two is reminiscent of what we know of conversations between the preternaturally verbose Edwina and her diffident son. The young man's dreamy, impractical nature is conjured as his mother compulsively corrects and harps on his inadequacies and weaknesses. Like Amanda Wingfield's in *The Glass Menagerie* (1944), Mrs. Fenway's speech is a variation on Edwina Williams's, although Mrs. Fenway's diction is snootier and more socially conscious than Amanda's. We learn that Mr. and Mrs. Fenway have recently separated, causing both a financial crisis and an impending lifestyle change, including the sale of the lakeside cabin that is their son's sole refuge. Mrs. Fenway repeatedly complains of headaches, the heat at the lakeside cabin, their stifling apartment back in the city, and the sale of the cottage. Meanwhile, she nags at her son to make something of himself. We learn through a letter that his absent father is pressuring Donald to leave school and start work at a factory, just as we know Cornelius did with Tom after he forced his son to withdraw from the University of Missouri in 1932.

From the opening line of the play, "Why are you so restless, Donald?" Mrs. Fenway subjects her son to a barrage of questions concerning his lack of progress at school and his obliviousness toward the future, complaining about his lack of social skills: "People will say you're not like the other boys and they'll—avoid you." In the face of this merciless harangue, Donald cryptically replies that "time doesn't wait for people," informing her, "I don't care about time. Time's nothing" (*SatL*, 64). During Mrs. Fenway's rambling, self-absorbed monologue, Donald quietly slips away. Finally, Mrs. Fenway and her maid, watching from inside the house, realize that Donald is missing, that he has swum out into the lake, and that he will not return.

Despite the lakeside cabin's bucolic setting, this short play is notable for its insistence on St. Louis as a character in its own right. Confronted by the prospect of returning to the city from the isolated cottage, Donald remarks, "Oh, God, mother, I don't want to go home! I hate it! I hate it! It's like being caught in a hideous trap! The brick walls and the concrete and the—the black fire-escapes!" (*SatL*, 62). In other words, the Fenway apartment back in St. Louis is a prison. Unlike *The Glass Menagerie*, where a fire escape offers potential escape, the very words *fire escape* bearing "a touch of accidental poetic truth" (*GM*, 143), in *Summer at the Lake* the fire escape mocks the adolescent's desire to flee his urban prison: "Don't they think people who live in apartments need to escape from anything besides fire?" Donald recounts a vivid dream of running up and down an endless fire escape, yet being unable to set himself free: "At last I stopped running, I couldn't run any further, and the black iron thing started twisting around me like a snake! I couldn't breathe!" (*SatL*, 62).

As we shall see, images of suffocation and constriction are significant in Williams's work—and life. In *Summer at the Lake*, St. Louis and family clearly represent the "black iron thing" wrapping itself around the boy, threatening to ensnare him in a living nightmare that is only alleviated by the cabin at the lake, as Donald observes, "There isn't any time out there. It's night or morning or afternoon but it's never any particular time" (*SatL*, 64).

Interestingly, Kate Chopin, another St. Louis literary luminary who set some of her best works in New Orleans, created in *The Awakening* Edna Pontellier, a heroine who similarly evades the constricting, imprisoning forces of middle-class morality by swimming into the waters of the Gulf of Mexico. Like Canary Jim's in *Not About Nightingales* and Donald's in *Summer at the Lake*, Edna's choice to return to the sea in the novel's closing sentences offers something ambiguous—both death and renewal. Chopin describes

Edna's final moments ambiguously in terms that suggest both suicide and rebirth: "The foamy wavelets curled up to her white feet,
and coiled like serpents about her ankles. She walked out. The water
was chill, but she walked on. The water was deep, but she lifted
her white body and reached out with a long, sweeping stroke. The
touch of the sea is sensuous, enfolding the body in its soft, close
embrace."[20] In describing his revisions to "Escape" in his notebook,
Williams wrote forthrightly, if somewhat unconvincingly, "The boy
in it is *me*. More than any character I've ever created except of course
that he is capable of violent action and I am not—and of course at
the bottom of my heart I really love *life* very dearly" (*N*, 85).

Throughout his life, Williams was obsessed with the idea of the
martyrdom of the artist. As we shall see, he imagined his own death
as a kind of homage to Hart Crane's suicide by drowning in 1932,
and in *Suddenly Last Summer* (1958–1959) he created the character of the poet Sebastian Venable (referencing the martyred Saint
Sebastian), who is literally devoured by a pack of starving street ur-
chins. Although not a suicide like Crane's, Keats's early death from
consumption (the "Romantic disease" par excellence) clearly made
him seem a kindred spirit to Williams.

Early in *Nightingales*, this death wish is provisionally qualified by
the conviction that "intellectual emancipation" is possible. Canary
Jim claims, "And as long as man can think as he pleases he's never
exactly locked up anywhere. He can think himself outside of all their
walls and boundaries and make the world his place to live in" (*NAN*,
38). Williams came to realize that for him, like Jim, escape—whether
by physical change to another geographical location or by flight into
the imagination, as in Keats's poems—would be necessary. At the
time of the play's composition, his beloved sister, Rose, had been
institutionalized, and he saw himself and Rose as two halves of a
single self (they were familiarly described as "the couple" in childhood) rather than two distinct individuals. Her flight into madness
always stood before him as a terrifying prophecy of his own. Two
years older, she led the way when they were children; now she forecast what he perceived as his own inevitable descent. Throughout
his life, Williams's reality was shaped by obsessions—with sudden

flight when the threat of confinement grew too great, with a fear of insanity, and with the imminence of death. The only respite from this unholy trinity was found in his writing, which became both his salvation and his addiction. His lifelong addiction to writing spared him Rose's unhappy fate, but when he could no longer write, he knew the end was near.

* * * * *

In a letter written to his mother in April 1938, Williams expressed great optimism about another new project. This new play was to be a departure from what he saw as the overly dogmatic social content of some of his previous work, and was, in his own words, "well-constructed, no social propaganda, and . . . suitable for the commercial stage" (*SL*, 127). He was hoping to complete the play that spring while finally finishing his degree, at the University of Iowa. He also communicated with Willard Holland about this new play, first titled "April Is the Cruelest Month," hoping to see it included in the Mummers' 1938–1939 season. But when the Mummers were temporarily disbanded due to a dispute between Holland and the theatre's board, Holland advised Williams not to send him his new play, expressing hope of organizing a new company if the Mummers did not agree to his terms (*SL*, 130).

Williams decided instead to submit the play (now titled *Spring Storm*) to Professor Mabie's playwriting workshop at Iowa with the hope of having it performed in the university's new theatre. However, after reading it aloud, the young playwright received a discouraging verdict: "When I had finished reading," he said, "the good professor's eyes had a glassy look as though he had drifted into a state of trance. . . . There was a long and all but unendurable silence. Everyone seemed more or less embarrassed. At last the professor pushed back his chair, thus dismissing the seminar, and remarked . . . 'Well, we all have to paint our nudes!'"[21]

Mabie's disdainful response led to *Spring Storm*'s disappearance for more than half a century, until (as with *Nightingales*) it was discovered in a box of miscellaneous papers that Tom had stored with his mother in St. Louis and that Edwina donated to the Harry Ransom Center at the University of Texas at Austin in 1962 with the assistance of Andreas Brown, owner of the Gotham Book Mart in New York.[22] The play was first produced in 1999, some sixty years after it was written.

The fact that Williams apparently accepted Mabie's unfavorable judgment as definitive and abandoned the play does not negate the fact that *Spring Storm* is an extraordinary work, indispensable to anyone interested in the playwright's relationship to St. Louis and his state of mind at the time he was hoping to cut ties with the city. The play similarly offers valuable insights into many of his later works, including that quintessential St. Louis play, *The Glass Menagerie*.

Spring Storm is set in the small town of Port Tyler, Mississippi, in 1937, and while the setting undoubtedly draws upon the play-wright's childhood memories of Clarksdale, Mississippi, the play is far from being a work of nostalgia. Rather, despite the play's south-ern atmosphere, redolent with picnics along the Mississippi River, cake-baking contests, ball gowns, and black servants, the play is a thinly disguised opportunity for the writer to examine himself in the present. *Spring Storm* is a deeply autobiographical work, rooted in St. Louis—the place Tom still called home.

The play revolves around four young people, all of whom are de-fined by a single urge—Eros. As he described it in an unmailed letter to Willard Holland, "The idea of the play as I see it now is simply a study of Sex—a blind animal urge or force (like the regenerative force of April) gripping four lives and leading them into a tangle of cruel and ugly relations" (*SL*, 96). Of the two central plots, one focuses on the love between Dick Miles and Heavenly Critchfield. Dick is a wanderer seeking escape from the confines of the small, constricting community in which he lives. He begins the play sitting alone, perched on a windy bluff, looking down on the Mississippi River below. Williams describes him as possessing a "fund of restless energy and imagination which prevents him from fitting into the conventional social pattern" (*SS*, 5). Although intensely physical, there is also poetry to his longing; he craves "the dark warm smell of the water real close an' the sound that it makes that's so quiet it's scarcely a sound" (*SS*, 105). Dick is in love with Heavenly and wants her to join him in his quest, but she is unprepared to accompany him to his job working on a government levee project, reverting to her ingrained sense of white, middle-class prejudice ("I thought those levee workers lived with niggers," she exclaims [*SS*, 101]). As a result, Dick abandons her and seeks his freedom alone.

Heavenly is described as a sensuous young woman "of pure southern stock" who is deeply in love with Dick. They have already consummated their relationship, and word of the scandal has begun to spread. But despite their powerful physical bond, Dick is of a lower social station, one that does not allow him to fit into the Port Tyler society that the Critchfield family (especially her mother) wishes to be a part of. Although Heavenly is unconventional and "frankly sensuous without being coarse, fiery-tempered and yet disarmingly sweet" (*SS*, 5), she is a product of her southern upbringing and unable to resist her mother's insistence on social propriety. She is terrified of the fate of becoming a "front porch girl" in this small, provincial southern town, and recalls a woman who "went out all the time with a boy that's left town. Now she just sits on the front porch waiting!—waiting for nothing, getting to be an old maid!" (*SS*, 103).[23] This image foreshadows Heavenly's fate at the end of the play, sitting on the front porch, alone. The wild, sensuous creature thus becomes the very thing she most feared, a spinster.

If the relationship between Dick and Heavenly is filled with the bold, tempestuous passions of youth, the second pairing, between Arthur Shannon and Hertha Neilson, is written in a minor key; neither Arthur nor Hertha has yet figured out who they are, sexually or emotionally. Arthur is the obverse of Dick's sensuous masculinity. Whereas Dick says that "it takes a pair of boots and a flannel shirt to make [him] feel like a man," Arthur comes from a wealthy, cultivated family, and he enters the first scene wearing white flannel pants, sports coat, and a scarf about his throat as though he were still punting at Oxford, where we learn he has gone to study. Despite his wealth and social position, Arthur is tentative and shy. He apparently had one sexual experience in England but admits self-consciously, "I've never had normal relations with people. I want what I'm afraid of and I'm afraid of what I want" (*SS*, 69). Like Dick, he wants to possess Heavenly; but in his case, desire is based less on actual passion than on reinforcing his notion of "normal" heterosexuality. When they were children, Heavenly had delighted in teasing Arthur. Her laughing at him caused him great anguish, as he recalls: "That laugh, that was why I couldn't go back to school anymore—so they had to send me to Europe and say I'd had a nervous breakdown" (*SS*, 70). Arthur admits to feeling like a fake in her presence: "It wasn't the boys yelling sissy that hurt me so much. It was you—you standing there laughing at me the way you were laughing at me a minute ago when I caught your face in the mirror" (*SS*, 70). He hopes to regain a sense of his own masculinity by marrying Heavenly, to reclaim, he tells her, "what you took away from me—that afternoon in the recess yard!" (*SS*, 97). Arthur is also an aspiring writer, but as with his sexuality, his relationship to his vocation is equivocal: "You see, my poetry, it isn't a terrific volcanic eruption—No—it's just a little bonfire of dry leaves and dead branches" (*SS*, 25).

The fourth member of this quartet on the cusp of adulthood is Hertha Neilson. Hertha is poor, and we discover that her father is an abusive alcoholic. In contrast with the beautiful, sensual Heavenly, Hertha is bookish and sexually repressed. It is only with Arthur, for whom she harbors a secret flame, that she is able to be fully herself. In their scene in the first act, immediately following the opening scene with Dick and Heavenly, Hertha ascends to the summit of the bluff just as the spring storm threatens to break. She shouts down to Arthur, "I'd like to die in a storm!" calling it "the noblest death I ever heard of" (*SS*, 29), prefiguring her association with death. Just before her descent at the end of the scene, Hertha deliberately positions herself between two dead trees, pretending to throw a curse on the town below.

While *Spring Storm* undoubtedly revolves around Eros, "the biggest God of them all" (*SS*, 95), the play's true subject is less the characters' sexual desires than the uncertainties that plague the lives of four young adults suspended in a kind of adolescent limbo reminiscent of Frank Wedekind's *Spring's Awakening* (1891; first performed 1906)—they are neither children nor fully realized adults—just as the twenty-seven-year-old Williams was at the time. He had not yet graduated from college, was uncertain about his literary vocation, and had not yet come to terms with or fully recognized his sexual preferences.

All four characters embody one or more important aspects of Williams's own complex and conflicted nature—the restless desire for adventure and escape from a small, constricting community (Dick); the need to ostentatiously flout convention and flaunt one's sexuality in the face of a puritanical, socially respectable matriarch (Heavenly); the self-doubts of a young, timorous artist profoundly uncertain of the trajectory of both career and sexual orientation (Arthur); and finally, the dread of loneliness and the attraction to death (Hertha). In a sense, *Spring Storm* does not take place in any real geographical place; instead the play's true location lies within Williams's aching heart and fragile psyche on the cusp of leaving home. This makes the play entirely different from anything he had written previously, and vital to an understanding of Williams despite its relative obscurity.

From the brief descriptions of the characters above, it is apparent that both the male and female characters represent bifurcated aspects of Williams's own nature: The two men's names (Dick and Arthur) suggest their identities, one bold and sexually uninhibited, a physical adventurer; the other a sensitive, neurasthenic artist. Likewise, the names of the two women, Heavenly and Hertha, suggest a binary between heaven and earth, a dichotomy between the attraction to a transgressive sexuality and the fear of acting on forbidden urges.

In this context, it is important to remember that Williams had virtually no emotional contact with or physical affection from his father growing up. His mother, despite her tiny stature, was the dominant force in the house and embraced an extremely repressive and puritanical attitude toward all things sexual. Even taking into account the social norms of the 1930s, Edwina Williams was also extreme in her total aversion to any kind of physical contact, including a mother's tender touch. According to the playwright's brother, Dakin, their mother was "president of the anti-sex league" and shunned any physical displays of affection: "She just didn't touch you, . . . She didn't react well to anything physical. We never had it, and didn't expect it."[24] As a result, Williams often described his youthful self as "the little Puritan," and biographer John Lahr informs us that Williams did not even masturbate until the age of twenty-six and (except for a single tryst with a young woman at the

University of Iowa) remained celibate until the age of twenty-seven. Lahr concludes that "his writing became both a conscious and an unconscious attempt to chart the unlearning of repression."[25]

While the four characters in *Spring Storm* represent different aspects of Williams's own nature, the tragedies of the two women in particular reflect the playwright's perspective toward Rose, who by the time of the play's composition had been institutionalized. From this perspective, Heavenly represents the side of Rose whose youthful beauty, rebelliousness, and sensuality were systematically undermined by her mother's values. Mrs. Critchfield is a satirical portrait of Edwina Williams, a woman whose concerns with social standing, reputation, and family pedigree override her daughter's well-being: "Don't you think that having the finest blood in America imposes on you some obligations? I'm sure that you do. . . . A girl whose name is listed under five or six different headings in Zella Armstrong's *Notable Families* and every other good southern genealogy couldn't help but feel it her sacred duty to live up to the best that's in her" (*SS*, 49).

A large portrait of a heroic Civil War ancestor, Colonel Wayne, hangs prominently in the Critchfield home, and Williams's stage directions specify that it be "preferably in a position that seems to command the whole room" (*SS*, 35). Mrs. Critchfield has repeatedly forced Heavenly to apologize to this portrait as a child, her mother says, "because I wanted you to understand the responsibility of having fine blood in you" (*SS*, 54). The impact of the over-large portrait of Colonel Wayne owes a strong debt both to Henrik Ibsen's *Hedda Gabler* and to Williams's own Tennessee frontier ancestry on his father's side. Although Mrs. Critchfield is essentially a comic creation, her prioritization of social propriety above feeling informs Heavenly's tragedy in the play, clearly foreshadowing Amanda Wingfield's deleterious impact on her daughter in *The Glass Menagerie*.

In contrast with the satirical portrait of Mrs. Critchfield, the portrait of Heavenly's father is surprisingly sympathetic. Oliver Critchfield is almost a cliché of the henpecked husband suffering from indigestion and gas. In the first scene in their home, he "flops wearily into the big chair under the floor lamp and unfolds the evening paper to the market reports" (*SS*, 56), only to have his wife charge into the room, "shooting Olympian bolts" at him, and, "like a predatory hawk," snatch the newspaper from his hands. The portrait of this unhappy marriage is an obvious reflection of the domestic circumstances Williams saw at home, and the chair and lamp are clear allusions to the overstuffed chair and floor lamp that graced the Williams home, and that the author memorably anthropomorphized in his autobiographical essay "The Man in the Overstuffed Chair":

> My father was never willing to part with the overstuffed chair. It really doesn't look like it could be removed . . . , as if it had absorbed in its fabric and stuffing all the sorrows and anxieties of our family life. . . . Over this chair stands another veteran piece of furniture, a floor lamp that must have come with it. . . . It rises from its round metal base on the floor. . . . Then it curves over his head one of the most ludicrous things a man has ever sat under, a sort of Chinesey-looking silk lamp shade with a fringe about it, so that it suggests a weeping willow. Which is presumably weeping for the occupant of the chair. (*CS*, x–xi)

A benign, put-upon figure, Oliver Critchfield shares a glass of whiskey with his daughter in a beautiful and tender scene that was not included in the only surviving draft of the full manuscript of *Spring Storm*, found in the Harry Ransom Center.[26] In response to Heavenly's cry of despair, "Why is everything so crazy, so mixed up!?" Mr. Critchfield is able to offer a kind of laconic sympathy: "I guess those things are sort of natural phenomena. Like these spring storms we've been having. They do lots of damage. . . . What for? I don't know" (*SS*, 81).

The other, terrifying side to Williams's own father's nature (epitomized by his having had his ear chewed off in a bar fight) is found in Arthur's description of Hertha's father, notorious in Port Tyler as "the terrible Swede": "He comes home polluted on Saturday nights, so I hear. Makes a big scene, throws things, calls you names" (*SS*, 119). In her memoir, *Remember Me to Tom*, Edwina Williams reflects on the impact her husband had upon their daughter. She

describes an incident where Rose wanted to invite a young man over
to the house, with Cornelius adamantly refusing to leave the living
room, forcing a confrontation:

> He stayed stretched out on the sofa, listening to the radio. . . .
> She phoned the young man and told him not to come over.
> Then she walked into the living room and evidently said some-
> thing her father considered saucy. He slapped her.
>   She burst into tears and ran out into the street.

When her grandmother asked her where she was heading, Rose replied, "To find a policeman to come and lock up my father. . . . He's
crazy!"[27]

If Heavenly is doomed to life as a "front porch girl," Hertha's
tragic fate may be what the playwright feared would become of
Rose: suicide. Hertha's solitary, morbid nature is signaled in the
play's opening scene as she stands poised between two dead trees.
In the third act, she reflects on her own nervous instability after
attempting to shush two young lovers in the town library, where
she works. After they call her a "cranky old maid," Hertha (precisely
Rose's age at the time, twenty-eight) reflects on her predicament,
even mentioning "dementia praecox," the diagnosis that had just
been given to Rose: "Maybe I'm losing my mind. . . . Lots of girls
do at my age. Twenty-eight. Lots of them get *dementia praecox* at
about that age, especially when they're not married. I've read about
it. They get morbid and everything excites them and they think
they're being persecuted by people. I'm getting like that" (*SS*, 114).
Although Hertha is already emotionally unstable, it is Arthur's
violent physical assault and rejection of her that send her over the
edge. Arthur arrives at the library drunk after being punched by
Dick ("Wrap him up in tissue paper and send him back to Mama
with my regards!" Dick leers to Heavenly after knocking Arthur
down [*SS*, 107]) and tries to reassert his masculinity at the virginal
librarian's expense. He grabs Hertha, telling her that her lips "have
been in the ground so long, not even April can make them warm,"
and predicting, "If I touched you with my lips you'd think you'd
been scorched by fire. You'd crumple up like a little white moth

that's flown into the candle flame" (*SS*, 122), and then forcibly kiss-
es the struggling Hertha, who goes limp in his arms. These words
would reappear some ten years later, in a play originally titled "The
Moth," later known as *A Streetcar Named Desire*. However, instead
of crumpling, Hertha is suddenly liberated from her faintheartedness
by Arthur's display of sexual desire and shocks him by responding in
kind, "Arthur! Now I can tell you!—I love you! So much that I've
nearly gone mad!" (*SS*, 123). Having awakened a dormant sexuality
in the fragile girl, Arthur is appalled. He tries to recant what he has
said, but when he cannot, he tells Hertha, "I didn't know you were
like that. I thought you were different. . . . You—you *disgust* me!"
(*SS*, 123).

This scene, directly precipitating Hertha's suicide, appears to read
as though it had been lifted from an incident between Williams and
his sister when Rose betrayed his trust and tattled to their parents
about a party Tom had held without permission at their home, then
located on 42 Aberdeen Place in St. Louis. Williams faithfully re-
corded the incident some forty years later in *Memoirs*: "We passed
each other on the landing and I turned upon her like a wildcat and
I hissed at her: 'I hate the sight of your ugly old face!' Wordless,
stricken and crouching, she stood there motionless in a corner of the
landing as I rushed out of the house" (122).

Although virtually unknown to most theatergoers, *Spring Storm*
is perhaps the closest thing we have to a psychological "portrait of
the artist as a young man" at the end of 1938. Despite the fact that
the play is set in the deep South, *Spring Storm* offers a remarkable
portrait of the playwright's fragmented psyche just prior to his departure from St. Louis. It depicts a young man profoundly insecure
emotionally, artistically, and sexually. Williams was then twenty-seven
years old, but (like his alter ego in this play, Arthur) certainly not yet
an adult.

* * * * *

Stairs to the Roof (1941), the final play of this seminal early period, is,
like *The Glass Menagerie*, explicitly set in St. Louis during the period
1933–1936. This was about the time that Williams was sent to work
at the International Shoe Company by his father after failing ROTC
at the University of Missouri. When he found out his son had (to

his way of thinking, deliberately) failed the compulsory course, C.C. Williams refused to allow him to return to Columbia for his senior year, insisting that he instead go to work as a stocking clerk at the same company where he was a manager.

In *Remember Me to Tom*, Edwina describes what Tom's failure at ROTC meant to his father, a Spanish-American War veteran—as well as what it meant to her son:

> Tom's failing ROTC was like a slap in the face to his father. "I told you he's not doing any good in college," Cornelius stormed at me. "I'm going to take him out and put him to work." This was the third year of the Depression and Cornelius constantly felt the financial bottom dropping out of his world. . . . He insisted Tom not return to the university for his final year. Tom wanted with all his heart to get a degree, to keep learning, to be able to write more effectively . . . but he did not defy his father. I can only guess what this must have cost him psychically.[28]

At the time of Tom's employment at the International Shoe Company, St. Louis was home to both the nation's largest footwear manufacturer (International Shoe, founded in 1911) and the third largest (Brown Shoe Company). By 1934, St. Louis manufacturers boasted the production of one-fifth of all the shoes in the United States.[29]

The nearly three years Williams spent at International Shoe were profoundly unhappy ones; his unhappiness is portrayed in great detail in *The Glass Menagerie*. But whereas *Menagerie* reveals the impact of Tom's sense of emotional confinement on his mother, his sister, and himself from a personal perspective, *Stairs to the Roof*, fueled by the political leanings of the Mummers and the Living Newspaper seminar he took with Professor Mabie at Iowa, is an expressionistic portrait of the socially constricting forces and intolerable working conditions that led its hero to despair.

Unlike the other full-length plays Williams had written to this point, *Stairs to the Roof* is a comedy—of sorts. More accurately, the play might be described as an expressionistic fantasy in which the

Figure 24. Tom dressed in business attire while working at the International Shoe Company (1932–1935). Courtesy of the Tennessee Williams Collection, Harry Ransom Center, University of Texas at Austin.

then thirty-year-old playwright tried to convert the claustrophobia he had felt during those earlier years into a quest for the freedom he thirsted for. Relying on nonrealistic staging more than in any previous work, *Stairs* combines the lessons of Proletarian Theatre already learned from the Mummers with the German expressionist techniques he was now quickly absorbing at the new institution he began attending in 1940, the New School for Social Research in New York, where the German émigré Erwin Piscator was head of the Dramatic Workshop.

Stairs was written at a time when Williams was beginning to feel liberated. He had experienced New Orleans, and had acquired the prestigious literary agent Audrey Wood, with whom he was to remain deeply connected not only as an agent, but as a dear friend (and surrogate mother) for more than three decades. He also felt financially more secure, having successfully applied for a $1,000 Rockefeller Fellowship, at Wood's prompting, which allowed him the freedom to study at the New School under both Piscator and the esteemed writer, critic, and playwriting professor John Gassner.

The play, then, reflects a time when Williams had stepped out of his personal darkness and into the light. He was no longer the "deadbeat son," the phrase his father used to browbeat him with.

Instead, he was an aspiring New York playwright with a new identity ("Tennessee Williams from Memphis") and a promising professional future ahead of him. In order to submit his work to a Group Theatre contest for writers under twenty-five, he liberated himself from his past still further by deducting the three years he had spent at International Shoe. In keeping with this new spirit of optimism, Williams called *Stairs to the Roof* a "play for tomorrow," although the work's crucial subtitle maintains its reflection on past sorrows: *A Prayer for the Wild of Heart That Are Kept in Cages.*

Several of the play's scenes refer directly to its protagonist's dreary past life in St. Louis—especially the mechanistic office scenes where the young hero, Benjamin Murphy, works at Continental Shirtmakers under his boss, Mr. Gum. Williams meticulously described this period of monotonous drudgery in an earlier, unpublished story with nearly the same title, "Stair to the Roof." The short story was written shortly after Williams's nervous collapse in St. Louis, and in this tragic precursor to the play he depicts a young poet, Edward Schiller (perhaps an allusion to the German Romantic poet-playwright Friedrich von Schiller). The story begins with Schiller's suicide, jumping to his death from the roof of the warehouse where he works. In this preliminary "sketch" for the play, Williams described his clerical labors in grotesque terms: "The duplicating machine is a monster with gaping jaws that will . . . crush him between its gelatined rolls, if he doesn't feed it fast enough. . . . the ticking clock that might have brought deliverance is now an axe hanging over his head."[30]

In the play version of "Stair to the Roof," in keeping with the optimism he now felt in New York as opposed to his feelings in St. Louis, Williams transformed the story's suicidal gloom into fantasy. However, the play's opening stage directions reveal the horribly regimented and mechanistic world of Continental Shirtmakers (where Benjamin Murphy has worked for the past eight years), reminding us that the dehumanizing effects of the soul-destroying work remained closely tied to the playwright's vision:

> The curtain rises on a department of Continental Shirtmakers. There is only the minimum equipment on the stage, such as Mr. Gum's desk and the enormous clock at the front of the

office. The rest is suggested by the movements of the workers. They sit on stools, their arms and hands making rigid, machine-like motions above their imaginary desks to indicate typing, filing, operating a comptometer, and so forth. Two middle-aged women are reciting numbers to each other, antiphonally, in high and sing-song voices. . . . There is a glassy brilliance to the atmosphere: one feels that it must contain a highly selected death ray that penetrates living tissue straight to the heart. (*SttR*, 3)

Employing the literary trope of the *Aufbruch* (breakthrough) typical of early German expressionist drama, *Stairs* chronicles Benjamin's liberation from constraints that hem him in at work and in his unhappy marriage at home. Through short, staccato, cinematic scenes accompanied by titles (indicating the influence of Bertolt Brecht, whom Williams would have been exposed to at the New School under the émigrés Gassner and Piscator), Benjamin suddenly quits his job, leaves his wife, and meets the Girl, who, as in many German expressionist dramas, goes unnamed. The Girl parallels Benjamin's struggle; she too is oppressed by her job in a legal office, where she is employed by a boss on whom she has a crush but who is oblivious to her longing.

In his escape from the constraints of job and wife, Benjamin visits a number of familiar St. Louis landmarks, including Washington University and its historic Quadrangle, the Grand Basin with its lagoon, and the zoo (where the two lovers free the foxes from their cages), culminating in a carnival scene in Forest Park. The play moves farther and farther away from realism, and the carnival scene builds the play to its climax. Along the way, each scene is punctuated by a series of offstage responses by "Mr. E." (a homophone of the word *mystery*), a shadowy, godlike figure. At the end of the play, Williams creates a deus ex machina as Mr. E. allows Benjamin and the Girl to disappear, eluding the clutches of Mr. Gum and the other Continental stockholders who pursue the two young fugitives up to the roof. With a blinding flash of lightning followed by thunder, the lovers vanish, accompanied by martial music, bells, and Roman candles in a celebration of "The Millennium."

In *Stairs to the Roof*, Williams celebrated his own liberation from the oppressive forces that threatened him in St. Louis. With the play's mixture of expressionism, science fiction, and utopian optimism, Williams hoped to parlay his new good fortune as a New York playwright into commercial success. Unfortunately, the moment was not right, and success still evaded his grasp. The manuscript of *Stairs to the Roof* was finished around Christmas of 1941, just as the United States entered World War II following the Japanese bombing of Pearl Harbor. Although Williams felt that the play "shines . . . about as well as I am able to say it right now," he realized that its buoyant optimism put it out of touch with the times. He confessed to Wood in a letter that *Stairs* might be "more a play for tomorrow than today. . . . Today is pretty dreadful, isn't it?"[31] The young writer's longing for commercial breakthrough ended in disappointment as the world he was writing about suddenly changed overnight on December 7th.

By the time the play was first performed at the Pasadena Playhouse in 1947, Williams was a very different sort of writer. Although he now considered the work "unskilled and awkward," he wrote in an afterword to the play's program that he envied his hero's optimism:

> I wish I still had the idealistic passion of Benjamin Murphy! You may smile as I do at the sometimes sophomoric aspect of his excitement but I hope you will respect the purity of his feeling and the honest concern which he had in his heart for the basic problem of mankind which is to dignify our lives with a certain freedom. (quoted in *SttR*, 101)

A few years after the completion of *Stairs*, however, Williams finally became the playwright he had always dreamt of being. He finally created a play that seamlessly combined commercial success and poetry in a way that *Stairs to the Roof* had not. That play, of course, was *The Glass Menagerie*, the young writer's confessional play about his life in St. Louis.

Chapter Four

More Faithful Than I Intended to Be

NO SINGLE WORK underscores Tennessee Williams's painful, complicated relationship with St. Louis more plainly than *The Glass Menagerie* (1944). Williams himself said of this play, which made him famous virtually overnight, "[It is] the saddest . . . I have ever written. It is full of pain. It's painful for me to see it."[1] The work's capacity to evoke deep feelings of melancholy in audiences explains why, more than seventy-five years after its Chicago premiere in 1944, *Menagerie* still resonates today with a lyrical power unmatched on the American stage. Indeed, the play carefully avoids the overtly violent images found in so many of Williams's other plays and stories, the inclusion of which he himself described as a "tendency toward an atmosphere of hysteria and violence" in his works, "an atmosphere that has existed since the beginning" (*NSE*, 94).

It is hardly surprising that Williams would have chosen to write a play set in his own family, or that his first sustained effort in that genre would reach back into the period of his youth in St. Louis in the 1930s. Classmate A. E. Hotchner recalled that various drafts Williams submitted for workshopping in Professor William G. B. ("Pop") Carson's spring 1937 playwriting class at Washington University were vignettes set in Williams's family. "During the semester, he wrote fragments of a play about his mother and sister, fragments which bore a strong resemblance to what was to be *The Glass Menagerie*," Hotchner said.[2] He also wrote a sketch (likely in 1938) titled "Apt. F, 3rd Flo. So.," concerning a brother and sister set in the sister's ivory-colored bedroom.[3]

More significantly, the very first play Williams wrote and saw produced upon his arrival in New York in 1940 was a direct antecedent of what would become *Menagerie*. This one-act, *The Long Goodbye*, clearly anticipates the later play in both subject matter (a young writer on the cusp of leaving his childhood home) and form (relying heavily on flashbacks disrupting the narrative arc) to convey the agonizing process of letting go of the claims of the past. The play was first produced at the New School for Social Research, where Williams was then studying, eagerly looking forward to what he was sure would be his first big break with *Battle of Angels*.[4] In a February 1940 letter to his agent, Audrey Wood, written from the YMCA where he was living, Williams adopts a somewhat condescending tone toward the production, directed by fellow student John O'Shaughnessy, who had taken the step of adding a socially conscious speech of his own to "improve" the script: "Saw a *stinking* rehearsal of my one-act—Student actors at the School for the Feeble-minded! (Malicious remark). Hope no one is there unless it improves vastly. John wrote a soap-box oration himself and inserted it in the script to give it a social message" (*SL*, 230). Although the play is supposedly set in a tenement in the "washed out middle of a large mid-western American city" (*LG*, 161), Williams makes no effort to mask the actual location as anything other than St. Louis, and the script is sprinkled with local references to such St. Louis landmarks as Sportsman's Park (then home to the St. Louis Cardinals), Bellerive Country Club, the Old Courthouse, Ladue, and the Chase Hotel Roof.

The setting of the play is identified as "apartment F, third floor south," a detail emphasizing the importance of the author's memory upon the work as a whole. Below, the shouts of children playing "Fly, Sheepie, Fly" are accompanied by the sound of the radio blaring out the Cards game. Joe, a twenty-three-year-old aspiring writer, is preparing to move out of the apartment where he has spent his childhood. We learn that his mother has recently died of cancer and that she has left him a small inheritance to make his way. During the course of the play, Joe is visited by a friend, Silva, and the two watch the movers come and go, removing various articles of furniture from Joe's past, including the bed on which he and his sister were born. In scenes of flashback, we not only meet his (surprisingly sympathetic) mother, who is not afraid of dying and sees death as "being let out of a box" instead of being interred in one; we are also introduced to the writer's sister, Myra, formerly a champion swimmer who "got kicked off the Lorelei team" for breaking training rules and has grown increasingly morally lax and reckless. As the last pieces of furniture are removed, "the yellow stains on the walls, the torn peeling paper with its monotonous design, the fantastically hideous chandelier now show up in cruel relief" (*LG*, 179), illuminating the ugliness of the writer's environment. Finally, all that remain are the sounds of the playing children's voices shouting "Olly-olly-oxen-free!" and Joe's paroxysms of nostalgia—followed by a valedictory salute to the now-empty apartment.

Despite the fact that Silva has told Joe, "This place is done for. . . . You can't help it" (*LG*, 178), the overall tone is one of nostalgia and loss, rather than anger. As in *Menagerie*, the key relationships are with the young man's mother and sister, although they are obviously portrayed very differently. There is also the trope of the absent father—not as a "telephone man who fell in love with long distance," as in *Menagerie*, but as a brooding, silent figure who sat in a big overstuffed chair, then "just got tired of living a regular middle-class life" and suddenly departed (*LG*, 177).

Although the play's final image is one of nostalgia, the children's shouts of "Olly-olly-oxen-free!" and Joe's ironic salute perhaps best express the feelings of hard-won freedom the playwright was attempting to articulate in *The Long Goodbye*. In a letter from February 21, 1940, to Alice Lippmann,[5] a patron of the arts and friend, Williams expressed his feelings unambiguously, employing the familiar image of the newly released bird: "Freedom is ruthless because it makes us forgetful of other things. For the past few weeks I've been like a bird let out of a cage. I've felt as though I'd just inherited the sky. It has made me a little dizzy" (*SL*, 231). In *Menagerie*, Williams took the subject matter and elements of the form of *The Long Goodbye* and adapted and developed them much further. More importantly, he was able to directly access the pain, anger, and guilt with infinitely more honesty and introspection than he could have in 1940, when the one-act was completed. He had attained much greater experience as well as a measure of distance in the intervening years. After leaving St. Louis for the French Quarter in December of 1938, he had greater financial independence, thanks to a $1,000 Rockefeller Fellowship secured with the aid of his prestigious agent and mentor, Wood. Before resuming the family drama that would become *Menagerie*, he had also traveled to places as disparate as California, Mexico, Provincetown, Taos, and New York; he had grown harder and had developed more resilience after his 1940 failure in Boston with *Battle of Angels*.

Williams took up residence in Los Angeles in 1943, working for MGM as a screenwriter while simultaneously hoping to peddle his screenplay, a preliminary version of *Menagerie* known as *The Gentleman Caller*. Although working for MGM initially seemed promising, Williams quickly discovered that he was not so much writing screenplays as constructing "celluloid brassiere[s]" (*SL*, 455), his pet term for Hollywood screenplays like *Marriage Is a Private Affair*, the vehicle for Lana Turner to which he was assigned. In August he wrote to Wood in protest, saying, "Let's face it!—I can only write for *love*," concluding that he needed to "adhere very strictly to the most honest writing, that [he was] capable of" (*SL*, 476).

In Williams's "provisional film story treatment" of *The Gentleman Caller*, the character of the mother is described as a conventional woman with a "heroic fighting spirit concentrated blindly on trying to create a conventionally successful adjustment for two children who are totally unfitted for it," suggesting that at this point she was the writer's primary focus. She represented "the natural elegance in the Old South," and the main thrust of his screenplay was "a defense of the romantic attitude towards life, a violent protest against the things that destroy it,"[6] which indicates that he was thinking about the prototype for the character who would become Blanche DuBois in *A Streetcar Named Desire*.

Months earlier, on January 13, 1943, after spending nearly six years confined at the state mental institution in Farmington, Williams's sister, Rose, had been subjected to a prefrontal lobotomy, performed by Dr. Paul Schrader. Edwina Williams arranged for the operation without offering any advance warning to Tom, and he never forgave his mother for consenting to the surgery that was to radically change the course of his sister's life (and his own) without consulting him. More than anything else, this devastating event altered the playwright's perspective toward his family, and the play he was working on.

At the time of Rose's surgery, the prefrontal lobotomy was not considered the act of barbaric medical malpractice it is seen as today; rather, it was advertised as a miraculous treatment giving hope to people with apparently incurable mental illnesses such as schizophrenia by pacifying the person in distress. Rose had been diagnosed with schizophrenia (then more commonly known as dementia praecox) as early as 1937, and references to dementia praecox appear in several early works by Williams, including *Spring Storm* (1938), in which Hertha's psychological state was modeled on Rose Williams's increasing paranoia and sexual repression, as discussed in chapter 3. A Portuguese doctor, Egas Moniz, invented the procedure, and it was developed in the United States by neurologist Walter Freeman and neurosurgeon James Watts. In November 1942, *Time* magazine outlined the procedure and its purposes in layman's terms:

> Purpose of the operation is to sever most of the nerve connections between the prefrontal lobes and the thalamus. The thalamus is lower, nearer the spinal cord. This part of the brain is widely believed to be the seat of emotions—fear, rage, lust, sorrow, and other purely animal instincts. All animals have a thalamus, but the higher animals—above all, man—developed superimposed layers of brain tissue which exercise some control over the thalamus.[7]

A significant phrase in this popular view of the operation is the one that marks the distinction between the thalamus of animals and of "the higher animals," that is, man. This distinction, so pointedly emphasized in the *Time* essay, is also a central issue in Williams's play. The binary of what it means to be animal versus human is present from *Menagerie*'s opening scene, when Amanda reminds her son, Tom, that "animals have secretions in their stomachs which enable them to digest food without mastication, but human beings are supposed to chew their food before they swallow it down" (*GM*, 146). Amanda's insistence on "higher" instincts is not there simply to provide color and authenticity to her speech, but reflects Williams's own literary and psychological preoccupations at the time with what it means to be human, especially in light of his discovery of this theme in the work of his hero, D. H. Lawrence.

After abruptly departing New Orleans early in 1939, a time when the nearly twenty-eight-year-old writer was still uncertain about his sexuality, Williams drove to California with a friend, and he found a copy of Lawrence's letters in a Laguna Beach library. The discovery was electrifying. In brief, Lawrence's writings offered Williams permission not only to acknowledge his not fully realized homosexuality but to embrace life, human instinct, and the world of the senses in ways that finally allowed him to separate himself from his mother's repressive, puritanical nature. This influence is present in numerous works written in the period beginning with Williams's departure from St. Louis near the end of 1938 through the early 1940s—the very time he was working on the various drafts of *The Glass Menagerie*. Among the most significant examples of this profound Lawrencian influence are his first professional production, *Battle of Angels* (1940); *You Touched Me!*, his stage adaptation (coauthored with Donald Windham) of the Lawrence short story "You Touched Me" (1942); and his one-act play written following his visit with Lawrence's widow, Frieda Lawrence, at their ranch in Taos, New Mexico. This last work, *I Rise in Flames, Cried the Phoenix* (1939–1941), is an account of Lawrence's final hours as well as his philosophy. Together with the previously discussed Williams poem "Cried the Fox" (1939), which carries the dedication "For D. H. L.," these works reveal the powerful influence of the English writer (who had died in 1930) upon Williams's psyche, an influence that is also palpably felt in *The Glass Menagerie*. Significantly, scene 3 of that play opens with Tom's anger at Amanda's confiscation of his books, a violation that she readily acknowledges: "I took that horrible novel back to the library—yes! That hideous book by that insane Mr. Lawrence. I cannot control the output of diseased minds or people who cater to them—BUT I WON'T ALLOW SUCH FILTH BROUGHT INTO MY HOUSE! No, no, no, no, no!" (*GM*, 161).

The reference here is to his mother's hostility to Lawrence's paean to instinctual, animal life and sexuality in the scandalous novel

Lady Chatterley's Lover (a work banned in Britain until 1961). It is also indicative of the underlying opposition in *Menagerie* between animal instinct and what it means to be human. In scene 4, after Tom has described to his mother his frustration with working at the warehouse and the utter absence of adventure in his life, Amanda criticizes him by saying, "Most men find adventure in their careers," and, "Not everybody has a craze for adventure." Tom's fiery rebuke reveals Williams's passionate embrace of Lawrence's philosophy: "Man is by instinct a lover, a hunter, a fighter, and none of those instincts are given much play at the warehouse!" Amanda's reply is equally significant: "Instinct is something that people have got away from! It belongs to animals! Christian adults don't want it!" (*GM*, 174).

For Williams, his mother's decision to subject Rose to the action that deprived her of agency and self-sufficiency for the rest of her life was entirely consistent with Edwina's narrow worldview that one's animalistic longings (including sex) must be rooted out in favor of "higher" aspirations, as suggested in the *Time* essay about lobotomy. The operation on Rose, therefore, was for Williams an expression of his mother's hostility to all that was wild and unruly about *both* of her children, Rose and Tom. To Edwina, it was a disorder that needed to be suppressed at any price, and in Rose's case, at least, it was.

In the months prior to her surgery, Rose made allegations of sexual advances made upon her by her father. These allegations were, at least for the playwright, demonstration that his mother's countenancing of the operation was a deliberate attempt to shut Rose up and avoid the possibility of a public scandal about Cornelius's possible sexual predations. While the veracity of these allegations was not proved, fifteen years later, in *Suddenly Last Summer* (1958), a play set not in St. Louis but in a tropical climate suggestive of the Key West he came to love and where he later built homes for both himself and Rose, Williams returned to his own family drama in a different guise. To prevent word getting out about her son Sebastian's mysterious death, Mrs. Venable shuts her niece Catharine up in a mental institution and threatens her with a prefrontal lobotomy if she continues to speak out about Sebastian's sexual indiscretions and subsequent violent death the previous summer.

In *Suddenly Last Summer*, Williams addressed his hostility toward his mother even more forthrightly than in *Menagerie*, where, for all Amanda's vanity and garrulousness, we are permitted to understand her desperation and caring for her children. In *Suddenly Last Summer*, Mrs. Venable demonstrates cold-blooded calculation in her scheme to cover up Sebastian's homosexual proclivities and grisly death at the hands of a band of starving village boys. She has engaged a prominent doctor who believes in the experimental surgery as a means of pacifying violent patients when all else fails, and she hopes to leverage her enormous wealth ostensibly in support of his medical research. He describes his pleasure when a formerly hopeless case whispers, "Oh, how blue the sky is!" and feels "proud and relieved because up until then her speech, everything that she'd babbled, was a torrent of obscenities!"[8] Despite his eagerness to pursue his research, the doctor has legitimate medical concerns: "There is a good deal of risk involved in—the operation" (*SLS*, 365). However, Mrs. Venable does not wish to heal her niece, merely to silence her. While the doctor remains cautious about the possible outcomes of the surgery, suggesting, "I can't guarantee that a lobotomy would stop her—*babbling*," Mrs. Venable cynically reveals that her true motive in encouraging the operation is, if not to buy her niece's complete silence, at least to render her speech nonsense: "That may be, maybe not, but after the operation, who would *believe* her" (*SLS*, 367).

In her memoir, *Remember Me to Tom* (1963), Edwina takes pains to place the blame for Rose's operation on others, most notably the doctor and her husband: "I now think the lobotomy for Rose was a grave mistake. We all believed at the time that this operation might completely cure Rose, as we relied on the advice of a local psychiatrist."[9] Edwina also argues, implausibly, that Cornelius feared for his own safety after a doctor told him, "Rose is liable to go down and get a butcher's knife one night and cut your throat."[10] However, Edwina surely realized that her daughter did not show a proclivity toward violence, and knew that much of Rose's fear and paranoia were due to the perpetual cloud of domestic violence that hung over the Williams home, where the sights and sounds of her parents' violent quarrels over money, liquor, and sex were almost certainly contributing factors, if not precipitating causes of her mental breakdown.

In her memoir, however, Edwina also suggests that Cornelius's stinginess (he apparently resented paying for a psychiatrist) was another inducement for having the surgery done at a bargain price:

> The psychiatrists convinced Cornelius the only answer was lobotomy. A noted surgeon was about to perform the operation on thirty selected patients at no cost to them, and the psychiatrists indicated Rose could be one of the chosen few, whereas if the operation were to be performed at a private hospital, it would cost thousands of dollars. They tried to make me believe this was the only hope for Rose, that otherwise she would spend the rest of her days a raving maniac in a padded cell.[11]

Only a full week after the surgery was completed, in a January 20, 1943, letter, did Edwina notify her son, then living in New York, about it: "Now that it's over, I can tell you about Rose who has successfully come through a head operation."[12] Williams's response indicates his utter bafflement about what had transpired; on January 25 he answered, "I did not at all understand the news about Rose. What kind of operation was it and what was it for?" (*SL*, 429).

Not surprisingly, Williams blamed his mother for consenting to Rose's operation without informing him beforehand. But unlike the blatant and explicit reference of Mrs. Venable's vindictively seeking a lobotomy for her niece in *Suddenly Last Summer*, the issue is delicately and symbolically approached in *The Glass Menagerie*, where the breaking of the unicorn's horn suggests the "normal" debutante Amanda wishes her daughter to be. Amanda has long tried to change her daughter into a version of herself by pretending her physical and emotional problems are not real. She will not even allow Laura or Tom to use the word *crippled* in the house. When Laura says, "I'm—crippled!" Amanda is appalled: "Nonsense! Laura, I've told you never, never, never to use that word. Why, you're not crippled, you just have a little defect—hardly noticeable, even!" Amanda encourages her daughter to compensate for her "slight disadvantage" with "charm—and vivacity—and—*charm*!" (*GM*, 158).

After Tom agrees to find a "gentleman caller" to have supper with the Wingfields so that Amanda can set her "pretty trap" for him,

Tom reminds his mother not to get her hopes up too high, suggesting that there is more to Laura's disability than the merely physical: "She's terribly shy and lives in a world of her own and those things make her seem a little peculiar to people outside the house" (*GM*, 187–88). In the play's exquisite final scene, the caller, Jim, delivers his banal armchair psychoanalysis, and (after removing his chewing gum and carefully wrapping it in paper) concludes, "You know what I judge to be the trouble with you? Inferiority Complex! Know what that is? That's what they call it when someone low-rates himself!" (*GM*, 220).

After dinner, when the electric lights have gone out (because Tom paid his Merchant Seaman's dues instead of the light bill), the mood of the play changes significantly. In the new, altered reality governed by the candelabrum that Jim carries into the front room, Jim and Laura meet absent the electric light that would have made their intimacy impossible. As they begin to speak more easily and move closer to one another, Laura shows him her collection of glass ornaments in what becomes "the climax of her secret life" (*GM*, 210). After they go over their past history at Soldan High School and Laura admits her insecurity about arriving late to assembly because of the sound made by the brace on her leg, she shares her favorite animal, the unicorn, with Jim, encouraging him to hold the animal to the light.

By having him look at the unicorn over the light ("Aren't they extinct in the modern world?" Jim asks), Williams allows Jim—and of course the audience—to perceive Laura's virginal beauty and fragility in a new way. Her disability, then, is transformed into something beautiful—like the imagery in the nickname "Blue Roses," which Jim called her in high school because he misunderstood the word in her description of her "pleurosis." When the couple dance and accidentally knock the glass unicorn off its shelf, breaking its horn, we expect her to be devastated. Instead, Laura smiles at the ostensible misfortune:

> LAURA: It's no tragedy, Freckles. Glass breaks so easily. No matter how careful you are. The traffic jars the shelves and things fall off them.

JIM: Still I'm awfully sorry that I was the cause.

LAURA [*smiling*]: I'll just imagine that he had an operation. The horn was removed to make him feel less—freakish! Now he will feel more at home with the other horses, the ones that don't have horns. (*GM*, 226)

For a moment, Laura herself no longer feels freakish—she is, if only for an instant, "normal."

In this powerful image born of his sister's tragedy Williams alludes directly to Rose's brain operation but reverses its consequences. Instead of robbing the unicorn of the very thing that made it unique, the accident has normalized the glass figure, and with it, Laura; it is now "just like the other horses" (*GM*, 226) and she feels like a normal woman. But when Jim announces he must rush off to pick up his fiancée and won't be returning, Laura bequeaths the now

Figure 25. Julie Haydon as Laura in the Broadway premiere of *The Glass Menagerie* in 1945. Courtesy of the Production Photographs Collection, Harry Ransom Center, University of Texas at Austin.

hornless unicorn to him as a "souvenir"—offering her suitor the sole remaining vestige of her normalized self.

In *Menagerie*, Williams employs autobiography to create a work of art that goes far beyond a retelling of the facts of his life in St. Louis during the 1930s. A play of escape, it is also a play about guilt, guilt that proved inescapable for both man and artist. No matter how much he tried to leave St. Louis behind in the years ahead, St. Louis would always be there; it was the place—literally and imaginatively—he was forced to return to.

Although Rose's lobotomy was the single most transformative event in Williams's entire life, his immediate response to it was surprising—he imagined he saw improvement in her condition: "The madness is still present—that is, certain of the Delusions—but they now have become entirely consistent and coherent. She is full of vitality! and her perceptions and responses seemed almost more than normally acute." His experience with Rose led to the playwright's renewed interest in the study of mental illness, a theme first evidenced in the character of the princess in *Me, Vashya* (1937) and one that became central to so much of his later work. "To me mental therapy is the most intriguing work there is," he wrote; "if I could make a fresh start, I'd take it up instead of writing. Unbalanced minds are so much more interesting than our dreary sanity is, there is so much honesty and poetry among them."[13] Perhaps Williams's most compelling examination of the secret wisdom he discovered in his visits to his sister at Farmington State Hospital is conveyed in the disturbingly beautiful poem "The Beanstalk Country," a work that anticipates several of *Menagerie*'s most important images (roses, light, and glass):

> You know how the mad come into a room,
> too boldly,
> their eyes exploding on the air like roses,
> their entrances from space we never entered.
> . . . .
> They see not us, nor any Sunday caller
> among the geraniums and wicker chairs,
> for they are Jacks who climb the beanstalk country,

a place of hammers and tremendous beams,
compared to which the glassed solarium
in which we rise to greet them has no light. (*CP*, 12–13)

What Williams discovered in his visits to his sister was a profound sense of kinship with the mentally ill. After one of these nightmarish yet illuminating visits to the hospital, Leverich notes, "Williams returned home with the intention of completing *The Gentleman Caller* as a full-length play," hoping to "weave together the threads of various writings about his family."[14] However, the play's trajectory was by no means a clear or smooth one. Consistent with his lifelong practice, Williams wrote draft after draft (amounting to several hundred pages) before completing the play in anything like the form we know now. Drafts and sketches were written over a period of years and were not always written with an eye to the stage. Williams typically constructed his material across various forms and in a variety of literary genres—stories, poems, one-act and longer plays, and even screenplays.

Because the material of *Menagerie* was so raw and personal, Williams had an inordinately difficult time controlling it. His process was a long and arduous attempt to simplify and untangle various knots and permutations, at the same time desperately trying to avoid the pitfalls of sentimentality. In September 1944, shortly before the Chicago premiere, he wrote to Margo Jones (who was eventually named assistant director on the Broadway production), complaining about "the terrible, compulsive struggle it was to do the thing and what a frightful, sentimental mess it might well have been, and was at some stages. It needs a good deal of pruning, condensing, possibly some rearranging even in this version" (*N*, 413).

In search of the work's elusive final form, Williams wrote the short story "Portrait of a Girl in Glass," as well as the aforementioned screenplay *The Gentleman Caller*. From these abundant drafts it is clear Williams was engaged in writing a vast, deeply personal work (strikingly different from the Proletarian plays he had written for the Mummers or the Living Newspaper productions he worked on at the University of Iowa). As originally conceived, the play was not merely cumbersome and unwieldy, it also lacked a clear dramatic focus. In one of the drafts Williams wrote, "The original play filled several hundred pages. The top-heavy structure collapsed. And I lay under the ruins like a caterpillar. After a while I picked myself up again. I looked about me. Here and there I picked up a sound particle, a piece that survived. I put these fragments together. Out of the ruins of a monument salvaged this tablet, these fragments of a play, *The Gentleman Caller.*"[15] Elsewhere, Williams, using his Narrator Tom as his mouthpiece, labels his work "The Ruins of a Play," in one draft confessing, "I've written this over ten times and torn it up, I've sweated over it, raged over it wept over it! I think I have it and then it gets all misty and fades away. . . . I must confine myself to a smaller ambition, not all but a little of it."[16]

If the multiple drafts of *The Gentleman Caller* indicate that Williams did not originally know what the true subject of his play might be, the short story "Portrait of a Girl in Glass" offers insight into one possible direction. Completed in June 1944, "Portrait" is a depiction of the poet character's sister, named Laura, as in *Menagerie*. His mother, whose previous history in Blue Mountain, Mississippi, was so precisely delineated in the many drafts of *The Gentleman Caller*, is now moved to the background and merely described as "Mother." Similarly, the mounting tension of the narrator's compelling desire to leave St. Louis is merely summarized in the story's brief, concluding paragraph, revealing that the writer's interest was becoming more narrowly focused around his sister. The story offers the basic situation of scene 7 of *Menagerie*, in which the gentleman caller arrives and soon makes his hasty retreat. Unlike Laura in *Menagerie*, however, the narrator's sister in the short story does not suffer from a physical impediment, but instead appears emotionally damaged, ill-equipped to handle the vicissitudes of life in the real world. The story's opening describes a daily struggle directly underneath Laura's window in which a vicious Chow dog corners the neighborhood alley cats against a brick wall, where they are forced to "spit at their death until it [is] hurled at them" (*CS*, 111). This alleyway, known in the story as "Death Valley," reveals the extent to which Laura is unable to cope with the daily struggles beneath her Maple Street window, let alone out in the wider world. The narrator (also called Tom in the story) describes Laura's sad serenade to her pieces of colored glass as a kind of self-induced trance, wherein she would look down upon her menagerie with "vague blue eyes until the points of gem-like radiance in them gently drew the arching particles of reality from her mind and finally produced a state of hypnotic calm" (*CS*, 112). This Laura asks her brother in all earnestness, "Do stars have five points really?" and he concludes, "I don't believe that my sister was actually foolish. I think the petals of her mind had simply closed through fear, and it's no telling how much they had closed upon in the way of secret wisdom" (*CS*, 112). This closed flower blooms for a brief instant in the play's final scene, when Jim appears, although in "Portrait" he is not the beloved high school hero who once sang the lead in *The Pirates of Penzance*; rather, he is the living embodiment of the character named Freckles from Laura's treasured novel about a one-armed orphan who lives in the mythical town of Limberlost. As in the play, Jim invites Laura to dance to "Dardanella," playing on her prized Victrola, and the narrator concludes of their blossoming romance, "To say it was love is not too hasty a judgment" (*CS*, 117).

Another of the preliminary versions of what would become *The Glass Menagerie* is the complete one-act play *The Pretty Trap* (its title referring to the pleasant deceit through which young women enticed their future husbands, some at the time may have said). As Amanda says, "All pretty girls are a trap, a pretty trap, and men expect them to be" (*PT*, 144). For audiences familiar with the pathos of *Menagerie*, *The Pretty Trap* ends, astonishingly, with Jim and Laura (following a kiss that possesses the "curious, hesitant intensity only possible between two people who have never really kissed before" [*PT*, 164]) heading off to Forest Park for a romantic stroll while Amanda and Tom happily celebrate their victory—having secured Laura's future happiness with Jim.

Not only does *The Pretty Trap* conclude on a note of optimism exceedingly rare in Williams's work, this version permits Laura to emerge from her mother's shadow and establish her own agency. As the two young people prepare to leave for the park, Amanda calls out to Jim, "Don't you think that Laura needs a wrap?" to which Laura herself defiantly interjects, "No, no! I won't need any!" (*PT*, 165). At the head of this play, Williams wrote the following note: "This play is derived from a longer work in progress, *The Gentleman*

Caller. It corresponds to the last act of that play, roughly, but has a lighter treatment and a different ending" (*PT*, 142). Of course, it is unclear whether Williams's motivation in creating this "lighter treatment" was merely to do a "five-finger exercise" to see if he could steer his work in a much different direction, or to see if a more optimistic treatment might ultimately prove more commercially successful. Regardless, it is interesting to think that the playwright at least considered the possibility of a Laura who independently emerges from her mother's formidable shadow in a way that he must have realized was impossible for his own sister after her surgery.

The final version of *Menagerie* is, of course, more than a play about the tragedy that befell Williams's sister; it is equally about the playwright's quest to extricate himself from the prison of St. Louis. The play tells the story of a young writer trapped during the day by his unrewarding job at Continental Shoemakers, based on Williams's experience at the International Shoe Company. But unlike *Stairs to the Roof* (1941), in which Williams also depicted this mechanistic, soul-crushing experience from his life, the focus in *Menagerie* is on memory, especially his recollection of the relationships between himself (the Narrator) and his mother and sister. While he employed nonrealistic, expressionistic devices in both works, *Menagerie* concentrates on his characters' interior states rather than on crushing external forces. In the play's final moments, Narrator Tom Wingfield announces his escape from the dreaded city: "I left St. Louis. I descended the steps of this fire escape for a last time and followed, from then on, in my father's footsteps" (*GM*, 236–37).

But while the play concludes with this explicit statement that the Narrator has departed, the audience is left unsure whether this is true. On one hand he has, like his father, "skipped the light fantastic" (*GM*, 145) out of town via the prominent symbol of the fire escape, with its "touch of accidental poetic truth" (*GM*, 143). On the other, it is arguable that the opposite is true, and Tom's escape is impossible. Although he seemingly abandons home at the end of *Menagerie*, his final monologue may also be read as an admission that leaving is, at least mentally, impossible. From this perspective, *The Glass Menagerie* is less the story of its hero's maturation and development (a kind of theatrical bildungsroman) than a ghost tale in the manner of Samuel Taylor Coleridge's *Rime of the Ancient Mariner* (1797–1798). Coleridge portrays a man who has committed a terrible crime: he has shot an albatross, the bird symbolizing purity and safe passage for his fellow sailors.

If we read the Narrator's abandonment of his mother and sister in analogous terms, his freedom cannot be acquired without continual expiation for his cruelty. Like Coleridge's Mariner, Williams's Tom is condemned to the purgatory of reliving his crime through memory. Narrating his tale in the theatre allows him to achieve momentary relief—but never full atonement. Coleridge's Mariner describes the continual torment in which he dwells:

> Since then, at an uncertain hour,
> That agony returns:
> And till my ghastly tale is told,
> This heart within me burns.[17]

In the final moments of *Menagerie*, the Narrator likewise describes the sensation of having his sister's spirit revisit him, taking possession of his being. The sight of Laura blowing out her candles may conclude the play in real time for the audience, but it is clear from Tom's monologue that his relief can only be momentary before the haunting begins again:

> Perhaps I am walking along a street at night, in some strange city, before I have found companions. . . . Then all at once my sister touches my shoulder. I turn around and look into her eyes. Oh Laura, Laura, I tried to leave you behind me, but I am more faithful than I intended to be! I reach for a cigarette, I cross the street, I run into the movies or a bar, I buy a drink, I speak to the nearest stranger—anything that can blow your candles out! (*GM*, 237)

This analogy with Coleridge's tale of cruelty, guilt, and attempted expiation is consistent with John Lahr's observation that "ghostliness is built into *The Glass Menagerie*" and that Rose's "lobotomy transformed her literally into a ghost of her former self."[18] *The*

Glass Menagerie may be the first of Williams's "ghost plays," but it
certainly was not the last. A number of later works, including *The
Two-Character Play* (1967, 1975), *Vieux Carré* (1977), and *Clothes
for a Summer Hotel* (1980), may be usefully examined in similar
terms. For Williams, as for the eponymous character in Christopher
Marlowe's play *Doctor Faustus*, there was no real escape from the
hell that was the city; its boundaries were not physical, its scope was
as vast as the imagination itself. As Mephistopheles tells Faustus, to
his horror,

> Why this is hell, nor am I out of it,
> . . . .
> Hell hath no limits, nor is circumscribed
> In one self place; but where we are is hell,
> And where hell is, there must we ever be.[19]

St. Louis, for Williams, was really never just a midwestern city at the
confluence of the Missouri and Mississippi rivers. Rather, it represented a dark place of the imagination from which he could never
fully extricate himself. He could never leave behind what his family
had done to him, or what they had done to his beloved sister.

* * * * *

While *Menagerie* is an autobiographical account of Tennessee
Williams's life in St. Louis, it is certainly *not* autobiography. The
play's deviations from biographical fact are myriad, but two aspects
emerge as particularly significant: the depictions of the role of the
playwright's father and of the family's economic circumstances. In
the Narrator's opening monologue, Tom describes the presence of a
character in the play who never appears: "There is a fifth character in
the play who doesn't appear except in this larger-than-life-size photograph over the mantel. This is our father who left us a long time ago.
. . . The last we heard of him was a picture postcard from Mazatlán,
on the Pacific coast of Mexico, containing a message of two words:
'Hello—Goodbye!' and no address" (*GM*, 145). Later in the play,
Tom confides to Jim, "I know I seem dreamy, but inside—well, I'm
boiling! Whenever I pick up a shoe, I shudder a little thinking how
short life is and what I'm doing!" (*GM*, 202). Revealing that he has

already paid his dues to the Union of Merchant Seamen instead of paying the family's light bill, he admits, "I'm like my father. The bastard son of a bastard!" (*GM*, 202).

In reality Williams's father was still very much at home during the period in which the play was set.[20] The fact that the Narrator, despite calling him a "bastard," chose to pattern his own behavior after his father's may seem surprising, particularly when we consider how Cornelius terrorized his son, ridiculing him as "Miss Nancy" and forcing him to withdraw from the University of Missouri at the end of his junior year. This deliberate contradiction of biographical facts as we know them anticipates Williams's later opinion of his father as a man who, like himself, was crippled by the restrictions of his desk job at International Shoe, and additionally by his wife's puritanical notions. In the later autobiographical essay "The Man in the Overstuffed Chair" (1960), Williams describes the "very deep kinship" he felt toward his father, wondering "if there wasn't more love than hate in his blood, however tortured it was" (*CS*, xvii). Adopting the sobriquet "Tennessee Williams," the author chose to align himself with his father's Tennessee background rather than his mother's Dakin ancestry, from Mississippi. Significantly, in *Memoirs* (1975) he notes with pride, "My father's lineage had been an illustrious one, now gone a bit to seed, at least in prominence. He was directly descended from Tennessee's first senator, John Williams, hero of King's Mountain; from the brother Valentine of Tennessee's first Governor John (Nollichucky Jack) Sevier; and from Thomas Lanier Williams I, the first Chancellor of the Western Territory" (12).

In scene 4 of *Menagerie*, Tom returns home drunk after witnessing a stage show featuring "Malvolio the Magician." The magician has performed a "coffin trick," extricating himself from a nailed-up coffin without removing a single nail. Tom informs Laura that this is "a trick that would come in handy for me—get me out of this two-by-four situation!" (*GM*, 167). By having Tom Wingfield say he could make use of that particular escape trick, Williams alludes to his own decision to align himself with the ancestry of his father, whose full name was—Cornelius *Coffin* Williams.

In addition to portraying the father in *Menagerie* as an example of how to escape, Williams disguises the reasonably comfortable economic circumstances he grew up in, depicting them as considerably worse than they actually were. The Wingfields live in a tenement in post-Depression St. Louis, as described in the opening stage directions: "The Wingfield apartment is one of those vast, hive-like conglomerations of cellular living-units that flower as warty growths in overcrowded urban centers of lower middle-class population and are symptomatic of the impulse of this largest and fundamentally enslaved section of American society" (*GM*, 143).

The apartment imagined in the play is a fictitious amalgam of several homes among the nine the Williams family lived in between 1918 and 1938, particularly the family's apartment at 6254 Enright Avenue, unit A. However, unlike the Wingfields, who are virtually without means and almost entirely dependent on Tom's meager warehouse salary for survival, the Williams family was, by post-Depression standards, comfortably middle-class. Williams's decision

Figure 26. One of the models for the Wingfield apartment, the building at 4633 Westminster Place (ca. 1960)—the Williamses' second home in St. Louis—is now known as the Glass Menagerie Apartments. Identifier: N21258. Courtesy of the Missouri Historical Society.

to alter his family's circumstances, making them far less prosperous than they really were, suggests not merely that issues of class conflict were still relevant to his vision; their poverty and the absence of a proper adult male breadwinner also makes the dramatic stakes higher when Tom abandons his mother and sister at the end of the play. His failure to support his family feels still more egregious in the theatre when we consider that his abandonment leaves the family literally without light, in a play where lighting and light symbolism are so crucial. Amanda has spent what little disposable money she has on new furnishings (including a new floor lamp) to captivate their gentleman caller, in the hope that Jim O'Connor may provide an opportunity to save Laura from the life of spinsterhood that almost certainly awaits. When Amanda calls after her son at the end of the play, "Go then! Go to the moon—you selfish dreamer!" (*GM*, 236), Tom is guilty as charged.

The absence of light at the end is an example of the way Williams skillfully manipulates light and dark throughout this play and others. Even his first full-length play, set in the Red Hills of Alabama, *Candles to the Sun*, depicts the miners' conflict in terms of an opposition between darkness belowground and light above. In *Menagerie* he carries this symbolism to a much more sophisticated and poetically satisfying level. Laura's menagerie is of course made of glass, and when she invites Jim to hold her unicorn, she enthusiastically remarks,

> LAURA: Go on, I trust you with him! . . . Hold him over the light, he loves the light! You see how the light shines through him?
> JIM: It sure does shine! (*GM*, 223)

Although Laura's menagerie may be associated with the delicate light refracted through the prism of her glass animals, it is also clear that the playwright wants light to work in a more complicated and expressive way than in a naturalistic play. Reminding us in his "Production Notes" that "the lighting in the play is not realistic," Williams insists that light is sometimes employed "in contradistinction to what is the apparent center" of the action, for example during Amanda and

Tom's quarrel scene, when Laura is lying silently on the couch yet
should remain the visual center of the action. Her illumination is
intended to contrast with the very different reality around her, and
the playwright refers to its having a "peculiar pristine clarity" comparable to that used in "early religious portraits of female saints or
madonnas" (*GM*, 133–34).

By ending the play with the reference that "nowadays the world
is lit by lightning!" (*GM*, 237), Williams accentuates the distinction
between electrical light, on one hand, and the delicate candlelight
associated with Laura, on the other. This difference between the
delicacy of Laura's light and the harsh glare of other characters'
reverberates through the entire play. Jim O'Connor's high school
exploits are chronicled in the school yearbook, *The Torch*, suggesting the more forceful illumination associated with Jim's nature;
similarly, his ambitions are in the field of radio and television, underscoring an association with the burgeoning electronics industry
of the future. Jim raves about the Century of Progress world's fair
in Chicago, particularly the Hall of Science, which illustrates how
distinct his goals are from Laura's: "I believe in the future of television! I wish to be ready to go up right along with it. Therefore I'm
planning to get in on the ground floor. In fact I've already made the
right connections and all that remains is for the industry itself to get
under way! Full steam—*Knowledge*—Zzzzzp! *Money*—Zzzzzp!—
Power!" (*GM*, 222).

Contrasting with Jim's America built on science and technologi-
cal initiative, Laura lives in a dimly lit world.

In the moments following dinner, but before Jim's entrance
near the beginning of scene 7, Laura is depicted huddled alone
on the sofa in the parlor. She is now reflected in the glow of the
new floor lamp that Amanda has improvidently acquired to beau-
tify their apartment in preparation for the gentleman caller. In a
lovely pun concealed in his stage directions, Williams alludes to the
"rose-colored silk shade [that] gives a soft becoming light to her
face, bringing out the fragile, unearthly prettiness which usually
escapes attention" (*GM*, 207). In this isolated image of the sister,
"eyes wide and mysteriously watchful," the playwright suggests the

vulnerability and solitude of his own sister, Rose, through the soft-ened light of the "rose-colored" shade.

Unlike Jim's interests, with his ambitions predicated on dynamism and progress, Laura's amusement is provided by her glass figurines and the wind-up Victrola that is a relic from her father. Laura is phys-ically unable to attend typing classes at Rubicam's Business College and must escape by taking long walks at the zoo, where (ironically for a family named the *Wing*fields) she opts to visit with the penguins— birds with flippers instead of wings, and hence unable to fly. She seeks shelter in the Jewel Box, a large Art Deco greenhouse made entirely of glass for the purpose of housing rare tropical flowers, flowers that, like Laura herself, are not like others. "But blue is wrong for roses," Laura tells Jim, who consoles her by pointing out, "Being different is nothing to be ashamed of. . . . They're one hundred times one thou-sand. You're one times one! They walk all over the earth. You just stay here. They're common as—weeds, but—you—well, you're—*Blue Roses*!" (*GM*, 227).

The Jewel Box, built by William W. C. Becker in 1936, at the time the play is set, and which still exists in Forest Park, is a remarkable metaphor for Laura. She is a "blue rose" in a world of ordinary weeds, seeking protection and warmth from the menacing world outside.

The symbolism of light and dark in the play is also on display in the electrical storm that temporarily knocks out the power in the Wingfield apartment, obliging Laura and Jim to sit in dim candle-light on the floor in the living room. Even the candelabrum itself has been threatened by the harsh and violent world of electricity outside; Amanda reveals that it was "melted a little out of shape when the church burnt down. Lightning struck it one spring" (*GM*, 210).

The play's final poetic image is most suggestive of the world that Laura inhabits—one that the Narrator has tried to leave behind, but which, as demonstrated above, he cannot. It is an image that Williams reveals in the stage directions should be viewed "as though through soundproof glass," combining the play's central metaphors of the menagerie, the Jewel Box, and of course Laura herself encased in her own glass world, where she can no longer be reached. Tom's final monologue, after which Laura blows out her candles, ending

Figure 27. The Jewel Box, in Forest Park. Photograph by W. C. Persons, 1930s. Identifier: N33556. Courtesy of the Missouri Historical Society.

Figure 28. The magical interior of the Jewel Box. Photograph by W. C. Persons. Identifier: N33555. Courtesy of the Missouri Historical Society.

the play, is a remarkable valedictory once more expressing the playwright's difficulty in disengaging himself from his St. Louis past,
reflecting the play's symbolic use of light and color in its references
to the leaves, bottles of perfume, and a shattered rainbow:

> I traveled around a great deal. The cities swept about me like
> dead leaves, leaves that were brightly colored but torn away
> from the branches. I would have stopped, but I was pursued by
> something. It always came upon me unawares, taking me alto-
> gether by surprise. . . . Perhaps it was only a piece of transparent
> glass. . . . I pass the lighted window of a shop where perfume
> is sold. The window is filled with pieces of colored glass, tiny
> transparent bottles in delicate colors, like bits of a shattered
> rainbow. (*GM*, 237)

A miraculous combination of reminiscence and guilt, the monologue captures the mixed feelings Thomas Lanier Williams had
about the loss of his sister, his own "blue Rose," who after years
of confinement in the state sanitarium in Farmington underwent
surgery on January 13, 1943, altering both of their lives forever.
Williams had left his family behind, at least physically, in St. Louis;
now Rose never could.

Perhaps Williams's most profoundly poignant evocation of that
event is not contained in the play at all; it is conveyed in the one simple notebook entry from March 24, 1943, the only specific reference
in his journals to what happened:

> A cord breaking.
> 1000 miles away.
> Rose. Her head cut open.
> A knife thrust in her brain.
> Me. Here. Smoking.
> My father, mean as a devil, snoring. 1000 miles away. (*N*, 361)

Chapter Five

I Never Left

AFTER THE DRAMATIC success of *The Glass Menagerie* on Broadway, one might assume that Tennessee Williams would have tried to put his St. Louis past firmly behind him, and in some ways he did exactly that. Certainly, if judged by the settings of his subsequent plays, one might well conclude that the writer had successfully left the city of his youth behind. In the nearly two decades immediately after *Menagerie*, the prolific playwright wrote play after play, most of which were critically successful and none of which is explicitly set in the city that had caused him so much pain throughout his younger years. These plays include *A Streetcar Named Desire* (1947—set in New Orleans), *Summer and Smoke* (1947—Glorious Hill, Mississippi), *The Rose Tattoo* (1950—a Sicilian immigrant village along the Gulf Coast between New Orleans and Mobile, Alabama), *Camino Real* (1953—an unnamed tropical seaport), *Cat on a Hot Tin Roof* (1955—a plantation on the Mississippi Delta), *Orpheus Descending* (1957—a dry goods store in a small southern town), *Suddenly Last Summer* (1958—the Garden District of New Orleans), *Sweet Bird of Youth* (1959—the Gulf Coast), *Period of Adjustment* (1960—Memphis), and *Night of the Iguana* (1961—a Mexican tropical resort).

However, as we have already observed, St. Louis was always more than a simple geographical location for Williams; it retained its permanent hold on his imagination through his family. The settings for his plays might become remote or exotic, but the circumstances that determined his vision of the world never left him. In a candid moment in 1974 when he was asked directly why he had left St. Louis behind, he replied simply, "I never left." Confessing that those unhappy years in St. Louis were far from wasted, he admitted, "I'm glad I spent those years there. . . . I was forced to become more and more introspective, and that made me a writer."[1]

There are many reasons why a writer chooses to set a work in one location rather than another. Choice of setting may be based on writers' concern for their survival at a risky political moment—Bertolt Brecht's situating his play about the rise of Adolf Hitler, *The Resistible Rise of Arturo Ui*, in the Chicago stockyards is one example; another is Arthur Miller's decision to set *The Crucible* in seventeenth-century Salem while writing about the McCarthy purges in America in the 1950s. Writers may also shift the setting within a single play to create a comparative perspective for an audience, as when Shakespeare moves the action in *Othello* from cosmopolitan Venice in act 1 to the remote island of Cyprus in acts 2 through 4. Or when he switches locations from Athens (associated with reason and rule of law) to a magical forest and then back to a transfigured Athens in *A Midsummer Night's Dream*. Settings for plays are never arbitrary, but neither should they be seen as absolutely determinative for a play's meaning, since the location of the play's action may not be intended literally by the author. Williams chose to set his plays in places he knew well, places he imagined, or some composite of both. He may even have chosen a particular location to deliberately mask another—one much closer to home. As a result, in the decades after *Menagerie*, we may still discover the presence of St. Louis in works ostensibly set elsewhere.

Considering the diverse locations in Williams's plays, it remains highly dubious whether anyone would seriously claim that Williams's masterpiece *A Streetcar Named Desire* might be understood as a St. Louis play. Just as *The Glass Menagerie* was the author's quintessential play about St. Louis, so *Streetcar* was his play about New Orleans, or so it would seem. Certainly, the play's opening stage directions suggest that the centrality of the "raffish charm" of New Orleans and the importance of its atmosphere are absolutely essential to the drama about to unfold:

You can almost feel the warm breath of the brown river beyond the river warehouses with their faint redolences of bananas and coffee. A corresponding air is evoked by the music of Negro entertainers at a barroom around the corner. In this part of New Orleans you are practically always just around the corner, or a few doors down the street, from a tinny piano being played with the infatuated fluency of brown fingers. This "blue piano" expresses the spirit of life which goes on here. (*SND*, 243)

Although when Walt Whitman visited the city in 1848 it already had a reputation as the "wickedest city in Christendom,"[2] in a certain sense one might argue that Williams "invented" the way we view New Orleans today—the city's sensuality, coarseness, musicality, and mysteriousness are all evoked and captured in his plays and stories.[3] His poem "Mornings on Bourbon Street" describes the Old Quarter's "sunny courtyard[s]," "innocent mornings," and "rotten-sweet odor" (*CP*, 72). In this poem, Williams observes "pigeons and drunkards coming together from under / the same stone arches," and in *Memoirs* he wrote, "I know of no other city where it is better to have a skylight," recalling the composition of *Streetcar* in a third-floor study where he felt "close enough to touch the clouds" (109).

In "The Decay of Lying" (1889) Oscar Wilde brilliantly and persuasively argued that it is art, not nature, that determines our perception of reality. Far from being our "great mother," Nature, Wilde concludes, "is our creation." His argument culminates in a wildly imaginative paradox—that it was the impressionist painters who actually "invented" the famous London fog: "There may have been fogs for centuries in London," he says, "but no one saw them, and so we do not know anything about them. They did not exist till Art had invented them."[4]

By analogy, we might argue that (despite the city's long history as a haven for artists, going back at least as far as Whitman in the mid-nineteenth century)[5] Williams "invented" New Orleans in *Streetcar*. However, the playwright's decision to set his play in New Orleans was anything but inevitable. The earliest draft of *Streetcar* is actually set in a neighborhood in the South Side of Chicago, where the Stanley Kowalski figure is an Italian named Lucio, and Stella and Blanche are called Rosa and Bianca, respectively. A second draft of the play (then called "The Primary Colors") shifted the play's location from Chicago to Atlanta, where its male lead was an Irishman, Ralph Stanley, sporting an emerald green bowling shirt. One constant in the three earliest drafts of *Streetcar*, however, was that the play was imagined taking place in an oppressive two-room apartment whose rear window looked out on a bleak urban landscape. In Atlanta, the view is of "a vacant lot with bill-boards to the skyline,"[6] suggesting that as he began writing the play Williams may have been thinking not of Chicago or Atlanta, but of St. Louis, the place he readily associated with stifling urban decay. This led Allean Hale to conclude that "even *Streetcar* began as a St. Louis play," suggesting that its imagined location was the kitchen table at one of the Williams family's many apartments, this one at 5 South Taylor.[7]

Another aspect of the play also reveals its indebtedness to St. Louis—its emphasis on poker games and the inextricable connection between card playing, liquor, and domestic violence—all of which Williams and Rose were witness to growing up in their St. Louis home. The play's penultimate title was "The Poker Night," and its third scene retains this title (significantly, the only titled scene in the play), creating an elaborate description of the mood and culminating in a *tableau vivant* in which the audience is encouraged to concentrate on the visual image of the poker players:

> There is a picture of Van Gogh's of a billiard parlor at night. The kitchen now suggests that sort of lurid nocturnal brilliance, the raw colors of childhood's spectrum. . . . The poker players— Stanley, Steve, Mitch and Pablo—wear colored shirts, solid blues, a purple, a red-and-white-check, a light green, and they are men at the peak of their physical manhood, as coarse and direct and powerful as the primary colors. . . . For a moment, there is absorbed silence as a hand is dealt. (*SND*, 286)

The atmosphere situates the men as card-playing, boozing, wearing the colorful emblems of an outsized masculinity—and they are epitomized, of course, by Stanley Kowalski himself, who is introduced in the play's stage directions as a "richly feathered male bird among hens" and a "gaudy seed-bearer" (*SND*, 265). Foreshadowing the poker-night scene's depiction of brutal maleness in conflict with vulnerable femininity is the play's opening image—Stanley heaving a "red-stained package from a butcher's" up at his wife, Stella, as the play begins:

STANLEY: Hey, there! Stella, baby!
STELLA [*mildly*]: Don't holler at me like that . . .
STANLEY: Catch!
STELLA: What?
STANLEY: Meat! (*SND*, 244)

Figure 29. C.C. Williams as branch manager at the International Shoe Company. Courtesy of the Tennessee Williams Collection, Harry Ransom Center, University of Texas at Austin.

This image of Stanley as the personification of a brutish, uncouth machismo (as opposed to Blanche Dubois's delicately refined, moth-like frailty), was precisely the image that dominated Williams's childhood in St. Louis in the constant quarrels between C.C. Williams and his wife, Edwina, the tiny but indomitable southern belle who routinely called for smelling salts and frequently threatened to faint. Explicit acts of domestic violence were all too familiar for Williams during his youth; indeed, Edwina describes in her diary a particularly savage incident from New Year's Day 1933, when Tom was twenty-one. Cornelius came home around seven in the morning, stumbling and drunk, causing Edwina, who was making breakfast, to upbraid him about his conduct. Instead of quieting down, C.C. flew into a towering rage and Edwina fled into the bedroom, locking the door in fear. C.C. began to shout that he was going to smash down the door if she did not come out. Before she could do so, he carried out his threat and the door flew open and knocked Edwina down, her nose bleeding profusely. The noise woke Rose, who, seeing her mother bleeding on the floor, rushed into the hall screaming hysterically for help.[8]

An even more bizarre and disturbing incident occurred on December 11, 1936, while Tom was studying at Washington University and Rose was in the early stages of being treated for mental illness at Barnes Hospital in St. Louis. At 3 a.m. Edwina received a call from the same hospital saying that Cornelius had had an accident. In his notebook that night, Williams noted, "Mother just received a call from Barnes' saying Dad had had an accident. Didn't say what kind. Frightened. Can't sleep. A terribly still night. I have taken a sleeping tablet and will read Ibsen. Hadn't enough things happened to us already? Apparently not. One thing and then another and another" (N, 69).

Counseled by her friend (and C.C.'s boss) Paul Jamison to wait until morning before visiting her husband at the hospital, Edwina wrote a letter to her mother the next day:

He [Cornelius] had been in a card game with one of the International Shoe salesman [sic] . . . who had been drinking heavily. They quarreled over the game, he cursed and hit Cornelius and C. knocked him down. . . . This infuriated him so that he bit a piece of Cornelius's ear off![9]

While Jamison apparently kept the scandal from spreading by swearing the other card players to secrecy and informing the other International Shoe employees that C.C. would be staying at home with an infected ear, it is clear that in a household rife with conflict, that particular "poker night" registered as memorable, and ten years later it likely provided inspiration for the inciting central event in *Streetcar*.[10]

Just as the violent clash between animalistic brutality and fading southern refinement was played out before the young writer's eyes in his own family in the 1930s in St. Louis, and then later became material for *Streetcar*, so the play *Suddenly Last Summer* and the short one-act *Something Unspoken*, originally produced together in 1958 under the title *Garden District*, offer examples of plays that were set elsewhere but were directly inspired by St. Louis.

Something Unspoken, originally included in the 1953 collection *"27 Wagons Full of Cotton" and Other One-Act Plays*, is a two-hander involving Miss Cornelia Scott, a wealthy and imperious spinster aged sixty, and her younger secretary, Grace, a faded figure in her forties. The plot of the play concerns Miss Scott's desire to be elected regent "by unanimous acclamation!" of the local chapter of the Confederate Daughters (*SU*, 283).

Although set in New Orleans, *Something Unspoken* is a satirical portrait of Williams's mother's long-standing quest for social prominence in St. Louis, specifically her desire for election to the Daughters of the American Revolution. Edwina had been elected to the Columbus, Mississippi, branch back in 1905, and after decades of being made to feel socially inferior, was finally nominated in 1936 to be regent of the Jefferson Chapter in St. Louis, a post she hoped would serve as vindication for the various slights she had received at the hands of St. Louis society. In scene 2 of *The Glass Menagerie*, we meet a much less wealthy and self-confident version of this character in Amanda, who returns from her DAR meeting to find her daughter guilty of "deception" since she has dropped out of Rubicam's Business College in favor of taking long walks in Forest Park (*GM*, 151).

Something Unspoken was included in the double bill entitled *Garden District* to fill out an evening-length performance rather than presenting *Suddenly Last Summer* (a long one-act) as a stand-alone play. In today's theatrical climate, where audiences are accustomed to sitting through a ninety-minute show without intermission, it has become usual to perform *Suddenly Last Summer* by itself. Although the two works are linked by their settings in the posh district of New Orleans filled with lovely mansions and broad, tree-lined alleyways, the location of both of these plays is really St. Louis, which serves as a reminder of how the city remained with the playwright long after he left home. And just as *Something Unspoken* is a portrait of Williams's mother in the guise of a wealthy southern matron concealing her many vulnerabilities behind a proud and pretentious exterior, so *Suddenly Last Summer* is a portrait of Edwina (now called Violet Venable) as a mother intent on maintaining the pristine memory of her poet son Sebastian, who died under mysterious circumstances the preceding summer. To preserve Sebastian's legacy, and her own preeminent position, Mrs. Venable is willing to sacrifice her niece Catharine Holly (modeled on Rose Williams) by consenting to have her lobotomized to prevent the young woman—hospitalized at St. Mary's, just as Rose was at St. Vincent's—from disclosing the sordid circumstances surrounding Sebastian's death at the hands of a band of starving boys near the Cabeza de Lobo, where Sebastian and Catharine had been vacationing the previous summer.

Since it is obvious that this play is intimately based on biograph-ical events concerning mother, son, and daughter connected with Williams's life in St. Louis, it is fair to ask why *Suddenly Last Summer* was set in the Garden District. The answer is found in the play's opening stage directions, which eschew *Menagerie*'s stylized realism in favor of fantasy. Instead of the tenement dwelling in *Menagerie*, the setting of *Suddenly Last Summer* is a "fantastic garden which is more like a tropical jungle," a jungle in which predatory, violent images abound. Describing the intended set as being as "unrealistic as the décor of a dramatic ballet," the play reveals a primitive world whose central image is introduced by the Venus flytrap in the garden, reflecting the play's obsession with the Darwinian forces that govern nature and human conduct, culminating in the play's terrifying image of the partially devoured body of Sebastian looking like "a big white-paper bunch of red roses" (*SLS*, 422).

In his stage directions opening the play, Williams chose not to paint a plausible replica of the Garden District or a real world of any kind; rather, "Sebastian's garden" is a steaming primordial jungle whose colors, heat, and fantastic shapes reflect the chthonic, savage world that exists just beneath the surface of civilized society. As Williams describes the scene, "There are massive tree-flowers that suggest organs of a body, torn out, still glistening with undried blood; there are harsh cries and sibilant hissings and thrashing sounds in the garden as if it were inhabited by beasts, serpents and birds, all of savage nature" (*SLS*, 349).

Only in a tropical climate similar to that of New Orleans could Williams have created a world that could plausibly contain elements of Mrs. Venable's extreme affluence covering the inchoate violence of a prehistoric jungle seething underneath. Early in the play, she describes her annual sojourn with her son to the Galapagos Islands, which Sebastian refers to as "Herman Melville's Encantadas," where (sailing on a four-masted schooner such as Melville would have known [*SLS*, 354–55]) they witness the Darwinian life cycle at its most elemental in the race to the sea by newly hatched sea turtles. Mrs. Venable and her son observe the baby turtles, having been left on the blazing sand beach by their exhausted, half-dead mother, in their desperate attempt to make it to the sea before flocks of carnivorous birds can devour them. This, in microcosm, is the Darwinian world depicted in *Suddenly Last Summer*. It is a godless, barbarous world in which benevolence or divine mercy are lacking—there are only the options of eating or being eaten.

In this world, Mrs. Venable's main purpose is to prevent her niece from desecrating her carefully curated memory of her son by revealing what truly happened to Sebastian. To do this, Mrs. Venable is willing to sacrifice Catharine on the altar of her illusion. In the play's opening scene, she attempts to bribe a surgeon into performing a lobotomy on her niece. "Oh, what a blessing to them, Doctor, to be

just peaceful, to be suddenly—peaceful," she says. "After all that horror, after those nightmares" (*SLS*, 366). When the doctor protests
that he can not guarantee a lobotomy would stop her from speaking
out, Mrs. Venable's chilling reply reveals her true intention, which
is not peace for Catharine but rather that "after the operation, who
would *believe* her, Doctor?" (*SLS*, 367). Just as Williams believed
his mother countenanced Rose's lobotomy with the design of sup-
pressing the scandal regarding C.C.'s possible sexual abuse, so Mrs.
Venable is willing to silence her niece at any cost, and the play trans-
poses events that played out in St. Louis into the luxuriant world
of the Garden District to accommodate the central visual metaphor
of Sebastian's primordial garden, which aptly sets the scene for this
Darwinian amorality play.

Around the time of writing of *Suddenly Last Summer*, Williams
underwent psychoanalysis, which radically shifted how he perceived his parents' marriage and his relationship with his mother.
Consequently, he depicted Mrs. Venable as a woman who literally
chose her son over her dying husband: "I made the hardest decision
of my life. . . . I stayed with my son," she says (*SLS*, 358). Williams
may have been thinking of the time his mother nursed him through
Bright's disease as a child, but he may also have been reflecting upon
the ways in which he saw his mother neglect her husband's sexual
and emotional needs throughout their marriage in favor of a smothering and ultimately destructive love for her son.

At the same time as Mrs. Venable rejects her husband, she takes
incestuous delight in her relationship with her son: "People didn't
speak of Sebastian and his mother or Mrs. Venable and her son, they
said 'Sebastian and Violet, Violet and Sebastian have taken a house
in Biarritz for the season'" (*SLS*, 362). Indeed, the very choice of
the names "Sebastian" and "Violet" alludes to the pair of siblings
repeatedly mistaken for one another in Shakespeare's *Twelfth Night*.
When Mrs. Venable picks up Sebastian's "Poem of Summer," the
play's stage directions suggest that she literally worships her son's
memory: "Her face suddenly has a different look, the look of a visionary, an exalted *religieuse*" (*SLS*, 353). If the relationship between
mother and son closely aligns with incest, Williams's analysis of Mrs.
Venable's response to her niece Catharine reflects the playwright's

critical view of his mother's interference in the relationship between himself and Rose, known as "the couple" during their childhood. Mrs. Venable views Catharine with jealousy, and sees her niece's relationship with Sebastian as a direct threat to her own possession of her son.

In reflecting upon her treatment of her niece, Mrs. Venable tells the doctor that "these people are not blood relatives of mine, they're my husband's relations," but "to please my son, . . . I went to the expense and humiliation, yes, public humiliation, of giving this girl a debut which was a fiasco. Nobody liked her when I brought her out. Oh, she had some kind of—notoriety! She had a sharp tongue that some people mistook for wit" (*SLS*, 391).

Figure 30. Rose in the year of her canceled debut, 1927. Photo reference: MS Thr 553 (69). Courtesy of the Harvard Theatre Collection, Houghton Library, Harvard University.

In 1927, when Rose (then beginning to demonstrate clear signs of mental illness) was eighteen, the family decided to send her to Knoxville for her debut under the watchful eyes of Cornelius's two sisters. Unfortunately, Rose's debut was called off because of the unexpected death of her aunt Isabel's (Cornelius's sister's) mother-in-law. In her memoir, Edwina's words about Rose's canceled debut seem to echo Mrs. Venable's callous indictment of the event she had arranged for Catharine: "The debut proved a fiasco from the first, as everything in Rose's life seemed destined to be."[11] Shortly afterward, Rose returned to St. Louis and attempted to go to secretarial school, where her mental state continued to deteriorate.

Both *Streetcar* and *Suddenly Last Summer* reveal how events and characters from the author's St. Louis past did not simply disappear in the period of great successes between 1944 and the early 1960s. For a profoundly autobiographical writer like Williams, setting and location should never be taken simply at face value; they remain secondary to the excavation and depiction of the writer's emotional history. Mrs. Venable reminds the doctor of this important inter-connectedness between a poet's life and work as she escorts him through Sebastian's garden, saying, "The work of a poet is the life of a poet and—vice versa" (*SLS*, 352). Her reminder about the inability of distinguishing place from consciousness is especially germane to the study of Williams—we separate the two at our peril. Even when writing about things that seem unconnected with his life, he was invariably writing about himself.

Chapter Six

In the Friggins Division

THREE DECADES AFTER believing he had abandoned St. Louis forever, Tennessee Williams found himself flung back onto the city he
hated. From mid-September to December 1969, he was confined
at the Renard Psychiatric Division of Barnes Hospital, the same
hospital where Rose had been treated for a variety of mysterious
gastrointestinal and psychiatric complaints at the onset of her own
terrible decline in the mid-1930s.

The fall for the prolific, Pulitzer Prize–winning playwright could
not have been more extreme or more astonishing. From *The Glass
Menagerie* (1944) through *The Night of the Iguana* (1961), Williams
had experienced the kind of phenomenal success achieved by very
few. More than a successful writer, he was a true American celebrity.
He was rich and famous; he had houses in New Orleans and Key
West and an apartment overlooking Central Park in New York. Each
new Tennessee Williams play on Broadway was eagerly anticipated
by audiences and critics alike. But now he had crashed and hit rock
bottom.

Cassandra-like, in an essay titled "The Catastrophe of Success,"
Williams had prophesied in 1947 what might happen to a young
artist enjoying great success in America. In a particularly revealing
anecdote about the dangers of sudden fame, he describes staying
at a luxurious hotel suite in New York, living on room service. He
ordered a rich meal of sirloin steak followed by a chocolate sundae.
However, he said, "everything was so cunningly disguised on the
table that I mistook the chocolate sauce for gravy and poured it
over the sirloin steak" (*NSE*, 33). Williams's embarrassing anecdote
suggests that he had learned his lesson—that he had learned the

difference between false and true: "The sort of life which I had had previous to this popular success was one that required endurance, a life of clawing and scratching along a sheer surface and holding on tight with raw fingers to every inch of rock higher than the one caught hold of before, but it was a good life because it was the sort of life for which the human organism is created" (*NSE*, 32). Published in the *New York Times* in late November 1947, just prior to the opening of his greatest triumph, *A Streetcar Named Desire*, "The Catastrophe of Success" sounds an ominous warning: "One does not escape that easily from the seduction of an effete way of life. . . . You cannot arbitrarily say to yourself, I will now continue my life as it was before this thing, Success, happened to me" (*NSE*, 35).

The essay implies that the writer had internalized a powerful lesson, "that not privation but luxury is the wolf at the door and that the fangs of this wolf are all the little vanities and conceits and laxities that Success is heir to" (*NSE*, 35). Sadly, in the months and years following the writing of that essay, Williams fell victim to a plethora of seductions so that by the late 1960s, each new work became grist for the sharpening of critical knives, and by 1977 he could plausibly author an essay with the sad title "I Am Widely Regarded as the Ghost of a Writer" (*NSE*, 184–86).

The events immediately precipitating his sudden return to St. Louis in the fall of 1969 were in some sense predictable. His brother, Dakin, responded to a mid-September emergency call from an alarmed friend in Key West, telling him that Tom, drinking very heavily and regularly injecting himself with amphetamines to stay awake and write during the day, had been taking sleeping pills at night and had slipped on his outdoor patio while carrying a Silex pot of hot coffee, scalding his shoulder. According to Dakin's recollection, "Tennessee was definitely on his last legs and badly panic-stricken. Seizing on this opportunity, I suggested to Tom: 'Don't you think we better get you to a hospital?'. . . Striking while the iron was hot—it was now or never—I immediately made reservations and we flew to St. Louis."[1] Dakin did manage to transport the fragile Williams back to his mother's home, but not before the intoxicated author made a scene on the plane when a stewardess would not let him exceed the two-drink limit. After waking up in Miss Edwina's

home in Clayton, a suburb of St. Louis, Tennessee refused to enter the hospital and abruptly announced he was returning to Key
West instead. Dakin finally persuaded him to enter Barnes Hospital,
where he checked in as Thomas L. Williams, a name he had not used
since December 1938. Dakin installed him in a suite in the hospital's luxurious Queeny Tower, where Dakin described his brother,
propped up on pillows, wearing a little stocking cap, and clutching
his little blue flight bag full of pills and alcohol, as thinking "he was
in full control."[2] In *Memoirs*, Williams acknowledged that paranoia
was a side effect of all the drugs he had been taking: "Every [TV]
program seemed to be directed at me with some thickly disguised
hostility, even Shirley Booth's soap opera [*Hazel*] struck me as a
personally menacing thing" (219); "I thought Shirley was making
veiled innuendoes about me," he said.[3] Feeling trapped and "totally
out of [his] mind," Williams decided to make a run for it: "I charged
into the corridor and down to the elevators. I started to enter one,
was blocked in this escape effort by a huge young man in hospital
uniform. He was blond, I remember, with a beefy, sneering face. I
somehow slipped past him into the elevator but he wouldn't let the
door close. Raging and storming invectives, I rushed back past him
to the room where Mother was asking for smelling salts. Jesus!"
(*M*, 219). After this attempted flight, Williams was strapped into a
wheelchair, and, he said, "clutching the flight bag that contained my
booze, my pills, my vial of speed" (*M*, 220), he was transferred from
posh Queeny Tower to room 9126 of the feared Renard Division,[4]
constructed in St. Louis in 1955 for the innovative treatment of
psychoses. There his precious flight bag was confiscated and he was
treated "cold turkey" for his various addictions.

For a month, Williams was kept in a lockdown ward, where his
"cell was checked every half-hour. . . . the door would open noisily
and a flashlight would be turned on [him]."[5] Dakin later acknowledged that he only had the right to legally commit his brother for a
maximum of ten days, arguing, "I determined that to save his life I
must intervene and keep him in the hospital, by force if necessary."[6]

Well, he could have walked out in ten days, but he didn't know
that. And I wasn't about to tell him his rights, even if I am

a lawyer. The doctors didn't either. He had four convulsions from drug withdrawals and blamed me. He kept asking when he could leave for three months, as the drugs gradually left his system. The doctors told him, "As soon as Dakin says so." He seethed with rage until I arrived one night, and then attacked me. He would ask me, "When can I get out of here?" and I would say to him, "When the doctors say you can." . . . His mail was opened and checked before he read it, and this made him furious.[7]

For some two months of his stay, Williams was not allowed to write letters, make phone calls, or receive unopened mail. For Dakin's part in what Williams later described as "legalized fratricide," he cut his brother out of his will, and he never forgave him for his incarceration at Barnes Hospital.[8]

During and immediately after this period at Barnes, Williams wrote a prose poem entitled "What's Next on the Agenda, Mr. Williams?" (*CP*, 150–58) describing his nightmarish experience in detail. The poem is part lament, part satire on the casual cruelty of the hospital staff, and part venomous attack on his brother and the attending physicians. In the first section of the four-part poem, "Apostrophe to Myself," Williams recalls his convulsions, those "pre-mature contractions of a heart-valve," comparing them with the childhood experience of riding the roller coaster at Forest Park Highlands in St. Louis, although the flashbacks were "hardly agreeable enough to be called nostalgic" (*CP*, 151). The Renard Division of Barnes Hospital in St. Louis on the Mississippi River is, in Williams's poem, the "Friggins Division of Barnacle Hospital in the city of Saint Pollution on the gobble-nobber of waters" (*CP*, 151, 156, 157). The idiom *gobble-nobber* is only explained in the poem's concluding lines—it is a translation of the phrase "boat-load of mothers," which he picked up from an unnamed black musician whom Williams cites as "an authority on the idioms of his race and vocation" (*CP*, 157).

Many of the poem's cruelest—and funniest—lines are directed at Williams's physician, a mammoth neurologist (Dr. Levy) he calls "Dr. Leviathan," with whom he exchanges witty repartee about his treatment and whom he considered "the least inhuman of the triumvirate of neurologists" who treated him (*M*, 224). When asked about the confiscation of his wristwatch and reading glasses and the alacrity with which, he said, "I was strapped and catapulted up here in a wheel-chair that I think could give an antiballistic missile one good fucking run for its money," Dr. Leviathan replies, "Your wrist-watch had a glass front and everything having glass on it or in it is taken away from inmates of the acute ward to prevent their making any attempt at wrist-or-throat-slashing or self-castration," and as for the removal of his glasses, the doctor quips, "Naturally, yes, glasses do contain glass, and so does a whiskey bottle" (*CP*, 154).

The third section, "Dedications and Mornings," offers the poem's dedication to a resident physician "with Dracula sideburns" and a night nurse who sarcastically puts the question that becomes the poem's title, "What's next on the agenda, Mr. Williams?," with "a vicious slow-growing smile" (*CP*, 155). Williams saves some of his most splenetic attacks for the brother who put him in the hospital, reminiscing about the fact that he and Rose had nicknamed their toddler brother "Sunny," with the vowel *u* not *o* "because he wore on his puss an all but perpetual gap-toothed grin" that he and Rose had "romantically misinterpreted as the token of a benevolent na-ture," concluding that "yes, the dedications of this bitch of a thing [the poem] should be extended to him" (*CP*, 156). The final section of "What's Next on the Agenda, Mr. Williams?" is written in com-memoration of his release: "I want to wash the slate clean and then scrawl on it in luminous chalk '*En avant!*', the command with which I concluded all entries in my old journals of days and nights gained and lost" (*CP*, 157).

For days after being interned at Renard, the writer went through absolute hell. After being taken off the addictive sleeping pill Doriden cold turkey, he suffered convulsions and apparently a heart attack. In *Memoirs*, he describes this in detail: "I don't know how long the convulsions lasted. I know that there were three of them in one morning and there was the 'silent coronary,' which is the only thing during the apocalypse that is clear to me" (220).

Despite his undergoing the sort of horrifying experience that might well have been included in one of his plays, Williams's hos-pitalization in all probability saved his life. Miraculously, he was released in December and even managed to stay relatively sober and off of drugs for an extended period. But the question one must ask is how could this have possibly happened in the first place? How could the best and most celebrated playwright of his generation have become so entangled in a nightmare that left him a virtual prisoner in a psychiatric ward, mere blocks from the boardinghouse where the Williams family had resided when they first moved to St. Louis in the summer of 1918?

The proximate cause of Williams's collapse may be traced to the critical responses to his play *In the Bar of a Tokyo Hotel*, which opened in the spring of 1969. However, to speak of "critical response" is inaccurate. The reactions were vicious and ugly by any standard, moving beyond legitimate theatre criticism into personal invective. Critics attempted not to analyze or illuminate the play but to use it as a weapon to savagely eviscerate both the work and the man who created it. Following are three examples from among many:

> Tennessee Williams is lying on the sickbed of his formidable talent. Ever since *The Milk Train Doesn't Stop Here Anymore*, his work has become increasingly infirm—so grave that *In the Bar of a Tokyo Hotel* seems more deserving of a coroner's report than a review.[9]

> [*In the Bar of a Tokyo Hotel*] is a play by a man at the end of, not his talent (that was long ago), but his tether—a man around whom the last props of the dramatic edifice have crumbled, and who, in an impotent frenzy, stamps his feet on the few remaining bricks.[10]

Easily among the most vituperative and vindictive of the responses was written by Stefan Kanfer and published in *Life* magazine, then boasting a circulation of eight million subscribers. The review, "White Dwarf's Tragic Fade-Out," was even reprinted in a full-page advertisement in the *New York Times* (accompanied by a photograph of the playwright) as a demonstration of *Life*'s "honest" reporting:

Tennessee Williams appears to be a White Dwarf. We are still receiving his messages, but it is now obvious that they come from a cinder. . . . Gone are his sustained flights of rhetoric—which always bordered on hysteria. Gone, too, are his poetic tendencies which always risked ridicule. . . . Other playwrights have progressed: Williams has suffered an infantile regression from which there seems no exit.[11]

Fifty years after its premiere, *In the Bar of a Tokyo Hotel* would still be a difficult sell to mainstream audiences, and it is hardly surprising that this work was unpopular then and has had few enthusiasts since. It is an unremittingly dark play, and its main characters, the abstract expressionist painter Mark and his promiscuous, pretentious wife, Miriam, compel little sympathy from an audience. For theatergoers still thinking of the languid lyricism of so many of Tennessee Williams's memorable southern characters, *Tokyo Hotel* was indeed both shocking and bewildering. Nevertheless, as an important play by a major playwright, it is deserving of far more attention than it has received. To a great extent, the play was victimized by what Williams wrote himself in his essay "I Am Widely Regarded as the Ghost of a Playwright": "I suspect that what happened is that after *The Night of the Iguana* in 1961, certain radically and dreadfully altered circumstances of my life compelled me to work in correspondingly different styles. There has surely been sufficient exposure in print of my misadventures in the 60's for that subject to be no more than mentioned at this point" (*NSE*, 184). While not exactly an apology for the wayward lifestyle that may have contributed to his damaged reputation, this remark points to the fact that, whatever his reasons, Williams needed to write in a different key than before and that audiences and critics were unprepared to allow an artist the freedom to experiment and change. In this regard, the critical and popular responses to Williams's later work are similar to what they were toward that of his contemporary, Arthur Miller, and toward the work of the leading playwright of the next generation, Edward Albee. As audiences seemed to demand that Williams write another

Streetcar, they wanted Miller to reprise *Death of a Salesman* and Albee to write another *Who's Afraid of Virginia Woolf?*

When the playwrights could not or would not accommodate their requests, audiences and critics alike showed their displeasure. In Williams's case, the critical opprobrium may have been triggered by the critics' conscious or unconscious homophobia, or displeasure with what they considered his aberrant lifestyle. To paraphrase F. Scott Fitzgerald's comment in *The Last Tycoon*, there are no second acts in American lives, although of these three great playwrights, Albee did manage a true "second act" in which he lived to see the resurgence of his celebrity, with late plays such as *Three Tall Women* and *The Goat*.

As for *Tokyo Hotel*, the play should be viewed as an experiment in monodrama, its main characters representing the conflict between warring halves of the dramatist's psyche.[12] On one side is Mark, a painter, who is physically frail and has experienced "a total collapse of the nervous system," yet feels himself on the brink of a remarkable discovery: "I feel as if I were crossing the frontier of a country I have no permission to enter, but I enter this, this! I tell you it *terrifies* me!" (*TH*, 19). Mark argues that an artist must lay his life on the line, and he has thrown over the traditional painterly techniques that have brought him celebrity, now applying color with spray guns to canvases fixed to the floor, in the manner of Jackson Pollock. Mark murmurs with visionary zeal, "The possibilities of color and light, discovered all at once, can make a man fall on the street. . . . I know the last things, the imperishable things, are color and light" (*TH*, 24).

Miriam, by contrast, can see only Mark's pathology, not his vision: "Mark is mad! I am married to *madness!*" she says (*TH*, 39). Resentful and dismissive of the experiments in color she sneeringly describes as "circus-colored mud-pies" (*TH*, 19), Miriam attempts to hold onto life through random attempts at seduction like the one she tries initiating with the Japanese hotel barman at the beginning of the play. She wants to be rid of her husband, yet when he collapses and dies near the play's conclusion, it is evident there is nothing left for her. Her final words, "I have no plans. I have nowhere to go," reflect that her vaunted "vitality" has been utterly sapped now that Mark is gone from her life. Her final action is one of "abrupt violence" as she wrenches the bracelets from her arms and throws them to the floor as the stage darkens at the end of the play (*TH*, 53).

Tokyo Hotel is another in the long line of autobiographical works by Williams. The play is a fearfully honest glimpse into the abyss of an artist's deteriorating mental and physical health, and the warring elements of inspired artistic vision and weary sensuality, both important aspects of his nature, are presented in mortal and unresolved combat. The play is not the self-indulgent mess contemporary critics assumed, but it is a depressing and ambiguous account of a life approaching its end. What are we to make of Mark's visionary explorations into new artistic territory? We are not sure.

Even as his life was spinning out of control through his addictions to drugs and casual sex, Williams continued to write obsessively. He never lost the "fatal need" to write that his friend Clark Mills observed in him in their Literary Factory days at Washington University. In *Tokyo Hotel*, he created a frighteningly revealing portrait of his own downward, self-centered, self-destructive spiral, and it is not only painful but abhorrent to witness. "An artist has to lay his life on the line," Mark says, now acknowledging that he is "adventuring into a jungle country with wild men crouching in the bushes, in in in—trees, with poison arrows" (*TH*, 22, 23). By contrast, Miriam represents the artist's anti-self, driven by a relentless pursuit of sensuality, utterly terrified of being left alone. Miriam asks at the end of the play's first scene,

MIRIAM: Are we two people, Mark, or are we—
MARK: Stop there!
MIRIAM: Two sides of!
MARK: Stop!
MIRIAM: One! (*TH*, 30)

As this exchange illustrates, another of the reasons for the play's hostile reception was its use of broken language and incomplete sentences, mirroring its characters' lack of balance and inability to communicate with one another. In contrast with the poetic lyricism Williams's work had been associated with since *Menagerie*,

Tokyo Hotel deliberately employs a language of fragmentation and uses incomplete thoughts to express his characters' inability to ever reach one another—or even to connect with themselves.[13] In this, Williams demonstrates his awareness of a new kind of nonlinear dramatic writing that had been emerging in the American theatre since the early 1960s, a style profoundly influenced by what Martin Esslin calls "the Theatre of the Absurd" in his 1969 book by that title. A wave of European playwrights, Samuel Beckett, Jean Genet, Eugene Ionesco, and Harold Pinter, along with a younger generation of American playwrights including Albee and Arthur Kopit, began employing a style in which traditional logic and meaning were of secondary importance, and in which characters spoke in clichés, or past one another, instead of communicating in logically constructed sentences. Esslin notes in *The Theatre of the Absurd* that Albert Camus described the notion of the Absurd succinctly in *The Myth of Sisyphus*: "A world that can be explained by reasoning, however faulty, is a familiar world. But in a universe that is suddenly deprived of illusions and of light, man feels a stranger. . . . This divorce between man and his life, the actor and his setting, truly constitutes the feeling of Absurdity." Esslin delineates this new kind of theatre that developed as a logical extension of Camus's philosophy, arguing that to adequately mirror a world that no longer offers fixed coordinates, language must also be "radically devalued," tending toward a poetry "that is to emerge from the concrete and objectified images of the stage itself."[14]

In his essay "Which Theater Is the Absurd One?" Edward Albee articulated a call for a new kind of nonrealistic theatre based on the implications of Camus's thought as applied to the contemporary American stage: "I would submit that the Theater of the Absurd, in the sense that it is truly the contemporary theater, facing as it does man's condition as it is, is the Realistic theater of our time; and that the supposed Realistic theater—the term used here to mean most of what is done on Broadway . . . is really truly the Theater of the Absurd."[15]

Williams's technique in *Tokyo Hotel* relies heavily on Esslin's and Albee's new way of looking at the theatre, in which broken syntax mirrors Mark and Miriam's broken relationship:

MIRIAM: The image of your new work must be extremely.
MARK: No, not at all. They're so vivid they.
MIRIAM: You could hire a car with a chauffeur and a siren to.
MARK: Miriam, don't ridicule the—To doubt is necessary.
  (*TH*, 15)

It is easy to assume that the technique Williams adopted, as Walter Kerr suggested in a review in the *New York Times*, simply "made a fetish of the unfinished sentence,"[16] or, as critic John Simon sarcastically wrote, that scores of sentences such as those illustrated above were left "lying around supposedly pregnant and tremulous with the burden of the unsaid."[17] Perhaps most hurtful of all was the pity evinced for the writer, along with the assumption that at fifty-eight, Williams was finished as a playwright: "One must never forget that despite his present esthetic humiliation, Tennessee Williams is a thoroughbred."[18] The unspoken assertion was that the verbal technique at the heart of *Tokyo Hotel* was not a technique at all, but was simply the incoherent product of Williams's drug- and alcohol-addled mind, and that Mark's desperate search for a mystical "circle of light" was only a portrait of the chaotic approach to dramaturgy seen in Williams's heavily condemned recent work, including *The Milk Train Doesn't Stop Here Anymore* (1963) and the double bill he called *Slapstick Tragedy* (1965), comprising the one-acts *Gnädiges Fräulein* and *The Mutilated*, which fared badly with both public and critics.

It is true that slurred speech and loss of balance were physiological symptoms that Williams experienced at this time, and they are mirrored in Mark's unsteadiness and lack of control—Williams notes that "his hand is too tremulous to lift the glass to his mouth," forcing Miriam to order a new drink, and then she tells the barman, "I'll pour it down him" (*TH*, 15). Such moments in the play offer an open invitation to read Mark's illness as a form of grotesque self-portraiture, and critics pounced with alacrity on the opportunity to mercilessly criticize Williams's various frailties through an unnecessarily vicious critique of his work. A writer who once encouraged autobiographical readings of his work in plays from *The Glass Menagerie* through

Suddenly Last Summer, where Violet Venable argues that "a poet's life is his work and his work is his life in a special sense" (*SLS*, 352), now became the victim of invidious personal attacks using his work as ammunition. In the essay "Too Personal?" Williams justifies his relentless exploration of self as a necessity of any writer and, by extension, any creative artist. He puts the question "Is it or is it not wrong for a playwright to put his persona into his work?" and offers the following answer:

> My answer is: "What else can he do?"—I mean the very root-necessity of all creative work is to express those things most involved in one's particular experience. Otherwise, is the work, however well executed, not a manufactured, a synthetic thing? . . . It is [also] the responsibility of the writer to put his experience as a being into work that refines it and elevates it and that makes of it an essence that a wide audience can somehow manage to feel in themselves: "This is true." (*NSE*, 166–67)

Whether or not Williams managed to "refine and elevate" his personal experience into art that can be communicated to others in *Tokyo Hotel* may be debated. What is *not* debatable is the fact that even in his addicted state, Williams continued somehow to engage in the desperate search for the truth of his own experience. And perhaps no writer suffered more vitriol in return for probing the depths of his psyche. In a review of an American Masters television documentary titled *Tennessee Williams: Orpheus of the American Stage*, one critic concisely summarized his fate: "He was the first postwar American playwright to reach stardom, and the first to watch that star crash terribly to Earth. To this day, Williams' extraordinary string of artistic and commercial triumphs signifies a kind of watermark for the ambitious American writer. His demolition by a hostile press and his seemingly self-indulgent drug and alcohol excesses also signify the American writer's worst nightmare."[19]

Chapter Seven

Back to Saint Pollution

AFTER HIS TERRIFYING three-month incarceration at Barnes Hospital, Tennessee Williams gradually returned to life. However dreaded, his time back in "Saint Pollution" finally freed him from the addiction to the fantastic cocktail of drugs (Nembutal, Doriden, Luminal, Seconal) that the notorious Max Jacobson ("Dr. Feel Good" [*M*, 208, 209]) had prescribed for him, which Williams had somehow managed to have mailed to himself wherever in the world he was and which he had consumed in conjunction with his customary heavy use of alcohol.[1]

He had been able to return to what ultimately mattered most— typing compulsively each morning until his fingers were too tired to hit the keys of his typewriter. For relaxation, he swam daily and resumed painting—a passion of his dating back to the late 1930s, when he took lessons from the mother of his friend Jim Parrott, a woman who had been a painter with the WPA.

Williams's painting continued until just before he died in 1983, and he pursued it with special assiduousness in Key West, where he had a home and where a friend, the developer David Wolkowsky, encouraged him to paint on his private island off the Florida coast. According to Wolkowsky, Williams would bring his painting materials, a jug of red wine, and a stack of Billie Holiday records to the island and work virtually uninterrupted until nightfall.[2]

After his hospitalization, his reputation never returned to where it was prior to his "Stoned Age," as Williams referred to the decade of the 1960s (*M*, 212), as it suffered attacks and self-inflicted wounds in the following years. An essay by Tom Buckley in the *Atlantic Monthly* in 1970, "Tennessee Williams Survives," chronicled his lifestyle in

Figure 31. Williams's self-portrait from 1939. The inscription reads: "Very flattering, even *then*! Tennessee." Courtesy of the Tennessee Williams Collection, Harry Ransom Center, University of Texas at Austin. Printed with permission of The University of the South.

lurid detail—detail Buckley acquired by surreptitiously recording a conversation with Williams, apparently using a concealed tape recorder. The essay begins with long-time friend David Loovis's assertion "He's a new man. . . . it's the most wonderful thing I've ever seen,"[3] but proceeds to document his past drug and alcohol dependence and his present circumstances in unsavory terms, including descriptions of the myriad young men who clustered around him, jockeying with one another to become favored members of the great man's coterie. "Tennessee Williams Survives" not only failed to rehabilitate Williams's reputation—it accomplished just the opposite. The piece may have purported to show that the writer had undergone a healthy transformation; instead, it confirmed to a wider audience the narrative of his spiraling self-destruction through drugs, alcohol, and sexual promiscuity. Williams detested Buckley's article, calling it "the worst piece of character assassination that's ever been tried on me for size," and had to be dissuaded by his trusted friend Maria St. Just from filing a lawsuit.[4]

Earlier in 1970, Williams's reputation had suffered another devastating blow. Appearing obviously drunk on *The David Frost Show*, he initially evaded responding to an impromptu question about his sexual preference before responding with good-humored (if ill-advised) candor, "I guess you could say I've covered the waterfront."[5] The remark was broadcast internationally and confirmed both the public's and the critical establishment's perception of Williams as debauched and committed to a lifestyle of sexual depravity. Even after the Stonewall uprising and the stirrings of the gay liberation movement in the late 1960s, homosexuality remained a taboo subject that could not be publicly discussed on television in the early 1970s.

In 1975 his reputation was damaged even further. Williams published *Memoirs*, a work of haphazard reflections and uncertain structure written with honesty and replete with lurid disclosures about his promiscuous lifestyle. The impact of *Memoirs* was to convince people that its author was unrepentant and chose to bask in his scandalous reputation rather than repudiate it with a more restrained and respectable chronicle of his storied life.

Williams's major plays of this period were abysmal failures, both critically and at the box office. These disasters included the auto-biographical memory play *Vieux Carré* (1977), a work inspired by Williams's early days in the French Quarter of New Orleans in the late 1930s, just after his arrival from St. Louis. The play's retrospective technique of a young writer recalling his past was reminiscent of *The Glass Menagerie*, while its French Quarter setting evoked *A Streetcar Named Desire*.

Instead of seeing the work as a richly evocative autobiographical examination of the writer's past, critics saw it as Williams cannibalizing his own previously successful plays in a vain attempt at reversing his fading artistic and commercial reputation. Even a normally sympathetic reviewer, Walter Kerr, noted "the appalling stage direction, . . . and the monstrously shabby physical design" that marked the play's "irresponsible production."[6]

Given the downward trajectory of his career as the 1970s came to a close, and his well-known hostility toward "Saint Pollution," it is astonishing that Williams chose to revisit St. Louis in the play *A Lovely Sunday for Creve Coeur* (1979). Even more remarkable is the fact that the play is a comedy with a hopeful ending—so different from nearly all his other works and certainly in deep contrast with his other portrayals of the city in both his fiction and his plays. *A Lovely Sunday for Creve Coeur* was written in a style that perhaps comes closest to his 1942 romantic comedy written in collaboration with Donald Windham, *You Touched Me!*, or the 1960 play *Period of Adjustment*, which he subtitled *A Serious Comedy*.

Conspicuously absent from *A Lovely Sunday for Creve Coeur* is the nonrealistic architecture and fragmented dialogue characteristic of Williams's experimental plays written during the 1960s, including *The Milk Train Doesn't Stop Here Anymore*, *In the Bar of a Tokyo Hotel*, and *The Two-Character Play*. Likewise absent is the tendency toward cartoonish caricature employed in his absurdist mid-1960s plays such as *Gnädiges Fräulein* and *The Mutilated*.

A Lovely Sunday for Creve Coeur is a deliberately simple work, relying on domestic realism and devoid of self-conscious artifice. Originally commissioned as *Creve Coeur* by the Spoleto Festival in

Charleston, South Carolina, in 1978, the title refers both to a St. Louis suburb (locally pronounced "Creeve Core") and to its literal French meaning of "broken-hearted." The one-act was subsequently expanded into a full-length play and in January 1979 was presented off-Broadway at New York's Hudson Guild Theatre under its new title, *A Lovely Sunday for Creve Coeur*.

Set on a Sunday morning in the 1930s in the West End of St. Louis, the play examines the lives of a quartet of women who are unmarried, no longer young, and lonely. The play's straightforward plot revolves around Dorothea, a civics teacher at Ben Blewett (Williams's junior high school). Dorothea is in a relationship with Blewett's principal, Ralph Ellis, and expects an engagement proposal from him at any time. She rooms with her friend "Bodey" Bodenhafer,

Figure 32. Kelley Weber as Bodey Bodenhafer (*left*) and Julie Layton as Helena Brookmire (*right*) in *A Lovely Sunday for Creve Coeur* at the Grandel Theatre during the Tennessee Williams Festival St. Louis in 2019. Reproduced with permission of the Tennessee Williams Festival St. Louis, 2019. Photograph by Peter Wochniak, ProPhotoSTL.com.

a lower-middle-class woman employed at International Shoe (the same name as the company where Williams and his father worked) who has unashamedly decorated the apartment to her gaudy tastes. Bodey discovers the announcement of the principal's engagement to a prominent socialite in the *St. Louis Post-Dispatch* and attempts damage control to spare her friend inevitable disappointment; she hides the news and plans for Dorothea to spend that Sunday at Creve Coeur Lake with herself and her twin brother, Buddy, with whom she hopes Dorothea will strike up a romantic relationship and assure happiness for all three. Helena Brookmire, another Blewett colleague and shameless snob, has other plans: after learning of the principal's engagement herself, she arrives and attempts to convince Dorothea to leave the ugly apartment and room with her in a more fashionable Westmoreland Place home—presumably for better social prospects than tacky Bodey and her brother. As Bodey and Helena war over Dorothea's affections, each hiding the engagement news to serve her own ends, the upstairs neighbor, a lonely and grieving German immigrant named Miss Gluck, enters the scene and serves as a comic foil for Helena's snobbish predations. Near the conclusion of the play, the devastating announcement about the principal's engagement is revealed and Dorothea is crushed. However, she quickly rebounds from her disappointment and, informing Helena that she has decided not to move out of her apartment after all, calls the streetcar station to announce she will indeed be coming to meet Bodey and Buddy at Creve Coeur Lake that evening.

It is hardly surprising that this play is so little known. Having been conceived as a one-act, the play is almost disconcertingly modest in scale and aspiration, consisting of two scenes in a single location. Simple in its trajectory, it has proved disappointing both to traditional scholars longing for the playwright's return to the intricate symbolism, psychology, and lyricism of *The Glass Menagerie*, and to those who wish to argue that the playwright's later plays represent a revolutionary break with his past work. Because of its critical neglect, despite the play's abundant humor and appealing accessibility, *A Lovely Sunday for Creve Coeur* remains largely unknown to the public. It stands out from Williams's other, more celebrated work as

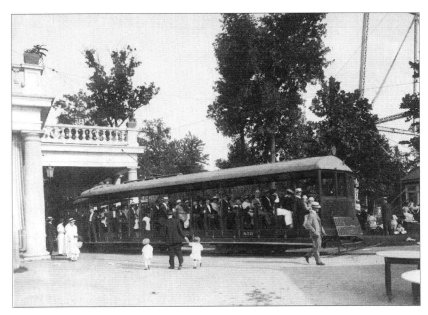

Figure 33. Passengers boarding a streetcar at Creve Coeur Lake, ca. 1915. Identifier: P0593-01-035. Courtesy of the Missouri Historical Society.

a simple, modest jewel in its avoidance of the melodramatic violence and tragic denouements that mark so many of his plays. Williams himself described the play as his "bijou." He seemed to desire, at least in this one play, a return to a quiet realism, although the play's very lack of ostentation and daring has paradoxically led both critics and the public to ignore its simple beauty. Charlotte Moore, the actress who played Helena in the original production in 1979, recalled in an interview that Williams had said despairingly, "I don't understand what they want. . . . I don't understand what they want from me anymore. I work hard and do my best and I do what I do like nobody else in the world does. I still do, but they hate it. Why do they hate it?"[7] Despite the anguish suggested by these words, *A Lovely Sunday for Creve Coeur* should not be dismissed as the inconsequential work many have perceived it to be. Rather, it represents neither regression nor compromise, but a truce between Williams and his St. Louis past, an act of humane reconciliation between the playwright and the city he so badly needed to hate.

A Lovely Sunday for Creve Coeur is Williams's most St. Louis–based play since *The Glass Menagerie*, and it is loaded with a remarkable number of specific references to sights and landmarks associated with the city's history. Among the many topical connections to St. Louis's past are the aforementioned Ben Blewett Junior High School and International Shoe Company; in addition, the play references the Anheuser-Busch brewery, Delmar Boulevard, the Olive Streetcar line, Art Hill (the city's highest spot, where Dorothea and Principal Ellis have had sex), the West End Lyric movie theatre, Tower Grove Park, Liggett's Drug Store, the First Lutheran Church on South Grand, the Scruggs, Vandervoort & Barney department store, the upscale residential area of Ladue, where Helena's wealthy cousin lives, and posh Westmoreland Place, where Helena hopes to convince Dorothea to share an apartment with her.

A Lovely Sunday for Creve Coeur should be seen as the comic obverse of *The Glass Menagerie*. Whereas the earlier play is centered on the necessity of escape from St. Louis, the latter work is about resilience and acceptance of it, despite the city's obvious insufficiencies. In their monumental biographical study of Eugene O'Neill, *O'Neill: Life with Monte Cristo*, Arthur Gelb and Barbara Gelb note that "*Ah, Wilderness!* and *Long Day's Journey into Night* should be regarded as two sides of a coin—one a genial glimpse of what the O'Neill family, at its best, aspired to be; and the other, a balefully heightened picture of his family at its worst." In O'Neill's case, the comedy *Ah, Wilderness!* (1932) was written while he was in his forties and at the height of his career, while *Long Day's Journey* was created nearly a decade later, when the playwright was "depressed, not only over his own failing health, but over the critical disparagement that had followed the 1934 production of *Days Without End*, as well as over the onslaught of fascism and the onset of World War II."[8]

In Tennessee Williams's case, these circumstances are almost precisely reversed. The tragic play, *Menagerie*, accompanied what he hoped would be his leave-taking from the city; it brought the young man his first popular and critical success, and made his name on Broadway. By contrast, the comedy *A Lovely Sunday for Creve*

Coeur was conceived and written during a period of protracted artistic failure. Gelb and Gelb's comment that "in *Ah, Wilderness!* the living room is seen through rose-colored lenses, while in *Long Day's Journey into Night* it is viewed through a glass darkly"⁹ is strangely apposite to the relationship between the two Williams plays. In *Menagerie*, the Wingfield apartment building is described with the imagery of disease; it is "one of those vast hive-like conglomerations of cellular living-units that flower as warty growths in overcrowded urban centers," and like all such buildings, it is "always burning with the slow and implacable fires of human desperation" (*GM*, 143). Superficially, Bodey and Dorothea's efficiency apartment, located only a few blocks away from the Wingfields', may seem similarly run-down, but in the roommates' case there has been an attempt to ameliorate and transform its shabbiness, however futile: "Attempts to give the apartment brightness and cheer have gone brilliantly and disastrously wrong, and this wrongness is emphasized by the fiercely yellow glare of light through the oversize windows" (*CC*, 119).

Both *Menagerie* and *Creve Coeur* focus on the unfulfilled desires of lonely young women, Laura and Dorothea. In *Menagerie*, Laura's isolation is made manifest by her physical handicap. Her difference from others is epitomized by the appellation "Blue Roses" and by the glass menagerie that is the center of her world.

By contrast, Dorothea is a fully functioning adult: she teaches civics at Blewett and has had a relationship prior to her current romance with Principal Ellis. However, Williams makes a point amid the comedy of drawing our attention to Dorothea's instability; her colleague Helena describes her as an "emotionally fragile type of person who might collapse, just suddenly collapse, when confronted with the disappointing facts of a situation about which she'd allowed herself to have—romantic illusions," and refers to an episode she has had at school as "neuro-circulatory asthenia" (*CC*, 146, 155). Later in the play, Dorothea does collapse, and after regaining consciousness calls for Mebaral anti-anxiety tablets, which she washes down with sherry straight from the bottle. If Dorothea's neurasthenia suggests that she descends from the long line of Williams's unhappy heroines stretching back to Laura, Blanche, and

Alma from *Summer and Smoke*, it is because they are all based on the same prototype, the playwright's sister, Rose.

* * * * *

Twenty years before composing *Creve Coeur*, Williams wrote a screenplay titled *All Gaul Is Divided*, which he cast aside and later discovered in his New Orleans apartment. In an author's note to the screenplay, Williams claimed he had "*totally* forgotten its existence when [he] wrote *Creve Coeur*" (*AG*, 3), a suggestion that would be met with extreme skepticism were the teller of this tale anyone but Williams, a man whose gargantuan appetite for writing was perhaps the most extreme feature of his compulsive, addictive personality. The screenplay mirrors the plot of the later play in myriad aspects. Like *Creve Coeur*, *All Gaul Is Divided* is set in a St. Louis school classroom (though set a bit earlier, in the late 1920s), and its central character is, like the "marginally youthful" Dorothea (*CC*, 119), Jenny Starling, over thirty, a "grown woman playing a little girl" (*AG*, 5). The unproduced screenplay, like the later comedy, revolves around a schoolteacher (she teaches Latin, not civics, as in the play), and she is in love with the school's physical education teacher, Harry Steed, who repeatedly teases her with the question "Well, Miss Starling, how many parts is Gaul divided into?" (*AG*, 17). As with *Creve Coeur*, the teacher has a sympathetic and maternal German roommate, named Beulah Bodenhafer (the same last name as Bodey), and a snobbish rival, Lucinda. A comparison between the screenplay and the stage play reveals that, despite strong similarities between both the two plays' plots and their characters, the neurotic aspects of the teacher's character are considerably heightened in the earlier work. The screenplay depicts Jenny Starling as lonely and mentally unstable, and we learn she has spent two years in an asylum and is the subject of repeated gossip among her colleagues. Her name, "Starling," suggests her delicacy and birdlike innocence for Williams, although her colleague Lucinda (a model for the catty social climber Helena in *Creve Coeur*) nastily remarks that Jenny is playing a part in dressing like a little girl: "You can't keep those little girl's curls forever, Jenny. They're sweet but I think the time has come for you to part with them. Mary Pickford has to keep hers to play child parts in pictures. Like Rebecca of Sunnybrook Farm. But you're not playing child parts in pictures, are you?" (*AG*, 20–21).

Jenny is also prone to fits of hysteria. When challenged in the classroom, she suddenly erupts in anger at an unruly student: "No, I—I WON'T BE TREATED LIKE THIS! NOW! GET YOUR SPONGE AND SPONGE THAT BLACKBOARD OFF!—and DON'T EVER!—FORGET TO, AGAIN!" (*AG*, 32).

Whether or not Williams was conscious of repeating the same characters, it is obvious that Jenny Starling became the prototype for Dorothea in *A Lovely Sunday for Creve Coeur*, written some twenty years later. The differences between the two, however, are also revealing. Whereas Jenny is presented as being on the verge of mental collapse, Dorothea's anxieties—her compulsive waiting for the phone to ring; her obsessive exercising—are mined for their comic potential, and are far less obvious markers of pathology.

Dorothea may remind us of such Williams heroines as Laura or Blanche, but it is also evident that she exists in a fundamentally comic world where neuroses may be safely contained and ameliorated. In Laura's case, her pathological shyness and physical disability are exacerbated by her domineering and competitive mother, who unintentionally increases her anxieties ("This is the prettiest you will ever be!" [*GM*, 192], Amanda tells her as she prepares for her gentleman caller); while in Blanche's, she is mercilessly destroyed by a predatory male adversary.

By contrast, threats to Dorothea's well-being come in the form of an unseen cad, Principal Ralph Ellis, and a nasty rival, Helena Brookmire, whose pretensions are so self-evident that Dorothea is easily able to see through them. Repeatedly described by Bodey as a bird of prey, Helena's threat to Dorothea's fragile stability lacks true destructive force, hinting at the playwright's more benign intentions. Williams even gives Helena an interior monologue, momentarily violating the play's consistently realistic form and allowing the audience to glimpse the pitiful loneliness lying beneath Helena's social aspirations. All the play's four women inhabit the world of "Creve Coeur," and all are terribly fearful of being left alone. When she overhears the grieving Miss Gluck moaning in German "*Allein,*

allein," Helena is allowed to reflect on her own heartbreak: "*Allein,
allein* means alone, alone. [*A frightened look appears in her eyes.*] Last
week I dined alone, alone three nights in a row. There's nothing
lonelier than a woman dining alone, and although I loathe preparing
food for myself, I cannot bear the humiliation of occupying a restaurant table for one. Dining *au solitaire!*" (*CC*, 161).

Helena's attitudes in the play may remind us of Edwina Williams's
overt hostility toward St. Louis, with its snobbish emphasis on money and social class, but her monologue undercuts the notion that she
is truly a dangerous adversary to Dorothea. In the world of *Creve
Coeur*, her social affectations are clearly less appealing to Dorothea
than Bodey's nurturing (if comically vulgar) maternal warmth.

Bodey is a character that in other plays Williams would almost
certainly have caricatured as a bovine German *hausfrau*. Both Linda
Dorff and Annette Saddik observe that in many later plays, Williams
employed stereotypes—particularly German stereotypes—as a means
of distancing himself from theatrical realism. Dorff argues that "the
outrageous late plays are bawdy, over-the-top farces that appropriate
systems of metadrama and the aesthetics of the cartoon,"[10] while
Saddik notes that in *Night of the Iguana* a group of German tourists who are Nazi sympathizers appear at Maxine's Mexican resort,
creating a "cartoonish, fantastical image" of grotesque excess, deliberately contrasting with the spiritual quests of the other characters.[11]

Both Dorff and Saddik rightly connect the birth of Williams's
anti-realist style with the influence of the Theatre of the Absurd and
the emergent wave of American dramatists whose most significant
representative was Edward Albee. Works such as *Kirche, Küche,
Kinder, Will Mr. Merriweather Return from Memphis?*; and *Gnädiges
Fräulein* all exemplify what Dorff terms Williams's "outrageous"
style and Saddik characterizes as his embrace of the "Rabelaisian
grotesque."[12] Williams himself endorsed this perspective in a short
essay published in *Esquire* in 1965, "*Slapstick Tragedy: A Preface,*"
in which he offered a comparison between his recent work and the
National Enquirer (ironically described as "the finest journalistic
review of the precise time we live in"), arguing that "the style of the
plays [was] kin to vaudeville, burlesque and slapstick, with a dash of
pop art thrown in" (*NSE*, 148).

However, while accurate, this view of Williams's late plays fails to take account of the unique position of *Creve Coeur*, where what might otherwise be seen as "outrageous" or "grotesque" is humanized into something oddly nurturing, compassionate, and redemptive. Craig Clinton argues that the "much maligned" *A Lovely Sunday for Creve Coeur* deserves both "reevaluation and far greater appreciation."[13]

As a way of underscoring this notion, it is essential to realize that it is Bodey, not Dorothea, who embodies the play's emotional core. Dorothea may be the work's ostensible heroine; it is she who undergoes change as she decides to abandon Ralph and Helena and join Bodey and her brother at the picnic. However, it is Bodey who functions as the play's beating heart. Her mundane, unrefined sensibility is represented in the set's ostentatiously vulgar color scheme, and her modest personal aspirations revolve around seeing Dorothea married to Buddy. Indeed, her name, Bodenhafer (deliberately mispronounced Boden-*heifer* by Helena), her vanity regarding her deafness—she wears a huge artificial chrysanthemum to conceal a hearing aid—all provide Williams with ample possibilities for verbal comedy, which is certainly aimed at her as its target but is never cruel. The following speech, which Bodey delivers as she is frying chicken for the picnic in their kitchenette, reveals the play's warm comic tone, unlike almost anything else Williams wrote:

So I went in Piggly-Wiggly's, I went to the meat department and I said to the nice old man, Mr. Butts, the butcher, "Mr. Butts, have you got any real nice fryers?"—"You bet your life!" he said, "I must have been expectin' you to drop in. Feel these nice plump fryers." Mr. Butts always lets me feel his meat. The feel of a piece of meat is the way to test it, but there's very few modern butchers will allow you to feel it. It's the German in me. I got to feel the meat to know it's good. (*CC*, 122)

Avoiding cynicism and nasty sarcasm, the passage allows us to enjoy the laugh at Bodey's unintentional double entendre about the butcher (Mr. Butts!) allowing her to "feel his meat" without dismissing her as simply foolish. Later, when she informs Helena that she will "tell Dotty, gentle, in [her] own way" (*CC*, 173) about Ralph's un-scrupulous behavior in stringing Dorothea along, we believe in her generosity toward her friend, in her selfless compassion as a woman who will not have the privilege of bearing children herself but who wishes more than anything to see her brother and her best friend happily united:

> And by Dotty and Buddy there will be children—children!—I will have none, myself, no! But Dotty and Buddy will have beautiful kiddies. Me? Nieces and nephews . . . I will slip away and Buddy will be alone with her on the lake shore. He will smoke no smelly cigar. He will just respectfully hold her hand and say—"I love you, Dotty. Please be mine," not meanin' a girl in a car parked up on Art Hill but—for the long run of life. (*CC*, 173–74)

Despite inching perilously close to sentimentality, Williams ends the play on a note of simple reconciliation with the city he had long reviled as "cold, smug, complacent, intolerant, stupid and provincial."[14] While Dorothea encompasses both Rose Williams and Tennessee in their neurotic and addictive behaviors, in this one play at least, the playwright offers a peaceful truce with landlocked, re-pressive St. Louis at last.

As previously noted, water functions as a symbol of freedom or escape in many of Williams's plays and stories. In *Summer at the Lake* it represents a place outside of time for young Donald Fenway, and in *Not About Nightingales* it is the only possible escape route for Canary Jim as the police move in. In the story "Oriflamme," a dried-up fountain is a harbinger of death. Even in *Streetcar* Blanche compulsively seeks "hydrotherapy" to calm her fraying nerves (*SND*, 374). Cornered by Stanley and her own impending break-down, Blanche screams for help in the only way she can: "Operator! Operator! Never mind long-distance. Get Western Union. . . . Take down this message! 'In desperate, desperate circumstances! Help me! Caught in a trap'" (*SND*, 400). Significantly, *Creve Coeur* also concludes with Dorothea's betrayal by a man, Ralph, an act that might have sent a more fragile psyche into a downward spiral analogous to that of Blanche, and Williams uses the identical device, the telephone, as a means of possible rescue: "Hello, operator, can you get me information, please?" (*CC*, 199).

But in the benign world of this comedy, instead of collapsing, Dorothea calls the operator about boarding a streetcar—not leading to "Cemeteries" or "Elysian Fields" (*SND*, 246), but to the lake, always for the playwright a place of solace and calm in the face of loneliness and heartbreak: "Can you get me the number of the little station at the end of the Delmar car-line where you catch the, the— open streetcar that goes out to Creve Coeur Lake?" (*CC*, 199).

Williams himself noted that *Creve Coeur* "is quite separate from [his] other work . . . almost a different genre."[15] Like O'Neill, who allowed imaginative wish fulfillment to counteract tragedy in *Ah, Wilderness!*, Williams discovered peace and reconciliation toward St. Louis in this rare "bijou" of a play.

* * * * *

If it is possible to infer reconciliation between the aging playwright and his loathed city near the end of his life, it is fascinating to imagine how this remarkable truce was brokered. Early in 1977, in an essay written for *Washington University Magazine* entitled "The Secret Year of Tennessee Williams," Shepherd Mead, Washington University alumnus and author of the book that inspired the celebrated musical *How to Succeed in Business Without Really Trying*, took Williams to task for omitting mention in *Memoirs* of any trace of the year he spent as a student at Washington University: "Tennessee Williams, now quite probably America's greatest living playwright, went to Washington University. I've always known it. . . . But Williams won't admit it; he hides the fact as though it were some kind of guilty secret. For years I've wondered exactly why." Mead recalls that, years before he began his formal studies at the university that was just blocks from his home, Williams would surreptitiously slip poems under his door when he was coeditor of the campus literary magazine *The Eliot*, and that these poems were "always first class."[16]

Mead praises *Memoirs* for its revelations about the intimate details of the author's personal life: "He hides almost nothing in this extraordinary book . . . includes intimate details of his homosexuality, his struggles against, as he calls it, 'lunacy,' and the time he spent in a mental hospital. Everything is there, everything but that one unspeakable secret: he went to Washington University." He also salutes his contemporary's literary talents, even recommending that he receive the Nobel Prize for Literature. Should he win the award, Mead says, "we'll all be proud of him" despite the fact that "his year at Washington U happened to coincide with, and perhaps helped to produce, one of his times of depression."[17]

Later in that same year something most improbable happened—on September 14, 1977, Tennessee Williams stood before a standing-room-only crowd at Washington University's Graham Chapel to offer a poetry reading. He had come to town to visit his mother and to offer (rather lukewarm) support for his brother's ultimately unsuccessful run for governor of Illinois.

Figure 34. Williams at Graham Chapel, Washington University, for a poetry reading in 1977, forty-one years after leaving "the stronghold of the Reactionaries." Courtesy of the Washington University Photographic Services Collection, Washington University Libraries, Julian Edison Department of Special Collections.

A suggestion in Mead's essay that Dakin had attempted to destroy the remaining copies of Tom's play *Me, Vashya* had led the playwright's brother to offer a lighthearted denial in the magazine's summer issue that year. This in turn resulted in an invitation to Williams from the director of Washington University's Assembly Lecture series, Trudi Spiegel, to offer a poetry reading at the university.

There, in the same Graham Chapel where forty-one years earlier prizes had been bestowed on the winners of William G. B. Carson's English 16 competition (including Thomas Lanier Williams's honorable mention, although he chose not to attend), the famous playwright came to read his poetry, followed by answering questions from students and faculty.

It is noteworthy that all the selections he read avoided the darkness that infused so much of the poetry he had published in *The Eliot* during those difficult years. He might, for example, have read from the first of his "Two Metaphysical Sonnets," entitled "The Mind Does Not Forget," published in December 1936, which contains the following lines:

The mind remembers still. Its memories live
In forms forever sifting through the sieve
Of water, earth, and air, becoming one
With memories inviolate of the sun! (*CP*, 183)

At the conclusion of the reading, which was warmly received, Williams agreed to be interviewed by the university's student newspaper, *Student Life*. The interviewer offered to drive Williams around parts of the city that were his familiar old haunts from his time at Washington University, hoping to assist him in reminiscing about his days there. Williams's responses to the student reporters who escorted him were invariably cheerful, befitting his altered perspective. To a question intended perhaps to provoke a quote about his well-chronicled dislike for the city of St. Louis, he simply offered, "Oh, I don't think we need to go over that." When further pressed by the same journalist, he admitted, "Why yass, I had some bad experiences here . . . which made for an unhappy family life," adroitly shifting the subject to his many fond memories of the poetry club he formed with Clark Mills and William Jay Smith.[18]

Only once, on the drive east along Kingshighway, did another sort of memory sweep across his consciousness, obliging him to furrow his brow and wave toward a large and imposing edifice just east of Forest Park. "Ah, my old friend Barnes Hospital," he said wearily.[19]

Chapter Eight

This House Is Empty Now

She knows not what the curse may be,
And so she weaveth steadily,
And little other care hath she,
The Lady of Shalott.

Tennyson, "The Lady of Shalott"

TENNESSEE WILLIAMS'S DESIRE regarding his burial was unequivocal—
he wished to be buried at sea. He said this often, and even spelled
it out with precision in a codicil to his will written in longhand on
June 21, 1972:

> I, Thomas Lanier (Tennessee) Williams, being in sound mind
> upon this subject, and having declared this wish repeatedly to
> my close friends—do hereby state my desire to be buried at sea.
> More specifically, I wish to be buried at sea at as close a possible
> point as the American poet Hart Crane died: . . . I wish to
> be sewn up in a canvas sack and dropped overboard, as stated
> above, as close as possible to where Hart Crane was given by
> himself to the great mother of life which is the sea.[1]

In making his plans clear, Williams demonstrated that his dying wish
was to leave landlocked, middle-class, puritanical St. Louis behind
forever; that he wished to leave the earth as "Tennessee," not as
Tom, the St. Louisan. The reference to Hart Crane was not merely
to a favorite literary antecedent but to someone who epitomized his
own struggle to first acknowledge and then fully accept his homosexuality. By requesting that his body be borne to the spot closest

181

to where Crane committed suicide, Williams expressed his fealty toward a fellow traveler and martyr in the cause of sexual freedom. In an unpublished letter to a young writer, Williams expressed his devotion to Crane's memory in quasi-religious terms:

> Crane remains closer to my heart than any other modern artist. I think he is a sort of archetype of the martyred artist in our times. Martyred is a sentimental word and yet in Crane's case it fits. I must confess his life is more meaningful to me, personally, than that of Christ, if only because he practiced my vocation in my time and suffered the same damnation that I and possibly you and so many others must suffer.

He then added this extraordinary postscript: "I carry [Crane's biography] with me along with Crane's Collected Poems, now. It brings Crane very close to me at times I feel the need of his singularly understanding companionship."[2]

But when Williams died, on February 25, 1983, instead of returning "to the great mother of life which is the sea," his body was brought back by his brother to the city in the Midwest where he may have been raised but never felt at home. The decision to commandeer his brother's body and transport it back to St. Louis has been harshly criticized, and one might question the motivations behind Dakin's decision: was it fraternal jealousy, the vindictive response of a sibling who had been cut out of his brother's will? Or was Dakin's decision to disobey his brother's intentions born of a just appreciation of Williams's international stature?

According to Dakin, both Williams's executor and his lawyer had already decided to ignore the playwright's intentions and bury him in Waynesville, Ohio, where his maternal grandparents, the Dakins, had been laid to rest. In this account, Dakin Williams chose to bring his brother back to St. Louis instead of to rural Waynesville out of respect for his brother's legacy: "I feel very strongly against disposing of the body of a person who had the giant literary stature of my brother. His remains should be placed in a readily accessible place."[3] And so Tennessee Williams was buried at Calvary Cemetery, a cemetery synonymous with traditional St. Louis, in the family plot, beside his beloved sister and his mother. His grave's proximity to that of his mother is particularly ironic in view of her outsized influence on him and the fact that Williams observed near the end of his life, "I still find her totally mystifying—and frightening," concluding, "it's best we stay away from our mothers."[4]

The ironies of his interment are manifold, compounded by the fact that Williams, born into the Episcopalian faith and only a convert to Roman Catholicism for a single day to please his brother, as Dakin said, "right before I committed him,"[5] is buried in one of the city's oldest and most revered Catholic cemeteries. And the accoutrements of Williams's burial were incongruous with its traditional surroundings. Dakin described Tom's simple pine casket as an "Orthodox Jewish coffin"—that is to say, a plain box lacking any adornment or even metal handles.[6] And Williams was interred holding a Russian icon and bearing a Russian Orthodox cross around his neck, markers of religiosity offered by his executor, Maria St. Just, the wildly eccentric Russian-born actress who became his executrix who was also responsible for the Russian Orthodox cross emblazoned on his headstone.[7]

Dakin freely admitted that his decision to bury Tom was in direct violation of his brother's wishes: "I'm sure he'd disapprove of being buried here. But I'm his only survivor and this is where I think he should rest. Where else would you put him? This way he'll be in a centrally located spot for people to pay their respects to the world's greatest talent since Shakespeare."[8] Biographer John Lahr suggests that Dakin had his eye on transforming Williams's grave into a tourist attraction, quoting Williams's friend Dotson Rader as saying that Dakin "planned a concession stand peddling refreshments, trinkets, souvenir key chains, and Dakin's books. . . . Good old Dakin was always trying to cash in. There'd be admission charged to visit the gravesite, like Graceland."[9] Not long after his brother's death, Dakin added a chapter to his self-published biography coauthored with Shepherd Mead, *His Brother's Keeper*, and changed the subtitle to *The Life and Murder of Tennessee Williams*, thus promulgating his unproven conspiracy theory that his brother's death at the Hotel

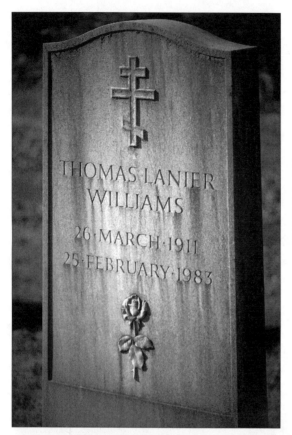

Figures 35a, 35b. Tennessee
Williams's headstone (*left*)
and Rose's grave marker
(*below*) at Calvary Cemetery
in St. Louis. Photographs
by Peter Wochniak,
ProPhotoSTL.com.

Elysée was the result not of his accidentally swallowing a medicine cap but of a murderous plot by Lady St. Just and Williams's attorney, John Eastman. Regardless of what one thinks of Dakin's decision about his brother's burial, the contrast between Williams's wish to have his body buried at sea off the Florida coast with its actual interment in St. Louis could not have been starker. Water, as we have seen in myriad instances, going all the way back to his experience at the Lorelei Natatorium in St. Louis as a boy and ending with his delight in taking daily swims at Key West in his late years, always represented freedom for Williams, in opposition to the landlocked Midwest of St. Louis.

* * * * *

Williams's ostensibly accidental death took place in the aptly named Sunset Suite of the Hotel Elysée in New York. If the name of the hotel might seem to allude to the mythical paradise of the dead in Greek mythology, Williams's pet name for his home away from home was less classical; he called his favorite hotel the "Easy Lay."

Biographical studies of Williams concur that his final months were spent in a frenzied attempt to elude a fate that he was all too aware was looming. Shortly before his death, he informed his secretary/companion, John Uecker, that he hoped to die on the big brass bed in his French Quarter apartment, "the site," he said, "of some of the happiest hours of my life,"[10] although his final weeks were spent in flight from whatever Furies were apparently pursuing him, forcing him to fly compulsively from one place to another in a frenzied quest for an unattainable peace. On Christmas Eve, 1982, friends were unable to reach Williams by telephone, so they summoned the police to come to his Key West home. What they discovered there was a man lying on the floor wrapped in a sheet and incoherently babbling, dehydrated, and surrounded by pills and wine bottles. He was rushed to the hospital and registered under an assumed name, but the doctor's attempts to get him to stay for a prolonged recuperation were in vain. As Uecker commented, "You couldn't tell him anything. He would only do what *he* wanted to do."[11]

After that incident Williams made plans to sell his home in Key West; when his longtime housekeeper, Leoncia McGee, asked when he would be returning, he informed her, "I won't ever be coming home again." As he left in a taxi, he handed Leoncia a check for one thousand dollars and kissed her on the cheek. "That's when I knew he wasn't coming back," she said. "He kissed me, and he was traveling alone, and he never done them things before."[12]

In February, Williams traveled companionless in seeming panic from New Orleans to New York, and from there on to London, Rome, and Sicily, ending up back in New York, exhausted, after only one week. Travel, which had once allowed him escape, now offered no respite. He sold his second-story flat in New Orleans, albeit with a leaseback provision to maintain it, and returned to the Elysée, in, as Lyle Leverich observes, "as much a surrender to the inevitable as it was evidently an accident."[13] On his deathbed, along with an empty prescription bottle, which had contained thirty Seconal sleeping pills, and two partially empty wine bottles, was a photocopy of a short story by James Purdy ("Some of These Days") upon which Purdy had inscribed two lines by the English poet Thomas Chatterton (1752–1770), whose suicide at age seventeen was an inspiration to the Romantic poets Keats and Shelley: "Water witches crowned with reeds / bear me to your lethal tides."[14]

* * * * *

The creative work Williams produced during this last period of his life reflects an imagination tormented by ghosts and whispers of mortality. It was a world he knew well and acknowledged from a young age. It is present in his very first short story "The Vengeance of Nitocris," written at age seventeen, and in adolescent poems such as "Dear Silent Ghost" (*CP*, 216) and "I See Them Lying Sheeted in Their Graves" (*CP*, 218), and is powerfully evoked in the unpublished "Blood of the Wolf": "When I was a boy / in the country between two rivers, / I lived on the margin / Of something not public domain. / I never went into / but always was ready to enter / the beanstalk country / where unseen presences are."[15] He captured this concept memorably in his poem "The Beanstalk Country," where the insane are described as "Jacks who climb the beanstalk country." The mad in Williams are usually possessed of far greater insight than we who are unable to grasp the unimaginable they have witnessed. In "The Beanstalk Country," he describes this forbidden world as

a place of hammers and tremendous beams,
compared to which the glassed solarium
in which we rise to greet them has no light.

The news we bring them, common, reassuring,
drenched with the cheerful idiocy of noon,
cannot compare with what they have to tell
of what they saw through cracks in the ogre's oven. (*CP*, 12–13)

Now sensing his impending end, Williams grew more and more obsessed with the beanstalk country, and chose to frequent it in virtually everything he wrote. On the Monday before his death, however, he announced to Uecker, "I can't write. And if I can't write, I don't want to live. I'm gonna get some Seconals. I know you don't approve, but you understand?" Uecker later observed, "You watched his vital forces leave. . . . He was interested in nothing. Not in meeting or being with young people. . . . He was removed from everything."[16]

The One Exception, a one-act dated January 1983 and likely the last piece of writing he completed, offers a remarkable window into Williams's state of mind as he approached the end.[17] Like so much of his late work, this play focuses on madness, confinement, and isolation. And, also like so much of his late work, it returns to the interconnectedness between his own ebbing life and that of Rose.

The play depicts Kyra, a woman in her thirties, who has been institutionalized. She is about to be moved to the Lodge, a private sanitarium, just as Rose Williams, who outlived her younger brother by more than a decade, spent her final years at Stony Lodge in Ossining, New York, before her death in 1996. Kyra is in the care of a nurse, May Svenson, who hopes that her patient may be able to reconnect with her former self by meeting a friend from her past. Since Kyra is withdrawn and "deathly afraid of institutions" (*OE*, 196), Miss Svenson's approach must remain covert. She cautions the painter friend she has summoned, "About the Lodge, not a word. She'd go into a panic" (*OE*, 199). When Kyra finally does appear near the end of the play, she is described as "almost apparitional . . . a woman in her middle thirties with the look of a frightened child" (*OE*, 202).

Kyra is unable to acknowledge her past friendship with the paint-er: "I—can't talk much. The past is—passed," she says, staring off into space, until she calls out for her nurse to remove the unwant-ed inquisitor (*OE*, 202). The play's tone is unremittingly cold and bleak, concluding with Kyra, who is frightened even by the sound of her own slippers on the floor, bolting the doors on either side of her room before sitting barefoot stage center and shutting her eyes as the lights fade for the end of the play.

The play's title refers to the fact that, unlike the rest of the com-mune of artists who have "come through with flying colors . . . [Kyra is] the one exception" (*OE*, 204). Exploring a bleak landscape more typically associated with Samuel Beckett than Williams, the play is a profound examination of the loneliness and fear of confinement Williams discerned both in his sister and in himself in those final months of withdrawal from all human contact. The supposed painter-friend who has come for a visit, Viola, turns out to be interested only in what she can extort from Kyra once the two of them are left alone, with Miss Svenson stationed outside. Ignoring Kyra's anxious, fragile state, Viola insists on trying to borrow money, leading to a remarkable exchange that demonstrates that, even in these last, sad days, the playwright's mordant wit did not completely desert him. Their conversation is loaded with darkly humorous misunderstand-ings revolving around Viola's request for "a loan":

> VIOLA: . . . You know how my absorption in my work has always made me indifferent to externals such as clothes. . . . I *must* purchase and remember to wear some smart new outfits now that this important new exhibition is about to open. . . . Kyra, I'm at the brink of a breakthrough but right now—I do need a loan . . .
>
> KYRA: Yes. Alone except for—
>
> VIOLA: L-O-A-N, a financial loan. You've always been so gen-erous. Could you get your accountant, the one with your power-of-attorney, to arrange that for me?
>
> KYRA: Alone.

VIOLA: Temporarily, only a month or two.
KYRA: Yes. Alone except for— (*OE*, 204–5)

Whereas Dorothea's final words in *A Lovely Sunday for Creve Coeur* suggest the importance of resilience in the face of loneliness: "We must pull ourselves together and go on. Go on, we must just go on, that's all life seems to offer and—demand" (*CC*, 199), *The One Exception* offers a portrait of hopeless isolation, as arid and skeletal as a Giacometti sculpture. Even the play's artist figure, Viola, is mercilessly exploitive toward the fragile being she has supposedly come to pay a friendly visit.

The final image of stasis, with Kyra rigidly seated stage center with her eyes closed, is even more pronounced and detailed in Williams's unproduced television play, *Stopped Rocking* (1977), written several years earlier. Like *Creve Coeur*, the teleplay is set in St. Louis, at St. Carmine's sanitarium, a place based upon St. Vincent's, where Rose was taken in 1937 before being moved to the state hospital in Farmington and where the Williams family first was informed of Rose's diagnosis of dementia praecox. Forty years later, the playwright returned to the very place where both his sister's life and his own were so cataclysmically altered. At the time of her diagnosis he wrote in a notebook,

Yesterday our worst fears about Rose were confirmed. Her trouble has been diagnosed as dementia Praecox. The doctor at St. Vincent's said Insulin shock was about the only hope—it is not decided yet whether to give her that—A catastrophe worse than death—I slept fitfully last night—that thought woven through my dreams—a living nightmare—Grandfather says "She is God's child and he will do what is best for her"—Why must a child of God have dementia Praecox? His ways are indeed mysterious— . . .

If only I can keep my sanity I shall count myself a fortunate man— (*N*, 95)

Evidently, Edwina was sufficiently concerned about Tom's instability that she sent him away for a week in the Ozarks, noting in a letter to her parents on August 3, 1937, that "Rose's trouble has been a blow to his already nervous system."[18] But prior to his departure, Williams wrote "Valediction," suggesting the inextricable link between himself and his sister. The poem opens with the haunting lines

> She went with morning on her lips
> down an inscrutable dark way
> and we who witnessed her eclipse
> have found no word to say. (*CP*, 198)

For the rest of his life—and particularly in his final years—Williams was still searching for the proper words to say, to apply them now as much to himself as to Rose.

The focus of *Stopped Rocking* is Janet Svenson, a woman who for the past five years has been confined to St. Carmine's asylum. During this time, her husband, Olaf, has become athletic director at a local community college and has begun living with Alicia Trout, a mathematics teacher at the same school. The plot of the teleplay concerns Olaf's attempts to finally free himself from his obligations toward his wife, at Alicia's insistence. Janet, on the other hand, lives for her husband's visits to the sanitarium. The teleplay opens with Olaf's evasive delivery of a pot of Easter lilies: "Would you please just give the flowers to her. You see, in five years' time, I've formed other attachments if she hasn't, I have—other commitments" (*SR*, 299).

We learn that Alicia is deeply jealous of what remains of Olaf's devotion to his wife and is embarrassed by living out of wedlock with her common-law husband. She accuses Janet of committing "moral blackmail": "Olaf, that woman is using her mental illness to keep a hold on you, and if it continues, I will have to bow out. Did you hear me? *Bow out, quit!*" (*SR*, 327). Olaf may be called "Stone Man" by Alicia, but he is a divided, weak character who, in spite of his sturdy physique and limited vocabulary (we later learn that Janet has in fact cured his speech disability), finds it difficult to sever his ties with Janet, certainly not with the precision that Alicia,

a "mathematical bombshell," is hoping for: "'Clear-cut decisions'—
they're a mathematical possibility, maybe, but in life?" Olaf helplessly
complains (*SR*, 305).

Threatened with losing Alicia, Olaf finally decides to inform Janet
that he is going to leave her, during a farewell outing to the Ozarks
in his camper. The wide shot with which the camera approaches St.
Carmine's in the teleplay's stage directions as Olaf goes to pick Janet
up is noticeably different from the grotesquely comic perspective
with which Bodey's efficiency apartment is depicted in *Creve Coeur*.
Whereas in Bodey's apartment, "brightness and cheer have gone
brilliantly and disastrously wrong" (*CC*, 119), the day room at St.
Carmine's is depicted with a somber gloom evocative of early Van
Gogh: it has "a poetic *tristesse*, on the surface, a stark desolation
of the spirit under" (*SR*, 306). As the camera approaches the day
room, where the patients congregate, Williams seems to rely heavily
upon his precisely engraved memories of the summer light in polluted 1930s St. Louis[19] as well as the specifics of Rose's lodgings at
St. Vincent's:

> The light is smoky as even fair summer light is often smoky in
> St. Louis, at least as I recall it. Through grated and screened
> windows, fast shut, the light slants, now, toward early dusk. The
> sisters move almost choreographically about the bleakly undec-
> orated, the sparsely furnished room, serving the evening meal
> from large metal carts on wheels; . . . There is no glassware since
> glass is a possible means of attack on the self or another; the film
> is in black and white or very, very unobtrusive color. (*SR*, 306)

The excursion into the Ozarks follows Janet's session with Dr.
Cash, a formidable specimen with huge stomach, narrow shoulders,
and rimless, glittering spectacles akin to those of "Dr. Leviathan,"
the acerbic doctor Williams encountered at Barnes Hospital in St.
Louis during his stay in the Renard Division there. While the trip is
intended to offer Olaf the opportunity to break the news to Janet
about his relationship with Alicia and move on from his conjugal
responsibilities with his wife, Janet sees their trip as "something of
transcendent importance," and her face is "luminous" as she prepares

to meet her husband (*SR*, 334). However, the journey that Janet hopes will offer her escape becomes instead a fatal descent into the abyss of mental illness.

Their trip to the Ozarks brings them to a "scene of strange desolation," where the camera closes in upon "a dead, almost skeletal creature" by a riverbank (*SR*, 363). Janet, terrified by the ill omen, begs Olaf to drive higher into the mountains, but he angrily dismisses her fears, saying, "Something is dead everywhere" (*SR*, 363). Olaf grudgingly disposes of the dead creature's carcass, savagely hurling it into the river, and symbolically prefiguring Janet's own fate.

At the start of their time together, Olaf tries to gently assure her that nothing can be the same as it once was: "In five years' time every cell of the body is replaced by others.—Physically you are a totally new person and you have to accept it" (*SR*, 372). Janet, on the other hand, attempts to reverse time's passage, reminding Olaf of the moment when she taught him to speak properly: "Loosen, don't tighten these muscles." At that time, he responded by taking her hand, saying, "Miss—Janet, thank you, I love you" (*SR*, 365). However, now all is changed.

Unable to find the means of convincing her of the merits of his new life with Alicia, Olaf grows first increasingly irritated and then sadistically cruel. He literally forces open her jaws to give her an overdose of Thorazine tablets so that she will remain passive and says to her, "Then I will tell you what I have to tell you and you will have to accept it" (*SR*, 375). He accuses her of living "in a world that's protected from any important changes. Almost a timeless world is what you live in" (*SR*, 368).

Under the influence of the antipsychotic Thorazine in Janet's system, the mood of the teleplay grows increasingly surreal. Williams describes the change: "Everything is now seen from Janet's POV as she hallucinates. Then the camera draws back but retains the hallucinated (visionary) view" (*SR*, 378). In *A Streetcar Named Desire*, Williams employed a similar technique; as Blanche DuBois's mental state deteriorated under the predations of Stanley Kowalski, the play's initial realism gave way to visual and aural hallucinations: "Lurid reflections appear on the walls around Blanche. The shadows are of a grotesque and menacing form. . . . The night is filled with inhuman voices like cries in the jungle" (*SND*, 398–99). Analogously, following Olaf's metaphorical "rape"—forcing the pills down Janet's throat—we begin to see the world increasingly through Janet's disoriented perspective. First, she encounters the specter of Father O'Donnell, a kindly priest from her past who has died and who now reappears to offer her absolution. Then, as the priest dissolves into the river's mist, she stumbles onward until the "margin between the shore and the river is indistinct" and she enters the river (*SR*, 379). Olaf saves her from drowning, but his figure becomes merged in her mind with that of the apparitional priest. Janet's last journey from land to river is depicted as a crossing of boundaries—from life to death, from release to confinement, and from relative calm into madness.

Janet is spared drowning, but her life essentially ends at the moment she enters the river. The teleplay's stage directions suggest her surrender: "The 'hallucinated' POV; Janet is in the river, her gown now swept about her breasts. She lifts her arms as if surrendering to the river—and then disappears beneath the rolling surface" (*SR*, 380). Although she survives, Janet has been transformed when she gets out of the water; she is "like a fountain figure, her wet gown clinging to her, hair twisted wet about her face and throat," and she is "quite still as if listening to something vocal in the river's murmur" (*SR*, 380). Passive and accommodating at last, she whispers that she is prepared to offer Olaf release from their past. The trailer now slowly passes "through spectral country, . . . a country of bleak landscapes and lightless buildings" as they head back toward St. Carmine's sanitarium (*SR*, 382, 383). It is fascinating to recall that in 1922, Tom (then age eleven) spent a half year at the Stix School in St. Louis. When his teacher asked the pupils to write an essay inspired by one of the pictures on the classroom walls, Tom wrote his based on an illustration of Alfred, Lord Tennyson's "Lady of Shalott." With its romantic references to water, drowning, and madness, he came upon three subjects that would preoccupy him for the entirety of his career.[20]

At the start of their journey up into the mountains, Olaf had maintained that people like Janet are "protected from any important changes," that they live in "almost a timeless world." Contradicting him, Janet described how time and change are present even in the day room of the sanitarium. People do change, she noted, even though their changes are slow and nearly imperceptible. In the beginning, the patients rock with a kind of fury, "racing to get somewhere in that rocker with the plaid cushion" (*SR*, 368), until they gradually slow down, and finally stop rocking altogether. After that, they are transferred from the day room to the ninth-floor "Vegetable Garden" (*SR*, 312).

As the couple returns to the asylum, Janet has lost her former zest and defiance and has become nearly catatonic. Asked for his account of what has happened, Olaf simply covers his face with his hands, and Janet, now completely unresponsive, is taken back—not to the day room, where she was previously, but to the dreaded ninth floor. Her rocking has stopped.

The spectral quality of Williams's teleplay was underscored at a read-through of scenes from the manuscript organized by director John Hancock at his home in Los Angeles. *Stopped Rocking* had been proposed as a Hallmark Movie of the Week, and Hancock invited Williams to attend a gathering with a number of distinguished actors reading key scenes. Hancock, however, observed, "I knew we were in trouble when I saw Tennessee get out of the car and stagger to the front door. Here was a ghost." Shortly afterward, instead of listening to what the actors might bring to their roles, Williams began to read from the script himself, "slurring wildly," according to Hancock. Later, after the actors began to read from the script as was intended, Hancock observed that Williams had fallen fast asleep: "I never heard from him again, . . . but in a way, he was vanishing even before he had gone."[21]

The terrain of ghosts, mental illness, and confinement to which Williams had become increasingly habituated in his waning years was also explored in another of his last plays, *Clothes for a Summer Hotel* (1980), directed by the distinguished José Quintero and with the legendary actress Geraldine Page, who had starred in such early triumphs as *Summer and Smoke* (also directed by Quintero, in 1952) and *Sweet Bird of Youth* (1959). Williams had high hopes for the play as a kind of redemption for a host of Broadway failures over the previous decades, most recently *Vieux Carré*, which ran only five performances on Broadway in 1977. As a pre-opening piece for the *New York Times*, Williams wrote "I Am Widely Regarded as the Ghost of a Writer," an essay attempting to challenge the critical perception that his best work was behind him. The essay begins with the sentence "Of course no one is more acutely aware than I that I am widely regarded as the ghost of a writer, a ghost still visible, excessively solid of flesh and perhaps too ambulatory, but a writer remembered mostly for works which were staged between 1944 and 1961" (*NSE*, 184).

The play that opened on Williams's sixty-ninth birthday, March 26, 1980, *Clothes for a Summer Hotel*, served, ironically, to underscore the writer's apparitional status rather than to refute it. Ugly reviews titled "Slender Is the Night," "'Clothes' Needs Some Tailoring," and "Damsels Inducing Distress" were among many scathing notices, and the play closed after just seven previews and fifteen performances.[22] The play's subtitle, *A Ghost Play*, was mocked by the notoriously acerbic critic John Simon, who punned on Williams's assertion that "all plays are ghost plays," quipping savagely, "Especially, I daresay, when written by ghost playwrights."[23] Although honored later that year by President Jimmy Carter with the Presidential Medal of Freedom, "Williams never heard a major American critic praise a new play of his" during the rest of his lifetime, Lahr points out.[24]

Clothes for a Summer Hotel makes no explicit connection with St. Louis; the play is set at Highland Hospital near Asheville, North Carolina, and its ostensible subject is the relationship between F. Scott Fitzgerald and his wife, Zelda. However, its actual subject is at the heart of the playwright's early life in St. Louis—the writer's relationship with his sister, Rose. In this instance, Williams creates a fictional encounter between Scott and Zelda at an asylum where Zelda, like Rose, was committed during the final years of her life.

The Scott Fitzgerald depicted in the play bears no resemblance to the glamorous expatriate of the Jazz Age. Instead he is a "man with blurred edges" and "tentative manner" (*CSH*, 205), whose enormous talent has been all but squandered through debauchery and alcohol. He is the man who died at age forty-four of a heart attack with his reputation apparently in irremediable decline—in short, an artist very much like Williams himself appeared in 1980. Analogously,

Zelda in the play is not the dazzling beauty who inspired Daisy in *The Great Gatsby* and a host of other women in Fitzgerald's stories and novels, but a delusional middle-aged woman in a bedraggled, gray tutu taking ballet lessons, vainly hoping for an audition before the great Sergei Diaghilev. She is the woman who was confined to an asylum during her final years, and who perished in the Highland Hospital fire of 1948. However, while she is overweight and no longer in her right mind, Williams's Zelda nonetheless possesses the genius of those who have dwelled in "beanstalk country" and "the majesty of those purified by madness and by fire" (*CSH*, 213).

She is a modern-day Cassandra, all too conscious of her impending doom and subject to premonitions about the fire that will consume her body. This is suggested in the play by frequent allusions to the salamander, which according to myth is able to endure fire, and by a bush displayed on the set prominently decorated with "flickering red leaves" (*CSH*, 204), an obvious harbinger of the fire to come. In addition to the play's atmosphere of foreboding, the characters' words are often rendered unintelligible by the sound of the wind, a suggestion of the work's engagement with the apparitional so important in these late works.

"Are you my lawful husband, the celebrated F. Scott Fitzgerald, author of my life?" are Zelda's words of greeting to Scott at the top of the play (*CSH*, 213). By having her put them directly to her husband, Williams begins the play by announcing the fundamental question of appropriation of one person's life by another for the uses of art—clearly a concern central to Williams's use of Rose throughout his own work. In her biography *Zelda* (1970), Nancy Milford suggests not only that Scott used his wife as a model for his heroines but that he borrowed freely from her letters and diaries in doing so.[25] In her own review of Fitzgerald's *The Beautiful and the Damned*, the real-life Zelda noted that a portion of her diary had gone missing, leading her to speculate cheekily that "Mr. Fitzgerald . . . seems to believe that plagiarism begins at home."[26] The play endeavors to examine a writer's guilt at having robbed his subject of her authentic voice, just as Williams must have considered his "theft" of Rose's narrative in *The Glass Menagerie* and so many other works. In her final words before vanishing behind the asylum gates at the end of the play, Zelda shouts back at her lover/antagonist, who has brought along a ring, proffered as a symbol of reconciliation between the two lovers: "The gates are iron, they won't admit you or ever release me again. [*She enters; the gates close.*] I'm not your book! Anymore! *I can't be your book anymore! Write yourself a new book!*" Reaching desperately through the bars that separate the two, Scott pleads, "The ring, please take it, the covenant with the past—still always present, Zelda!" (*CSH*, 280).

As Scott's beloved disappears back into her gated asylum, the play ends with an extraordinary visual image of the two lovers separated forever by iron bars.

* * * * *

Were there any question that a powerful misanthropy had crept into Williams's psyche in the final years of his life, the one-act *The Chalky White Substance* would immediately resolve all doubt. As bleak as anything he ever wrote, the play is set in a dystopian world in which light and water are absent, the very air is filled with tiny granules of "something like old powdered bones," and the dialogue on stage is accompanied by a wind that "blows about an earth shriveled and desiccated as a terminally sick being" (*CWS*, 3), reminiscent of the ghostly wind that obscures the lovers' dialogue in *Clothes for a Summer Hotel*.

Set a couple of hundred years in the future, and "an almost equal time after a great thermonuclear war" (*CWS*, 3), the play is a bitter, grief-stricken testament to a world that is all but dead. Unsurprisingly, the play's simple subject is the betrayal of light by darkness, of youthful innocence by experience. The two-character play begins with Mark, an older man, watching Luke, his young protégé and lover, from atop the verge of a chasm. After a brief *tableau vivant*, Mark stealthily descends into the dried-up riverbed and clasps his large, powerful hands over young Luke's eyes before revealing his identity. In the brief interaction that follows, we discover that Mark has determined to betray the young innocent to the nameless, vicious authorities who rule this "brave new world" for profit. After forcing Luke to confess that he has violated the state's rules by bathing twice per day, and has hidden the location of an underground spring from the authorities, Mark slowly begins to strangle the young man before bearing him off to claim the bounty that rewards those who inform on enemies of the state.

The world depicted in *The Chalky White Substance* is one that has been abandoned by God. There is talk of a past time when "women were a comfort" and Luke refers to a picture on the wall "of the lady that was called the Madonna" (*CWS*, 6). But Mark describes such "old mythological pictures" as rarities and advises Luke that they can "be sold to the Center for special privileges, you know" (*CWS*, 6). As he drags the boy off the darkening stage at the end of the play, Mark rejects Luke's pleas of "Kill me, Mark!" and instead taunts him to call upon "the great protector called God. No breath? I'll call Him for you. PRO-TEC-TOR!" (*CWS*, 11). When there is only an echo in reply, the play's final words reflect a barren world where the only presence of divinity is the polluting "chalky white substance" that represents the desiccated bones of God: "What a huge creature, what an immense beast He must have been to have left such enormous white bones when He died. . . . Endlessly long ago, the bones of Him now turned to powder that blows and blows about His broken—creation" (*CWS*, 12).

Even if Williams's pessimism was nearly total at this final stage of his life, it is nonetheless remarkable to witness the aging playwright's astonishing range of theatrical strategies and techniques employed to roam the disparate corners of his inner wasteland. Thus, it should not be surprising that Williams's final full-length play, after the spectral *Clothes for a Summer Hotel* and the dystopian one-act *The Chalky White Substance*, was a black comedy, *A House Not Meant to Stand* (1980–1982). Williams described the play as a "kind of Southern Gothic Spook Sonata," referring to Swedish dramatist August Strindberg's *Ghost Sonata* (1907), adding that "probably it would astonish Strindberg as much as it does you and me" (*HMS*, xiii).

The play began as the one-act *Some Problems for the Moose Lodge*, first performed at Chicago's Goodman Theatre as part of a series of short plays under the title *Tennessee Laughs*. Later, the one-act was expanded (twice) into the full-length play *A House Not Meant to Stand*, also produced at the Goodman. As Eugene O'Neill did in his treatment of the Tyrone family in *Long Day's Journey into Night*,

Williams returned near the end to his own haunted St. Louis family to excavate material for this last play.

Mixing moments of realism with the expressionism he found in *Ghost Sonata*, Williams plumbed his family's genealogy. Always proud of his ancestry, Williams referred to it often in interviews, and described this habit as "the Southern weakness for climbing a family tree" (*M*, 12). Even the name "Tennessee," chosen to distinguish himself from "Tom," alluded to his father's proud frontier ancestry, and he briefly flirted with using the nom de plume "Valentine Xavier," tracing his family's connections all the way back to the nephew of the sainted Jesuit missionary Francis Xavier.[27] Williams wrote that his lineage comprised "a little Welsh wildness, a lot of Puritan English and a big chunk of German sentiment," attributing his wildly conflicting impulses to the mix of Puritan and Cavalier strains in his pedigree.[28]

Williams's exploration of his ancestral past is essential to understanding this last play. He took the first name of the family's crusty, mean-spirited patriarch, Cornelius, from his own father, although the character's political ambitions owe far more to his brother, Dakin, who unsuccessfully ran for political office several times (including a bid for governor of Illinois). The name of the family matriarch, Bella, in *A House Not Meant to Stand* is a composite of the names of two aunts on his father's side, Isabel and Ella. The surname "McCorkle" is also taken directly from Williams's past—Williams's paternal grandmother, Isabella Coffin, was the daughter of Nancy McCorkle and Cornelius Coffin. Similarly, the Dakins are known as the Dancies in *House*.

The location of the ramshackle, dilapidated house is Pascagoula, Mississippi, a nod to the playwright's Mississippi roots before the family's move to St. Louis in 1911; however, embedded in the work's bitter tone are the unmistakable sounds of hostility and verbal abuse the playwright and his siblings suffered at the hands of their father in St. Louis. No longer inhibited by his living under the roof of his in-laws in Clarksdale, Cornelius's fierce temper and bullying demeanor had free rein to express themselves. The move to St. Louis also meant that Cornelius's days of freedom on the road as a traveling salesman were over, locking him and Edwina together in a Strindbergian "dance of death" for the remainder of their marriage.

In keeping with Williams's notion of a "Southern Gothic Spook Sonata," the McCorkle house in *A House Not Meant to Stand* has the weight and significance of a character, and is not intended to resemble an actual place. The playwright calls it "a metaphor for the state of society" (*HMS*, 3), but it might just as easily be considered a metaphor for the state of his mind, like the drafty, abandoned theatre in *The Two-Character Play*.

The aging playwright's misanthropy notwithstanding, *A House Not Meant to Stand* is a meditation on Williams's past—specifically the St. Louis in the 1930s he captured so beautifully in *The Glass Menagerie*. One reviewer of the opening performance observed, "On viewing the set, a dilapidated living-room with a raised dining area to the rear, a playgoer is immediately reminded of *The Glass Menagerie*. The walls are made of scrim and melt away as Bella McCorkle, an obese Amanda Wingfield, loses touch with the present and romanticizes her past."[29]

Both plays are plays about families in extremis. The sense of desperation in *Menagerie* is evoked by the Narrator's description that the Wingfields dwell in one of those "vast, hive-like conglomerations of cellular living-units" where this "fundamentally enslaved section of American society" is forced to live (*GM*, 143).

For Tom in *Menagerie*, the portrait of his "gallantly smiling" father augurs the possibility of escape from the prison of home: when Tom asks, "Who in hell ever got himself out of [a nailed-up coffin] without removing one nail?" the smiling portrait of the departed Mr. Wingfield is illuminated "as if in answer" (*GM*, 167–68). At the end of the play, as we have seen, the Narrator descends "this fire escape for a last time and follow[s], from then on, in [his] father's footsteps" (*GM*, 236–37).

By contrast, there is not even a hint of escape in *A House Not Meant to Stand*, only imminent collapse and death. Even before characters enter this (literally) crumbling edifice, the audience is greeted by a kind of ghostly memento mori in the loud ticking of a large mantel clock—for about half a minute. Williams emphasizes in the stage directions that these sounds "are not vocal but mechanical" (*HMS*, 3). Ironically, this image of the ticking clock, although a universal symbol of mortality, is a poignant reminder of its usage in the essay "The Catastrophe of Success," written in 1947 just at the very moment Williams was poised to vault into the highest echelon of fame with *A Streetcar Named Desire*: "The time is short and it doesn't return again," he wrote. "It is slipping away while I write this and while you read it, and the monosyllable of the clock is Loss, loss, loss, unless you devote your heart to its opposition" (*NSE*, 36).

The play proper commences with Cornelius's direct address to the audience, explicitly referencing a decaying world inside the house that the playwright hopes the audience is "rightly appalled by" and doing so with black humor: "I tell you, entering this house from a cloudburst ain't exactly like coming in outa the rain" (*HMS*, 4).

Significantly, *House* begins and ends with death. Bella and Cornelius enter, returning home from the funeral of their eldest son, Chips, a gay alcoholic, obviously an allusion to the playwright himself. Even though Cornelius and Bella have just buried their elder son, the play opens with a scene of violent recrimination on Chips's supposedly effeminate behavior, evoking the furious epithets that Williams must have heard ad nauseam while growing up in St. Louis:

CORNELIUS: You encouraged it, Bella. Encouraged him to design girls' dresses. He put a yellow wig on and modeled 'em himself. Something—*drag* they call it. . . .

BELLA: He could have grown outa that.

CORNELIUS: Naw, naw, was in his blood. There was nothin' Mc-Corkle about him, he was pure Dancie and I didn't send him to Memphis, I told him to go stay with your folks, the Dancies, in Pass Christian where sex confusion and outrageous public behavior was not just accepted but cultivated among 'em. Considered essential! (*HMS*, 7–8)

Throughout the play, the elderly couple quarrel about the fate of the "Dancie money" that Cornelius imagines Bella has hidden somewhere in the house, and which is discovered at the end of the play, thanks to Chips's ghost, who appears and reveals to Bella where the money has been stashed.

The rather conventional plot of the play and the search for hidden money feel almost irrelevant in comparison with the bizarre, surreal, and decaying world Williams has created. The walls of the set in the original production "were painted with exaggerated designs, heightening the feeling of unreality which pervades the play," while the entire set was placed on raked platforms intended to emphasize the "off-center world of the McCorkle home" (*HMS*, 91). The characters in the play are sketched in broad, cartoonish strokes, bordering on caricature, until the very end of the play, when the stakes are suddenly and powerfully raised. Cornelius is a vulgar, abusive bully, claiming he is going to have his wife institutionalized. He is also bitter about his own declining health: "When a man's got to live off pills in the quantity at the price, extortionary, with only temporary relief at best, why I say it's time to quit hangin' on, it's time for a man to let go" (*HMS*, 16). His long-winded speeches have a certain comic effectiveness, but his animosity toward life and cruelty to Bella render him almost completely unsympathetic. Even his banter with Emerson, his equally cantankerous neighbor and drinking buddy, lacks warmth. As Williams describes their relationship, the two "have really stopped listening to each other" (*HMS*, 27). Emerson is losing his mind and hopes to establish a string of brothels called the "Nite-A-Glory" motel chain, equipped with vibrating mattresses (*HMS*, 52). His wife, Jessie, is an equally grotesque creation; she is addicted to plastic surgery and is on the prowl for young men. In the second act, she arranges to have her husband locked up and shipped off to a mental institution.

Only Bella, hardly able to breathe with cardiac asthma, is offered a degree of sympathy by the playwright. She is confused and wanders about trying to cook meals in a decaying house where both food and nurture are absent. At the same time, she lives in a state of perpetual mourning for her three children—Chips, who has just died; Joanie, who is confined in a lunatic asylum; and the youngest, Charlie, a loafer unable to hold a job and living with his born-again Christian girlfriend.

As the play progresses, Bella grows increasingly detached from reality; she drifts through the rooms, hallucinating, speaking to her children, inhabiting a past when things were different. At one point, her breathing increasingly labored, she addresses a long-absent black maid, Hattie, instructing her, "If supper is ready, call the children in, please.—Don't let them chase fire-flies, they—never—stop—chasing fire-flies" (*HMS*, 82).

As Bella lights the candelabrum for the family meal, ghostly outcries from her three children fill the scene, and Bella, mercilessly ridiculed by Cornelius for her weight and her dementia, now "moves with a slow, stately dignity into the dining room" to say grace (*HMS*, 82). The scene remains aligned with the grotesquely comic world of the play as Jessie filches the envelope filled with Dancie money and attempts to hide it in her frilly negligee, but the theft is foiled by Dr. Crane, a young physician who has come to the house to assist Bella in her final moments.

As the play concludes, a tone of lyrical sadness combines with the grotesque humor as Bella's dying hallucinations and her ghostly children's cries are interspersed with Jessie's crass denials about her theft of the money. The scene grows contrapuntally more somber, and the children's voices grow younger, their cries monosyllabic:

VOICE OF YOUNG CHIPS: —*Dark!*
VOICE OF YOUNG CHARLIE: *Mommy!*
VOICE OF YOUNG JOANIE: We're *Hungry!*
JESSIE: I'm gonna sit and remain here till responsible witnesses are summoned.
BELLA: That chair is—little—Joanie's . . . (*HMS*, 85–86)

These final moments of the play are tremendously evocative, offering a powerful—and deliberate—echo of the opening tableau of *The Glass Menagerie*: "We can't say grace until you come to the table!" (*GM*, 146). After the ghostly voice of young Chips intones, "Bless this food to our use and ourselves to Thy service," the concluding line of the play is the doctor's reprimand, "I think you might dismiss that subject in the presence of death" (*HMS*, 86). After Dr. Crane passes his hand gently across Bella's eyes, denoting her passing, the ghostly children "ceremoniously rise from the family table and slip soundlessly back into the dark" (*HMS*, 86).

* * * * *

The story of Williams's final months and days is one that is in keeping with both the history and the rhythm of his entire life. It is perfectly summed up by the motto he used to define himself—"En avant!" Hemmed in by his family and the city of St. Louis, he always relied on clever strategies of escape. As infirmity and death approached, he once more tried to go forth, avoiding boundaries and restrictions, just as he had managed to flee St. Louis for New Orleans in late 1938:

> Once again I feel dangerously cornered, cut off—wonder how I am going to fight my way through—A trip somewhere would be the best—Some external stimulus must be applied to snap me out of this. But what? . . . Soon as I gather my forces (and I shall!) I must make a definite break—because this stagnation is debilitating my will—making me weak and timid again. . . . Now is the time to make a break—get away, away—I have pinned pictures of wild birds on my lavatory screen—Significant—I'm anxious to escape—But where & how?— . . . What a terrible trap to be caught in! (*N*, 125, 127)

In 1969, following the appearance of the irresponsible and devastating reviews of *In the Bar of a Tokyo Hotel*, he fled once again, this time to Japan in the company of actress Anne Meacham and his bulldog, Gigi, ostensibly to see rehearsals of *Streetcar* by the Bungakuza Theatre Company. The dog's required quarantine sent him spiraling into a deeper depression and further regression, as author Yukio Mishima recalled: "I took care of him with Anne beside of his bed in order to give him a good sleep and sweet dream. He was just a big baby with beards [*sic*] drinking alcohol instead of milk."[30]

In the earlier instance, of course, Williams was incredibly fortunate, instantly recognizing that he and the French Quarter were a perfect match for one another. As he wrote in his notebook, "I am delighted, in fact enchanted with this glamorous, fabulous old town.

I've been here about 3 hours but have already wandered about the Vieux Carré and noted many exciting possibilities. Here surely is the place I was made for if any place on this funny old world" (*N*, 131).

But in his final few months of life, nothing worked—no escape was possible. His burial at Calvary Cemetery in St. Louis, however bizarre and ironic it might appear at first glance, was in fact not merely predictable but entirely appropriate. The writer who despised the city with unmatched ferocity was always destined to return to it in the end. Throughout his life, he had expressed his unequivocal hatred toward its repressive conventionality. But, as Stanley says to Blanche, the two had this date from the very beginning.

Appendix

Tennessee Williams Trail

by Jessie Hoagland

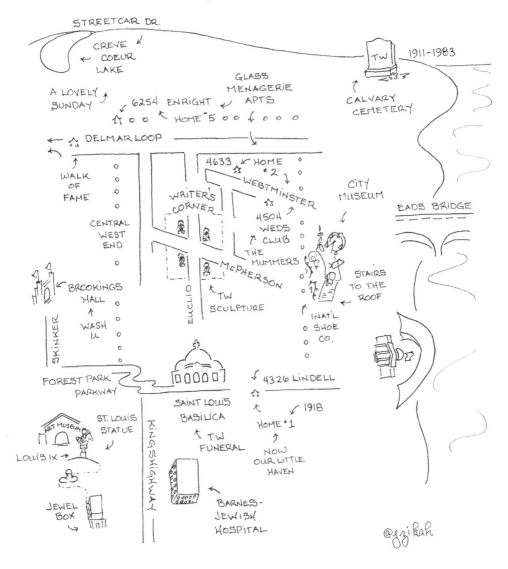

Notes

INTRODUCTION

1. However, the festival, under the dynamic artistic direction of Carrie Houk, has already done much to correct this perspective.

2. See the bibliography for biographical writings about Tennessee Williams.

3. Tennessee Williams, "What's Next on the Agenda, Mr. Williams?," in *CP*, 151, 156, 157.

4. John Lahr, *Tennessee Williams: Mad Pilgrimage of the Flesh*, 602.

CHAPTER ONE

Epigraph. In an exercise of poetic license, Williams added a shield, which the statue does not have.

1. The story is a revision of an unpublished piece from 1937 entitled "The Red Part of a Flag." It was published as "Oriflamme" in 1974 in *Vogue* and was later included in *Collected Stories*.

2. For more on Lawrence's influence on Williams, see my essay "After the Fox: The Influence of D. H. Lawrence on Tennessee Williams."

3. Robert Bray, foreword to "His Father's House," 3.

4. Edwina and C.C.'s third child, Dakin, was born in St. Louis in 1919.

5. Lyle Leverich, *Tom: The Unknown Tennessee Williams*, 37.

6. Leverich, *Tom*, 47.

7. Edwina Dakin Williams, *Remember Me to Tom*, 148.

8. Williams, *Remember Me to Tom*, 149.

9. Leverich, *Tom*, 181 (interview of Clark Mills by Leverich, August 27, 1983, New York).

10. William Jay Smith, *Army Brat*, 190–91.

11. Williams, *Remember Me to Tom*, 30.

12. Tennessee Williams, "'St. Louisans Cold, Smug, Complacent.' Also Intolerant, Stupid, Provincial, Says Tennessee Williams, Local Boy Who Made Good as Playwright—You Get Idea He May Be Chilly Toward City," interview by Virginia Irwin, 41.

13. Williams, *Remember Me to Tom*, 32.

14. Williams, *Remember Me to Tom*, 28.

15. Williams, *Remember Me to Tom*, 19.
16. Williams, *Remember Me to Tom*, 24.
17. Leverich, *Tom*, 43.
18. Kenneth Holditch and Richard Freeman Leavitt, *Tennessee Williams and the South*, 19.
19. Holditch and Leavitt, *Tennessee Williams and the South*, 14.
20. W. Kenneth Holditch, *The Last Frontier of Bohemia: Tennessee Williams in New Orleans*, 5.
21. Holditch, *Last Frontier of Bohemia*, 10.
22. Williams referred to this illness as a "heart attack" although this was never medically proven. In any event, this incident freed him from his bondage at the dreaded International Shoe Company.
23. F. Scott Fitzgerald, *The Great Gatsby*, 99.
24. Nancy M. Tischler, *Tennessee Williams: Rebellious Puritan*, 62.
25. Allean Hale, "Two on a Streetcar," 36.
26. William Blake, *The Marriage of Heaven and Hell*, plate 3.

CHAPTER TWO

Epigraph. Holditch and Leavitt, *Tennessee Williams and the South*, xi (interview of Williams, 1970s).
1. Tennessee Williams author biography, in *The Playbill for the Playhouse* (New York), program for *The Glass Menagerie*, August 26–September 1, 1945, 32 (in author's possession).
2. D. H. Lawrence, *Studies in Classic American Literature*, xx.
3. Shepherd Mead, "The Secret Year of Tennessee Williams," 9.
4. David Loth to Donald Spoto, October 9, 1983, quoted in Donald Spoto, *The Kindness of Strangers: The Life of Tennessee Williams*, 14.
5. Williams, *Remember Me to Tom*, 30.
6. Tennessee Williams, "Tennessee Williams," interview by Lincoln Barnett. In this 1948 interview in *Life*, Williams recalls "gangs of kids following [him] home yelling 'Sissy!'—and home was not a very pleasant refuge." In his foreword to the previously unpublished story "His Father's House," Robert Bray suggests Williams "may have been thinking back upon his tortured days at the Eugene Field Elementary School for the story's inspiration" (3).
7. Bernard Winer, "A Good Year for Fascinating, Maddening Tennessee Williams," 13; Robert Berkvist, "Broadway Discovers Tennessee Williams," 5, both quoted in Leverich, *Tom*, 9. After undergoing psychoanalysis in the 1950s, Williams had begun to view his hatred toward his father as sublimated love, Leverich says, while his feelings toward his mother, although perpetually conflicted, shifted in the direction of outright hostility (*Tom*, 9).
8. The Enright apartment, where the family lived for nearly a decade, undoubtedly provided much of the inspiration for the Wingfields' tenement in

Menagerie. Nonetheless, a different apartment building that had been the family's second home in St. Louis, at 4633 Westminster in the city's Central West
End, became known as "The Glass Menagerie Apartments."

9. Rose Williams to Tom Williams, May 25, 1927; Reverend Walter Edwin
Dakin to Tom Williams, April 12, 1927, both quoted in Leverich, *Tom*, 81.

10. Leverich, *Tom*, 89.

11. Allean Hale, "Tennessee Williams at Missouri."

12. Leverich, *Tom*, 111.

13. Edwina Williams reproduces this article in her memoir, *Remember Me to
Tom*, 51. The piece was reprinted in the *Columbia Missourian*, December 9,
1984, 10–11.

14. Williams, *Remember Me to Tom*, 50.

15. This phrase is attributed to C.C. Williams in Leverich, *Tom*, 29.

16. Leverich, *Tom*, 106.

17. William Jay Smith, *My Friend Tom: The Poet-Playwright Tennessee Williams*, 11.

18. Leverich, *Tom*, 112.

19. Tennessee Williams, "Tennessee Williams—A Self-Analysis," interview by
Eugene B. Griesman, 2, quoted in Leverich, *Tom*, 126.

20. Williams, *Remember Me to Tom*, 62.

21. Cardinal Le Gros to Williams, November 9, 1932; Robert L. Ramsay to
Williams, December 10, 1932, both quoted in Leverich, *Tom*, 137.

22. Leverich, *Tom*, 135.

23. Tennessee Williams, "Stair to the Roof" manuscript, n.d., one of several
in box 43, folders 3, 4, Tennessee Williams Collection, Harry Ransom Center,
University of Texas at Austin.

24. Williams, *Remember Me to Tom*, 70.

25. Emily Dickinson, "Elysium is as far as to," st. 2, ll. 5–8.

26. Smith, *My Friend Tom*, 19, 23. In *Memoirs* Williams describes an awkward meeting with Clark Mills outside his Manhattan apartment on East Sixty-
fifth Street in the early 1960s. When Mills saw his old friend and said hello,
Williams wrote, "All I could think of was: 'He must know I've turned queer.'
The conversation was pitiably brief and embarrassed." The two parted without
Williams's inviting his old friend inside (*M*, 123). Curiously, a very similar incident occurred between Williams and another close friend and mentor from
his St. Louis days, Willard Holland (discussed in chapter 3). Holland's wife described a chance meeting between the two on Hollywood Boulevard in 1943,
and recounted that Williams "almost cut Willard dead" on the street (Harriet
Holland Brandt to Lyle Leverich, August 11, 1985, quoted in Leverich, *Tom*,
516). The parallels between these two unfortunate meetings reinforce the idea
that Williams avoided anything that reminded him of his painful St. Louis past,
as well as showing his embarrassment over whether these former close friends
would accept his coming out as a gay man.

27. Smith, *My Friend Tom*, 22–23.

28. Leverich, *Tom*, 221 (interview of Clark Mills by Leverich, August 27, 1983, New York).

29. Leverich, *Tom*, 221 (Mills interview).

30. Smith, *My Friend Tom*, 23.

31. In *The Night of the Iguana* (1961), the painter Hannah Jelkes delineates how she tries to outwit her "blue devil," expressed as a journey that "spooked and bedeviled people are forced to take" through the "*unlighted* sides of their natures" (353). In describing this shadowy side to her apparently calm exterior, Hannah is speaking for Williams's lifelong battle with depression.

32. Leverich, *Tom*, 224.

33. Leverich, *Tom*, 223 (interview of Dakin Williams by Leverich, October 2, 1984, New York).

34. The play's title was later changed from "Escape" to *Summer at the Lake*, and it is published in *"Mister Paradise" and Other One-Act Plays*, edited by Nicholas Moschovakis and David Roessel. See chapter 3 for further discussion of this play.

35. "Blue Song" is the property of Washington University Libraries, Julian Edison Department of Special Collections. It was published in the *New Yorker*, December 25, 2006–January 1, 2007, 60. Since its publication in the *New Yorker*, I have concluded that one word in the poem was given incorrectly when it was printed: the final word in line 10, I now believe, is *no*. In previous publications of the poem, that word has been *is*.

36. Spoto, *Kindness of Strangers*, 55.

37. Dakin Williams and Shepherd Mead, *Tennessee Williams: An Intimate Biography*, 57; Martyl Schweig Langsdorf to Lyle Leverich, August 2, 1983, quoted in Leverich, *Tom*, 216.

38. Tennessee Williams, *Me, Vashya*, 46, 50.

CHAPTER THREE

1. For more information on the politics of the Mummers, see Tom Mitchell's informative essay "Tennessee Williams and the Mummers of St. Louis: The Birth of a Playwright." Mitchell also offers helpful details on the configuration of the Wednesday Club Auditorium, where the Mummers performed, and the major influence of working-class theatre on Williams.

2. Tennessee Williams, "Tennessee Williams," interview by Walter Wager (1966), 129.

3. Tennessee Williams, "Tennessee Williams," interview by Charles Ruas (1975), 292.

4. Arthur Miller, "Tennessee Williams' Legacy: An Eloquence and Amplitude of Feeling," 204.

5. J. P. Hollifield to Tom Williams, November 7, 1935, quoted in Dan Isaac, introduction to *Candles to the Sun*, xxiv.

6. Smith, *My Friend Tom*, 38.

7. Colvin McPherson, review of *Candles to the Sun*.

8. The name "Luke," derived from the Latin "Lucius," means "the bright one" or "born at dawn." Williams, who studied Latin and Greek, in part to please his grandfather, would certainly have been conscious of this meaning. Indeed, in the much later dystopian one-act *The Chalky White Substance* (1980), a character named Luke is admired for his "eyes being so clear" by his lover, Mark (*CWS*, 4).

9. Robert Rice, "A Man Named Tennessee," M2, quoted in Leverich, *Tom*, 209.

10. See Vanessa Redgrave, foreword to *Not About Nightingales*, vii–xii, for details on the discovery of that play.

11. Edwina Williams to the Reverend Walter and Mrs. Rose Otte Dakin, September 28, 1938, quoted in Leverich, *Tom*, 270.

12. *Look*, October 11, 1938, quoted in Redgrave, foreword to *Not About Nightingales*, ix–x.

13. See Allean Hale's introduction to *Not About Nightingales*, "A Call for Justice," for more detail on the genesis of this play and the film's influence on it.

14. John Keats, "Ode to a Nightingale," st. 3, ll. 1–4.

15. Tennessee Williams, *Orpheus Descending*, 265. *Orpheus Descending* is a revised version of Williams's 1940 *Battle of Angels*.

16. It is interesting that Eva's surname is "Crane," not only because she is another example of a "bird" in the play but because she summons the wisdom of another poet, Hart Crane, to come to the aid of Jim, bringing him back to the world of his imagination.

17. The prison was notorious for a number of atrocities in addition to the one that took place in 1938. See Hale, "A Call for Justice," xv–xvi.

18. Williams, *Remember Me to Tom*, 68.

19. Leverich, *Tom*, 163.

20. Kate Chopin, *The Awakening*, 109.

21. Dan Isaac, introduction to *Spring Storm*, xiv–xv.

22. Isaac, introduction to *Spring Storm*, xvii.

23. "The Front Porch Girl" was one of the preliminary titles for *The Glass Menagerie*, further demonstrating the connections between *Spring Storm* and the later St. Louis play.

24. Lahr, *Tennessee Williams*, 53 (interview of Dakin Williams by Lahr, 2004).

25. Lahr, *Tennessee Williams*, 77, 73.

26. This short scene was found among the outtake pile of notes for the play but was not in the surviving complete manuscript. It was added to the published version of the play by Dan Isaac, editor of the New Directions edition. For more information on this scene, which Isaac describes as "something akin to reflective mood music," see Isaac's "Textual Notes" in *Spring Storm*, 158.

27. Williams, *Remember Me to Tom*, 57.

28. Williams, *Remember Me to Tom*, 61–62.

29. Jon C. Teaford, *Cities of the Heartland: The Rise and Fall of the Industrial Midwest*, 179.

30. Williams, "Stair to the Roof" manuscript.

31. Hale, "A Play for Tomorrow," introduction to *Stairs to the Roof*, xvii.

CHAPTER FOUR

1. Tennessee Williams, interview by Vivien Goldsmith, quoted in Robert Bray, introduction to *The Glass Menagerie*, x, xv.

2. Dakin Williams and Shepherd Mead, *His Brother's Keeper: The Life and Murder of Tennessee Williams*, 56.

3. Tennessee Williams, "Apt. F, 3rd Flo. So." manuscript, n.d., box 1, folder 14, Tennessee Williams Collection, Harry Ransom Center, University of Texas at Austin. Leverich calls this story about a brother and sister named Arthur and Valerie the earliest of Williams's various writings about his family. The ivory-colored furniture in Valerie's bedroom is clearly connected with Williams's memory of his sister's bedroom (Leverich, *Tom*, 489n).

4. Produced by the prestigious Theatre Guild, *Battle of Angels* seemed headed for Broadway until its Boston premiere. The play emphasizes the playwright's regenerated self in the person of its protagonist, Valentine Xavier, a character named after one of Williams's own Tennessee forebears. However, the opening night in Boston ended catastrophically when smoke from a fire intended as the play's denouement (and Val's tragic apotheosis) ended up billowing out into the audience, forcing people to head for the exits, sputtering and coughing, before the curtain call. Williams described the scene as being "like the burning of Rome" in "The History of a Play (With Parentheses)" (*NSE*, 23), while biographer John Lahr succinctly observed, "If ever the professional debut of a major playwright was a greater fiasco, history does not record it" (*Tennessee Williams*, 25).

5. It was Lippmann who encouraged the *St. Louis Star-Times* to send a reporter to interview the budding playwright. As a result, she was responsible for initiating the meeting and later friendship between Williams and then *Star-Times* reporter William Inge.

6. Tony Kushner, introduction to *The Glass Menagerie: Deluxe Centennial Edition*, 19.

7. "Medicine: Psychosurgery," 48.

8. This quotation appears only in the British edition of *Suddenly Last Summer*, not in the standard American edition published by New Directions, which I cite elsewhere. See Williams, *Suddenly Last Summer*, in *"Baby Doll" and Other Plays* (Harmondsworth, UK: Penguin, 1968), 119.

9. Williams, *Remember Me to Tom*, 85.

10. Williams, *Remember Me to Tom*, 85.

11. Williams, *Remember Me to Tom*, 85.

12. Leverich, *Tom*, 480.

13. Both quotations are from Williams to Paul Bigelow, unsigned and unmailed typewritten letter, ca. April 10, 1943 (*SL*, 437).

14. Leverich, *Tom*, 489.

15. Brian Parker, foreword to *The Pretty Trap*, 6.

16. Parker, foreword, 5.

17. Samuel Taylor Coleridge, *The Rime of the Ancient Mariner*, pt. 7, st. 16.

18. Lahr, *Tennessee Williams*, 59.

19. Christopher Marlowe, *Doctor Faustus*, 1.3.76, 2.1.121–23.

20. Edwina and Cornelius Williams separated only in 1948, once Edwina gained financial independence from her husband after acquiring half the rights for *The Glass Menagerie*, bestowed upon her by her son.

CHAPTER FIVE

1. Tennessee Williams, "A Visit with Tennessee Williams," interview by Lois Timnick, quoted in Allean Hale, "Tennessee Williams's St. Louis Blues," 623.

2. Justin Kaplan, *Walt Whitman: A Life*, 139.

3. For more on the importance of New Orleans in Williams's work, see for example Holditch's pamphlet *The Last Frontier of Bohemia*; Holditch and Leavitt's book *Tennessee Williams and the South*; and my essay "'The Place I Was Made For': Tennessee Williams in New Orleans."

4. Oscar Wilde, "The Decay of Lying," 1086.

5. For more on New Orleans as an early haven for artists and poets, see T. R. Johnson, ed., *New Orleans: A Literary History*.

6. Vivienne Dickson, "*A Streetcar Named Desire*: Its Development through the Manuscripts," 158–59.

7. Hale, "Tennessee Williams's St. Louis Blues," 612.

8. Leverich, *Tom*, 138.

9. Leverich, *Tom*, 191.

10. In addition to the brutality and domestic violence at the heart of the play, there are other significant connections between *Streetcar* and Williams's Missouri past. During his second year at the University of Missouri, Williams befriended a freshman from a small Missouri farming town named Harold A. ("Mitch") Mitchell. Mitchell would become the model for Blanche's beau, Mitch, in *Streetcar*. In his earliest days at International Shoe in 1932, Tom also became friends with a young Polish fellow. Williams later wrote that this experience gave him "first-hand knowledge of what it means to be a small wage earner in a hopelessly routine job" (Tischler, *Tennessee Williams*, 38). That young man's name was Stanley Kowalski.

11. Williams, *Remember Me to Tom*, 55.

CHAPTER SIX

1. Williams and Mead, *His Brother's Keeper*, 292.

2. Lahr, *Tennessee Williams*, 499 (interview of Dakin Williams by Lyle Leverich).

3. Spoto, *Kindness of Strangers*, 283.

4. It seems particularly ironic that Williams, who as we have seen in his early

poem "Cried the Fox" styled himself an artist in the mold of "Reynard the Fox," the medieval trickster figure prominent in so much European literature, was now captive in a hospital wing bearing the name "Renard" (the French word for "fox"). As he wrote in that strangely prophetic poem, the fox had thus far evaded capture, but now his brush indeed "[hung] burning / flame at the hunter's door."

5. Tennessee Williams to William Glavin, n.d., quoted in Lahr, *Tennessee Williams*, 501.

6. Williams and Mead, *His Brother's Keeper*, 292.

7. Dakin Williams, "An Interview with Dakin Williams," interview by Robert Bray, 784.

8. Lahr, *Tennessee Williams*, 501, 502.

9. T. E. Kalem, "New Plays: Torpid Tennessee."

10. John Simon, "The Eighth Descent of Tennessee."

11. Stefan Kanfer, "White Dwarf's Tragic Fade-Out."

12. For more on *Tokyo Hotel* as a representation of Williams's divided self, see Allean Hale's essays "Tennessee's Long Trip" and "*In the Bar of a Tokyo Hotel*: Breaking the Code."

13. For more on Williams's use of language in *Tokyo Hotel*, see Ruby Cohn, "Tennessee Williams: The Last Two Decades."

14. Martin Esslin, *The Theatre of the Absurd*, 5 (Camus quote), 7. For more on the relationship between *Tokyo Hotel* and the Theatre of the Absurd, see William Prosser, *The Late Plays of Tennessee Williams*, 71–76.

15. Edward Albee, "Which Theater Is the Absurd One?," 10.

16. Walter Kerr, "The Facts Don't Add Up to Faces."

17. Simon, "Eighth Descent."

18. Kalem, "New Plays."

19. Robert Koehler, "Tennessee Williams: A Fragile Master."

CHAPTER SEVEN

1. Spoto, *Kindness of Strangers*, 262.

2. Author's conversation with David Wolkowsky, Key West, 2016.

3. Tom Buckley, "Tennessee Williams Survives," 162.

4. Tennessee Williams, *Five O'Clock Angel: Letters of Tennessee Williams to Maria St. Just*, 217–18.

5. Tennessee Williams, "Will God Talk Back to a Playwright? Tennessee Williams," interview by David Frost, 146.

6. Walter Kerr, "A Touch of the Poet Isn't Enough to Sustain Williams's Latest Play," 266, 268.

7. Charlotte Moore, "Working with Tennessee: Charlotte Moore Discusses the Production of *A Lovely Sunday for Creve Coeur*," interview by Craig Clinton, 101 (including "bijou" quote).

8. Arthur Gelb and Barbara Gelb, *O'Neill: Life with Monte Cristo*, 192.

9. Gelb and Gelb, *O'Neill*, 192.

10. Linda Dorff, "Theatricalist Cartoons: Tennessee Williams's Late, 'Outrageous' Plays," 13.

11. Annette J. Saddik, "'Drowned in Rabelaisian Laughter': Germans as Grotesque Comic Figures in Williams' Plays of the 1960s and 1970s," in *Tennessee Williams and the Theatre of Excess: The Strange, the Crazed, the Queer*, 27.

12. Dorff, "Theatricalist Cartoons," 13; Saddik, "'Drowned in Rabelaisian Laughter,'" 28.

13. Moore, "Working with Tennessee," interview by Clinton, 97.

14. Williams, "'St. Louisans Cold, Smug, Complacent,'" interview by Irwin.

15. Moore, "Working with Tennessee," interview by Clinton, 103.

16. Mead, "Secret Year," 9.

17. Mead, "Secret Year," 9, 11.

18. Christopher Looby, "Tennessee Williams: Return to the Menagerie at Last," 8.

19. Looby, "Tennessee Williams," 8.

CHAPTER EIGHT

1. Dotson Rader, *Tennessee: Cry of the Heart*, 345.

2. Tennessee Williams to Konrad Hopkins, March 1952, letter in author's possession.

3. Rob Rains, "Despised Brother Buries Williams in a Place He Didn't Like," quoted in Leverich, *Tom*, 10.

4. Berkvist, "Broadway Discovers Tennessee Williams," 5, quoted in Leverich, *Tom*, 9.

5. Dakin Williams, "Interview with Dakin Williams," interview by Bray, 781.

6. Peter Hoffman, "The Last Days of Tennessee Williams," 41, quoted in Lahr, *Tennessee Williams*, 589.

7. For more on this woman and her bizarre relationship with Williams, see John Lahr, "The Lady and Tennessee."

8. "Playwright Is Buried in City He Hated," sec. 1, p. 23.

9. Lahr, *Tennessee Williams*, 590 (interview of Dotson Rader by Lahr, 2011). Lahr's biography also cites esteemed Williams scholar Robert Bray's interview with Dakin as evidence that the self-described "First Brother" had plans to exploit "the Williams franchise." In an interview by Lahr, Bray said these included "digging up the coffin in St. Louis and repatriating TW back to New Orleans, in order to establish a TW theme park. He'd say, 'You know, we could have Brick hobbling around on a crutch. Amanda strolling about with her jonquils, Shannon looking for a drink'" (Lahr, *Tennessee Williams*, 721n591).

10. Leverich, *Tom*, 1 (interview of John Uecker by Leverich, n.d.).

11. Lahr, *Tennessee Williams*, 580 (interview of John Uecker by Lyle Leverich, 1983).

12. Rader, *Tennessee*, 338.

13. Leverich, *Tom*, 1.

14. See Leverich, *Tom*, 1–11, for a description of the days before and after Williams's death. The Chatterton lines Purdy inscribed are from *Aella, a Tragical Interlude* (ll. 898–99), one version of which may be found in *The Complete Poetical Works of Thomas Chatterton* (Bristol, UK: Ragged Hand, 2020), 201–324.

15. The poem "Blood of the Wolf" is housed in the Harry Ransom Center and reproduced in the explanatory notes of *CP*, 226.

16. Lahr, *Tennessee Williams*, 585 (interview of John Uecker by Lahr, 2010).

17. The play was originally published in the *Tennessee Williams Annual Review*, no. 3 (2000), along with an editorial note by Robert Bray, and is included in *"The Traveling Companion" and Other Plays*, ed. Annette J. Saddik.

18. Leverich, *Tom*, 224.

19. Later Alicia says to Olaf, "Stay out here and admire the polluted sky, there may be a visible star" (*SR*, 328).

20. See Hale, "Tennessee Williams's St. Louis Blues," 615.

21. Lahr, *Tennessee Williams*, 558 (interview of John Hancock by Lahr, 2012).

22. Jack Kroll, "Slender Is the Night," *Newsweek*, April 7, 1980; Clive Barnes, "'Clothes' Needs Some Tailoring," *New York Post*, March 27, 1980; John Simon, "Damsels Inducing Distress," *New York*, April 7, 1980.

23. Simon, "Damsels Inducing Distress," 273.

24. Lahr, *Tennessee Williams*, 567.

25. Nancy Milford, *Zelda*, 89.

26. Zelda Fitzgerald, review of *The Beautiful and the Damned*.

27. He used "Valentine Xavier" or "Val Xavier" (pronounced "Savior") as the name of his protagonist in both the ill-fated *Battle of Angels* (1940) and its rewritten version, *Orpheus Descending* (1957).

28. Tischler, *Tennessee Williams*, 16.

29. Albert E. Karlson, *"A House Not Meant to Stand,"* 283.

30. Yukio Mishima to Robert MacGregor, July 3, 1969, quoted in Lahr, *Tennessee Williams*, 494.

Bibliography

Albee, Edward. "Which Theater Is the Absurd One?" In *Stretching My Mind: The Collected Essays of Edward Albee*, 5–13. New York: Carroll & Graf, 2005.

Bak, John S. *Tennessee Williams: A Literary Life.* New York: Palgrave Macmillan, 2013.

Berkvist, Robert. "Broadway Discovers Tennessee Williams." *New York Times*, December 21, 1975.

Blake, William. *The Marriage of Heaven and Hell.* 1793. London: Oxford University Press, 1975.

Bray, Robert. Foreword to "His Father's House." *Tennessee Williams Annual Review*, no. 7 (2005): 2–4.

———. Introduction to *The Glass Menagerie*, by Tennessee Williams, vii–xv. New York: New Directions, 1999.

Buckley, Tom. "Tennessee Williams Survives." In Devlin, *Conversations with Tennessee Williams*, 161–83.

Cardullo, Bert. "The Blue Rose of St. Louis: Laura, Romanticism, and *The Glass Menagerie*." *Journal of American Drama and Theater* 10, no. 2 (Spring 1998): 1–25.

Chopin, Kate. *The Awakening.* 1899. Edited by Margo Culley. New York: W. W. Norton, 1994.

Cohn, Ruby. "Tennessee Williams: The Last Two Decades." In *The Cambridge Companion to Tennessee Williams*, edited by Matthew C. Roudané, 232–43. Cambridge: Cambridge University Press, 1997.

Coleridge, Samuel Taylor. *The Rime of the Ancient Mariner.* 1798. In *Wordsworth & Coleridge: Lyrical Ballads*, 2nd ed., edited by Derek Roper, 115–37. London: MacDonald and Evans, 1976.

Crandell, George W., ed. *The Critical Response to Tennessee Williams.* Westport, CT: Greenwood, 1996.

Devlin, Albert J., ed. *Conversations with Tennessee Williams.* Jackson: University Press of Mississippi, 1986.

Dickinson, Emily. "Elysium is as far as to." In *The Complete Poems of Emily Dickinson*, edited by Thomas H. Johnson, 712. New York: Back Bay Books, 1976.

Dickson, Vivienne. "*A Streetcar Named Desire*: Its Development through the Manuscripts." In *Tennessee Williams: A Tribute*, edited by Jac Tharpe, 154–71. Jackson: University Press of Mississippi, 1977.

Dorff, Linda. "Theatricalist Cartoons: Tennessee Williams's Late, 'Outrageous' Plays." *Tennessee Williams Annual Review*, no. 2 (1999): 13–33.

Esslin, Martin. *The Theatre of the Absurd*. New York: Anchor, 1969.

Fitzgerald, F. Scott. *The Great Gatsby*. 1925. New York: Scribner, 1953.

Fitzgerald, Zelda. Review of *The Beautiful and the Damned*, by F. Scott Fitzgerald. *New York Tribune*, April 1922.

Gelb, Arthur, and Barbara Gelb. *O'Neill: Life with Monte Cristo*. New York: Harper & Row, 1962.

Hale, Allean. "A Call for Justice." Introduction to *Not About Nightingales*, by Tennessee Williams, xiii–xxii.

———. "*In the Bar of a Tokyo Hotel*: Breaking the Code." In *Magical Muse: Millennial Essays on Tennessee Williams*, edited by Ralph F. Voss, 147–62. Tuscaloosa: University of Alabama Press, 2002.

———. "A Play for Tomorrow." Introduction to *Stairs to the Roof*, by Tennessee Williams, ix–xix.

———. "Tennessee's Long Trip." *Missouri Review* 7, no. 3 (Spring 1984): 201–12.

———. "Tennessee Williams at Missouri." *Missouri Alumnus* 74, no. 3 (January–February 1986): 18–19.

———. "Tennessee Williams's St. Louis Blues." *Mississippi Quarterly* 48, no. 4 (Fall 1995): 609–25.

———. "Tom Williams, Proletarian Playwright." *Tennessee Williams Annual Review*, no. 1 (1998): 13–22.

———. "Two on a Streetcar." *Tennessee Williams Literary Journal* 1, no. 1 (Spring 1989): 31–43.

Hoffman, Peter. "The Last Days of Tennessee Williams." *New York*, July 25, 1983, 41.

Holditch, W. Kenneth. *The Last Frontier of Bohemia: Tennessee Williams in New Orleans*. 1987. Pamphlet reprinted from *Southern Quarterly* (1987): 10.

———. "South toward Freedom: Tennessee Williams." In *Literary New Orleans: Essays and Meditations*, edited by Richard S. Kennedy, 61–75. Baton Rouge: Louisiana State University Press, 1992.

Holditch, Kenneth, and Richard Freeman Leavitt. *Tennessee Williams and the South*. Jackson: University Press of Mississippi, 2002.

Isaac, Dan. Introduction to *Candles to the Sun*, by Tennessee Williams, xix–xxviii.

———. Introduction to *Spring Storm*, by Tennessee Williams, vii–xxv.

Johnson, T. R., ed. *New Orleans: A Literary History*. Cambridge: Cambridge University Press, 2019.

Kalem, T. E. "New Plays: Torpid Tennessee." Review of *In the Bar of a Tokyo Hotel*, by Tennessee Williams. *Time*, May 23, 1969.

Kanfer, Stefan. "White Dwarf's Tragic Fade-Out." Review of *In the Bar of a Tokyo Hotel*, by Tennessee Williams. *Life* 66, no. 23 (June 13, 1969): 10.

Kaplan, Justin. *Walt Whitman: A Life*. New York: Simon and Schuster, 1980.

Karlson, Albert E. "*A House Not Meant to Stand*." Review of *A House Not Meant to Stand*, by Tennessee Williams. In Crandell, *The Critical Response to Tennessee Williams*, 283–84.

Keats, John. "Ode to a Nightingale." 1819. In *The Poetical Works of John Keats*, 230–33. Oxford: Oxford University Press, 1924.

Kerr, Walter. "The Facts Don't Add Up to Faces." Review of *In the Bar of a Tokyo Hotel*, by Tennessee Williams. *New York Times*, May 25, 1969.

———. "A Touch of the Poet Isn't Enough to Sustain Williams's Latest Play." Review of *Vieux Carré*, by Tennessee Williams. In Crandell, *The Critical Response to Tennessee Williams*, 266–69.

Koehler, Robert. "Tennessee Williams: A Fragile Master." Review of *Tennessee Williams: Orpheus of the American Stage*, American Masters film, PBS. *Los Angeles Times*, December 12, 1994.

Kushner, Tony. Introduction to *The Glass Menagerie: Deluxe Centennial Edition*, by Tennessee Williams, 1–48. New York: New Directions, 2011.

Lahr, John. "The Lady and Tennessee." *New Yorker*, December 19, 1994.

———. *Tennessee Williams: Mad Pilgrimage of the Flesh*. New York: W. W. Norton, 2014.

Lawrence, D. H. *Studies in Classic American Literature*. New York: Thomas Seltzer, 1923.

Leverich, Lyle. *Tom: The Unknown Tennessee Williams*. New York: W. W. Norton, 1995.

Looby, Christopher. "Tennessee Williams: Return to the Menagerie at Last." *Student Life* (Washington University), September 16, 1977, 8–9.

Marlowe, Christopher. 1592. *Doctor Faustus*. London: Ernest Benn Limited, 1965.

McPherson, Colvin. Review of *Candles to the Sun*, by Tennessee Williams. *St. Louis Post-Dispatch*, March 19, 1937.

Mead, Shepherd. "The Secret Year of Tennessee Williams." *Washington University Magazine* 47, no. 3 (Spring 1977): 8–11.

"Medicine: Psychosurgery." *Time*, November 30, 1942, 48–50.

Milford, Nancy. *Zelda*. New York: Harper and Row, 1970.

Miller, Arthur. "Tennessee Williams' Legacy: An Eloquence and Amplitude of Feeling." In *Echoes Down the Corridor: Collected Essays: 1944–2000*, 203–4. New York: Penguin Books, 2000.

Mitchell, Tom. "Tennessee Williams and the Mummers of St. Louis: The Birth of a Playwright." *Tennessee Williams Annual Review*, no. 10 (2009): 91–104.

Moore, Charlotte. "Working with Tennessee: Charlotte Moore Discusses the Production of *A Lovely Sunday for Creve Coeur*." Interview by Craig Clinton. *Tennessee Williams Annual Review*, no. 9 (2007): 96–106.

Paller, Michael. "A Playwright with a Social Conscience." *Tennessee Williams Annual Review*, no. 10 (2009): 105–10.

Parker, Brian. Foreword to *The Pretty Trap*. *Tennessee Williams Annual Review*, no. 8 (2006): 5–7.

"Playwright Is Buried in City He Hated." *New Orleans Times-Picayune*, March 6, 1983, sec. 1, p. 23.

Prosser, William. *The Late Plays of Tennessee Williams*. Lanham, MD: Scarecrow, 2009.

Rader, Dotson. *Tennessee: Cry of the Heart*. New York: Doubleday, 1985.

Rains, Rob. "Despised Brother Buries Williams in a Place He Didn't Like." *Miami Herald*, March 6, 1983.

———. "Williams Buried in City He Criticized as 'Cold' and 'Smug.'" *St. Louis Post-Dispatch*, March 15, 1983.

Rasky, Harry, dir. *Tennessee Williams' South: A Film by Harry Rasky*. Canadian Broadcasting Corporation, Color/80 min., 1973.

Redgrave, Vanessa. Foreword to *Not About Nightingales*, by Tennessee Williams, vii–xii.

Rice, Robert. "A Man Named Tennessee." *New York Post*, April 29, 1958, *Daily Magazine*, M2.

Saddik, Annette J. *The Politics of Reputation: The Critical Reception of Tennessee Williams' Later Plays*. Madison, NJ: Fairleigh Dickinson University Press, 1999.

———. *Tennessee Williams and the Theatre of Excess: The Strange, the Crazed, the Queer*. New York: Cambridge University Press, 2015.

Schvey, Henry I. "After the Fox: The Influence of D. H. Lawrence on Tennessee Williams." *Tennessee Williams Annual Review*, no. 17 (2018): 115–46.

———. "'Getting the Colored Lights Going': Expressionism in Tennessee Williams's *A Streetcar Named Desire*." In *Critical Insights: Tennessee Williams*, edited by Brenda Murphy, 58–79. Pasadena, CA: Salem, 2011.

———. "'The Place I Was Made For': Tennessee Williams in New Orleans." In *New Orleans: A Literary History*, edited by T. R. Johnson, 225–41. Cambridge: Cambridge University Press, 2019.

———. "The Road to Tennessee." *River Styx* 81/82, no. 35 (2010): 40–51.

Simon, John. "Damsels Inducing Distress." Review of *Clothes for a Summer Hotel*, by Tennessee Williams. *New York*, April 7, 1980.

———. "The Eighth Descent of Tennessee." Review of *In the Bar of a Tokyo Hotel*, by Tennessee Williams. *New York* 2, no. 21 (May 26, 1969): 56.

Smith, William Jay. *Army Brat*. New York: Persea Books, 1980.

———. *My Friend Tom: The Poet-Playwright Tennessee Williams*. Jackson: University Press of Mississippi, 2012.

Spoto, Donald. *The Kindness of Strangers: The Life of Tennessee Williams*. New York: Da Capo, 1997.

Teaford, Jon C. *Cities of the Heartland: The Rise and Fall of the Industrial Midwest*. Bloomington: Indiana University Press, 1993.

Tischler, Nancy M. *Tennessee Williams: Rebellious Puritan*. New York: Citadel, 1961.

Vidal, Gore. Introduction to *Collected Stories*, by Tennessee Williams, xix–xxv.

Wilde, Oscar. "The Decay of Lying." In *The Complete Works of Oscar Wilde*, 1071–92. New York: Collins, 2003.

Williams, Dakin. "An Interview with Dakin Williams." By Robert Bray. *Mississippi Quarterly* 48, no. 4 (Fall 1995): 776–88.

Williams, Dakin, and Shepherd Mead. *His Brother's Keeper: The Life and Murder of Tennessee Williams*. Collinsville, IL: Dakin's Corner Press, 1983.

———. *Tennessee Williams: An Intimate Biography*. New York: Arbor House, 1983.

Williams, Edwina Dakin. *Remember Me to Tom*. As told to Lucy Freeman. New York: Putnam, 1963.

Williams, Tennessee. "The Accent of a Coming Foot." In *Collected Stories*, 32–42.

———. *All Gaul Is Divided*. In *"Stopped Rocking" and Other Screenplays*, 1–95. New York: New Directions: 1984.

———. "Apt. F, 3rd Flo. So." Unpublished manuscript, n.d., box 1, folder 14, Tennessee Williams Collection, Harry Ransom Center, University of Texas at Austin.

———. *Auto-da-Fé*. In *The Theatre of Tennessee Williams*, 6:131–54.

———. "The Beanstalk Country." In *Collected Poems*, edited by Roessel and Moschovakis, 12–13.

———. *Beauty Is the Word*. *Missouri Review* 7, no. 3 (1984): 185–95.

———. "Birth of an Art (Anton Chekhov and the New Theatre)." In *New Selected Essays*, edited by Bak, 246–54.

———. "Blue Song." *New Yorker*, December 25, 2006–January 1, 2007, 60.

———. "Can a Good Wife Be a Good Sport?" In *New Selected Essays*, edited by Bak, 223–24.

———. *Candles to the Sun*. New York: New Directions, 2004.

———. "The Catastrophe of Success." In *New Selected Essays*, edited by Bak, 32–36.

———. *The Chalky White Substance*. In *"The Traveling Companion" and Other Plays*, edited by Annette J. Saddik, 1–12. New York: New Directions, 2008.

———. *Clothes for a Summer Hotel*. In *The Theatre of Tennessee Williams*, 8:201–80.

———. *The Collected Poems of Tennessee Williams*. Edited by David Roessel and Nicholas Moschovakis. New York: New Directions, 2002.

———. *Collected Stories*. Introduction by Gore Vidal. New York: New Directions, 1985.

———. "Comments on the Nature of Artists with a Few Specific References to the Case of Edgar Allan Poe." In *New Selected Essays*, edited by Bak, 254–58.

———. "Cried the Fox." In *Collected Poems*, edited by Roessel and Moschovakis, 6–7.

———. "Demon Smoke." In *Collected Poems*, edited by Roessel and Moschovakis, 214.

———. "Desire and the Black Masseur." In *Collected Stories*, 205–12.

———. *Five O'Clock Angel: Letters of Tennessee Williams to Maria St. Just*. New York: Knopf, 1990.

———. "Foreword to *Sweet Bird of Youth*." In *New Selected Essays*, edited by Bak, 93–96.

———. *Fugitive Kind*. New York: New Directions, 2001.

———. *The Glass Menagerie*. In *The Theatre of Tennessee Williams*, 1:123–237.

———. "His Father's House." *Tennessee Williams Annual Review*, no. 7 (2005): 5–13.

———. "The History of a Play (With Parentheses)." In *New Selected Essays*, edited by Bak, 15–24.

———. *Hot Milk at Three in the Morning*. *Missouri Review* 7, no. 3 (1984): 196–200.

———. *A House Not Meant to Stand*. New York: New Directions, 2008.

———. "I Am Widely Regarded as the Ghost of a Writer." In *New Selected Essays*, edited by Bak, 184–86.

———. "In Memory of an Aristocrat." In *Collected Stories*, 79–92.

———. Interview by Vivien Goldsmith. *London Daily Standard*, June 8, 1977.

———. *In the Bar of a Tokyo Hotel*. In *The Theatre of Tennessee Williams*, 7:1–53.

———. *The Long Goodbye*. In *"27 Wagons Full of Cotton" and Other One-Act Plays*, 161–79. New York: New Directions, 1966.

———. "Look Both Ways Crossing Streets." In *Collected Poems*, edited by Roessel and Moschovakis, 215–16.

———. *A Lovely Sunday for Creve Coeur*. In *The Theatre of Tennessee Williams*, 8:117–200.

———. *The Magic Tower*. In *"The Magic Tower" and Other One-Act Plays*, edited by Keith, 11–38.

———. *"The Magic Tower" and Other One-Act Plays*. Edited by Thomas Keith. New York: New Directions, 2011.

———. "The Man in the Overstuffed Chair." In *Collected Stories*, vii–xiii.

———. *Me, Vashya*. In *"The Magic Tower" and Other One-Act Plays*, edited by Keith, 39–59.

———. *Memoirs*. 1975. New York: New Directions, 2006.

———. "Mornings on Bourbon Street." In *Collected Poems*, edited by Roessel and Moschovakis, 72–73.

———. *New Selected Essays: Where I Live*. Edited by John S. Bak. New York: New Directions, 2009.

———. *The Night of the Iguana*. In *The Theatre of Tennessee Williams*, 4:247–376.

———. *Not About Nightingales*. New York: New Directions, 1998.

———. *Notebooks*. Edited by Margaret Bradham Thornton. New Haven: Yale University Press, 2006.

———. "Old Things." In *Collected Poems*, edited by Roessel and Moschovakis, 213–14.

———. *The One Exception*. In *"The Traveling Companion" and Other Plays*, edited by Annette J. Saddik, 193–207. New York: New Directions, 2008.

———. "Oriflamme." In *Collected Stories*, 128–33.

———. *Orpheus Descending*. In *The Theatre of Tennessee Williams*, 3:217–342.

———. "Portrait of a Girl in Glass." In *Collected Stories*, 110–19.

———. *The Pretty Trap*. In *"The Magic Tower" and Other One-Act Plays*, edited by Keith, 141–66.

———. *The Selected Letters of Tennessee Williams*. Edited by Albert J. Devlin and Nancy M. Tischler. Vol. 1, *1920–1945*. New York: New Directions, 2000.

———. "*Slapstick Tragedy*: A Preface." In *New Selected Essays*, edited by Bak, 147–48.

———. *Something Unspoken*. In *The Theatre of Tennessee Williams*, 6:273–96.

———. "Something Wild . . ." In *New Selected Essays*, edited by Bak, 43–47.

———. *Spring Storm*. New York: New Directions, 1999.

———. *Stairs to the Roof*. New York: New Directions, 2000.

———. "Stair to the Roof." Unpublished manuscripts, box 43, folders 3, 4, Tennessee Williams Collection, Harry Ransom Center, University of Texas at Austin.

———. "'St. Louisans Cold, Smug, Complacent.' Also Intolerant, Stupid, Provincial, Says Tennessee Williams, Local Boy Who Made Good as Playwright—You Get Idea He May Be Chilly Toward City." Interview by Virginia Irwin. *St. Louis Post-Dispatch*, December 22, 1947, *Everyday Magazine*, 41.

———. *Stopped Rocking*. In *"Stopped Rocking" and Other Screenplays*, 293–384. New York: New Directions, 1984.

———. *A Streetcar Named Desire*. In *The Theatre of Tennessee Williams*, 1:239–419.

———. *Suddenly Last Summer*. In *The Theatre of Tennessee Williams*, 3:343–423.

———. *Summer at the Lake*. In *"Mister Paradise" and Other One-Act Plays*, edited by Nicholas Moschovakis and David Roessel, 55–74. New York: New Directions, 2005.

————. *Sweet Bird of Youth.* In *The Theatre of Tennessee Williams*, 4:1–124.

————. "Tennessee Williams." Interview by Lincoln Barnett. *Life*, February 16, 1948.

————. "Tennessee Williams." Interview by Charles Ruas. 1975. In Devlin, *Conversations with Tennessee Williams*, 284–95.

————. "Tennessee Williams." Interview by Walter Wager. 1966. In Devlin, *Conversations with Tennessee Williams*, 124–33.

————. "Tennessee Williams—A Self-Analysis." Interview by Eugene B. Griesman. *San Francisco Chronicle*, February 28, 1983.

————. *The Theatre of Tennessee Williams.* 8 vols. New York: New Directions, 1971–1992.

————. "The Tomb of the Capuchins." In *New Selected Essays*, edited by Bak, 225.

————. "Too Personal?" In *New Selected Essays*, edited by Bak, 165–67.

————. "Two Metaphysical Sonnets." In *Collected Poems*, edited by Roessel and Moschovakis, 183.

————. "The Vengeance of Nitocris." In *Collected Stories*, 1–12.

————. *Vieux Carré.* In *The Theatre of Tennessee Williams*, 8:1–116.

————. "A Visit with Tennessee Williams." Interview by Lois Timnick. *St. Louis Globe Democrat*, September 10, 1974, 84.

————. "What's Next on the Agenda, Mr. Williams?" In *Collected Poems*, edited by Roessel and Moschovakis, 150–58.

————. "Will God Talk Back to a Playwright? Tennessee Williams." Interview by David Frost. In Devlin, *Conversations with Tennessee Williams*, 140–46. Edited version of Frost's conversation with Williams on *The David Frost Show*, WNEW-TV, New York, January 21, 1970.

Winer, Bernard. "A Good Year for Fascinating, Maddening Tennessee Williams." *San Francisco Chronicle Datebook*, January 18, 1976.

Index

Note: unattributed works are by Tennessee Williams

About the Author

Henry I. Schvey is Professor of Drama and Comparative Literature at Washington University in St. Louis and the author of three books, including *Oskar Kokoschka: The Painter as Playwright*. He lives in St. Louis, Missouri.

Joe Angeles/Washington University